I0818855

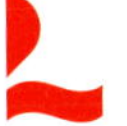

ANDREW
ROVENKO

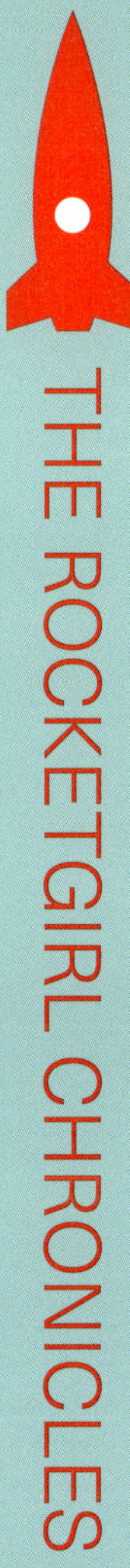

Lannoo

A girl in a homemade spacesuit.

She stands in an empty street, in front of a house or under an overpass. Is she visiting us from another world, or is she 'one of us' exploring an alien landscape?

It was during the lockdowns of the Covid-19 pandemic that the Rocketgirl Chronicles were born. Andrew Rovenko's daughter was four years old, and soon lockdown became almost all she knew. Her innate childhood curiosity was supercharged by the restrictions placed on us all – what blossomed was a fascination with space and all that existed beyond her lived experience.

In a spacesuit made by her mother, the 'Rocketgirl' would head out on short, permitted walks with her father and his camera. She was an astronaut setting out from her moonbase to explore the desolate world of the 'outside'. This game became a project and a shared experience for both parent and child.

So many of us wanted to be astronauts when we were kids. It's a totally unremarkable childhood fantasy, but that sense of wonder – of imagining yourself weightless on a spaceship or stepping out onto the surface of an uncharted planet – is not something that ever really leaves us. Few people, on the rare occasion that they remember to look up at the night sky, remain unmoved. Stars arranged into constellations by ancient astronomers, planets named after the gods of mythology, 20th-century satellites blinking and beeping away, representing the best of human ingenuity – science, mythos and humanity are all bundled together here. That sense of possibility and that wonder at the cosmological infinite, lived in direct opposition to life during the pandemic.

It was a very specific time. A virus spread, uncertainty about transmission and death rates followed, governments fumbled, and we were told to stay indoors. The world felt more precarious overnight; those of us in relative stability had our comforting routines upended. Governments locked down their populations and many facets of modern life simply ceased to function. We masked up, we stockpiled hand sanitiser and toilet paper, and we were limited to how much time we could spend outside each day. Those who lived alone were now utterly isolated. Those with young children had to multitask as parent, teacher and friend. So many of us, left to our own devices, fell down internet rabbit holes, the effects of which we are still struggling to overcome today. Social skills flaked away. Marriages and relationships were put under immense strain. We had to adapt – and essential to adaptability is imagination.

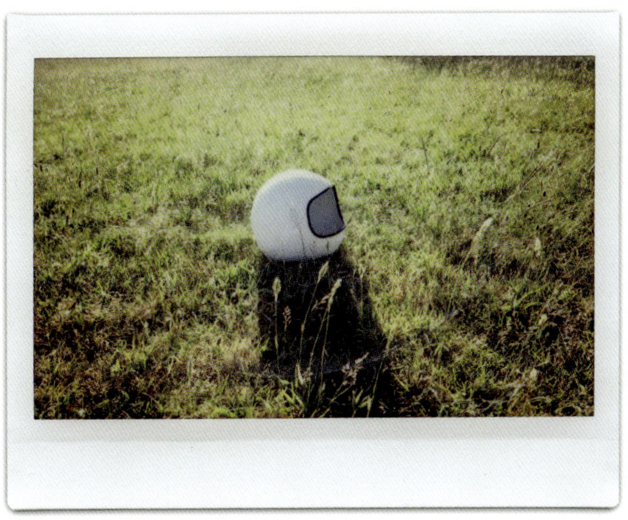

Embracing their daughter's interest in space, Andrew's wife, Mariya, crafted the 'Rocketgirl' spacesuit. Having studied theatrical costume design, she was able to employ those skills to make an outfit that allowed for immersive imaginative play. It's clearly reminiscent of the cosmonauts and astronauts of the Space Race. But combined with the papier-mâché helmet with its open face and her long blonde hair creeping out from beneath, it invites the observer to join in with the Rocketgirl's game.

The retro-futuristic design, the handcrafted aesthetic – it's like looking at production stills from any number of mid-century science-fiction shows. The landscapes are often decaying, rusting and empty – what was once futuristic is now old. And they were old long before this young humanoid was born. She is an explorer, an archaeologist and a scientist. She is a Victorian opening the Pharaoh's tomb.

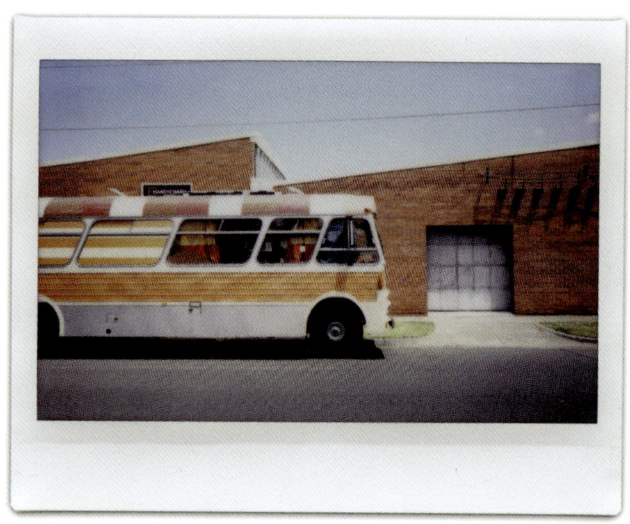

What these photographs capture is not only a particular moment in time, but the exact moment when we were all forced to take another look at the world.

Our streets became alien landscapes, our homes became cocoons, our friends and relatives became pixels – messages sent from light years away. The joy of these photographs is in the sharing of the imaginative play of a father and his daughter, attempting to take something unprecedented and make it normal. A game. A story. An adventure.

I think in many ways what I see when I look at Andrew's photographs is the emptiness of those locations. All that's there is his daughter, a curious expression on her face, and the relics of humanity – there's something post-apocalyptic about the industrial buildings, the vehicles, the laundrettes. It's not just the lack of people, but the choices of subject – the scrapyards and fire escapes, the graffiti-covered abandoned warehouses, these forgotten places, these liminal spaces. The decaying, rusting hulks of cars and fly-tipped sofas.

Of course, that's me looking at them with my tired adult eyes, because to a child they are not liminal – they are playgrounds. They are spaceships and climbing frames and adventure. What these photographs capture is the meeting of interests of child and parent – that it came about during a time when children were unable to mingle and play together, a time when families were forced to (oh the horror) spend so much time together, only adds to their bittersweetness.

When you look at these images you see two at a time – the reality of it, but also the imaginative world of the game. It is because of that friction that these images speak to us. The world falls apart sometimes. It is often empty of people. Metal rusts. Plastic toy buggies are abandoned beneath flyovers. Ice cream melts. Someone once cared for those cars – washed them, polished them, kissed in them, tinkered with their engines – and now they are abandoned. Our interstellar archivist hopes they will learn something of this long dead civilisation from the ruins it left behind.

My personal experience of lockdown is intrinsically entangled with the birth of my son. So much of what we wanted, hoped and/or expected of that experience was denied us. He was delivered by C-section and I was allowed to be present for that, though no one was one hundred percent sure of what the new guidance meant. I was permitted to stay with them in the recovery room, but after forty or so minutes, when my wife and son were taken up to the maternity ward, I was sent home. No other family members were allowed to come and be with me. No friends could hug and congratulate and reassure me. No cigars were handed out. I was unable to hold my son or my wife. I felt like an astronaut on a spacewalk who had become untethered from the mothership. Eventually, five days later, when they were allowed to come home, we settled into our new life – only without the flurry of support and human contact that would ordinarily manifest after the birth of a child. We lived in South London, where people were everywhere but everyone was alone.

I look at my son now – he's five years old – and he laughs so much at so little. How easy it is to be silly and happy when you are young. How delightful to run around in a circle and take joy in the dizziness of it. How fun it is to take a plastic dinosaur and have it storm a toy castle and fight a wizard. To recognise the names of the planets from a book of Greek mythology. To look up at the moon and try to see a face, or a bunny making mochi. How fun to learn that the solar system's biggest volcano is on Mars. How joyous to know that Mercury's days are longer than its years. That there's an ocean beneath Enceladus. That Titan's atmosphere smells of farts. That every star is a sun. I forget sometimes how amazing the universe is. Spending time in the company of a bright and curious child will always remind you of how fascinating and weird the world is. How special that Andrew has captured that sense of wonder in these photographs.

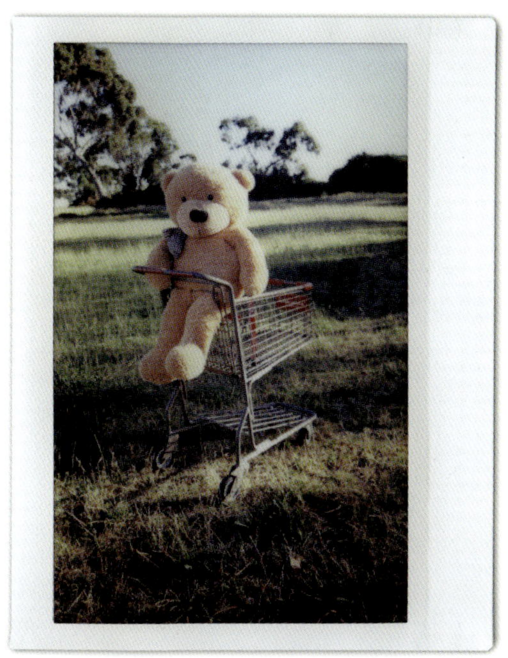

But these images are more than nostalgia for lost childhood days and are in many ways greater than a testament to the relationship between a father and his daughter. They speak to the strangeness of our modern world, and of how so many of us live in the in-between places of cities and suburbs that are both highly populated and often neglected. These images offer an escape – into the imagined worlds of our childhood, the intergalactic adventures of our daydreams and away from the grief, fear and uncertainty of a world ravaged by pandemic, climate breakdown and hatred. We see ourselves in the Rocketgirl, but we also envy her – her curiosity is allowed to be impartial. She remains a visitor, ready to be teleported to her orbiting spaceship at the first sign of trouble.

The best art grants us permission to see our world anew. A child dressed as an astronaut moving through otherwise mundane, quotidian locations allows us to see them again for the first time. As though these roads and suburbs were alien to us. How strange a thing a caravan is. Or a wall of tyres stacked up in a scrapyard. How peculiar to sell sweetened frozen milk sprinkled with coloured sugar out the back of a gaudily painted van.

Why has somebody threaded these tin cans together and hung them in a doorway like a braid of onions – to ward off evil spirits perhaps, or to act as a rudimentary alarm system, or maybe it's art? By placing his daughter, dressed as an interplanetary explorer, alongside these objects and locations, Andrew Rovenko invites us to look again at the world we live in. And to find beauty in it.

Looking at this collection I am struck by the beauty of their composition. The figure of the Rocketgirl draws our attention and from her our gaze radiates outwards to take in the whole scene, building the story for it as we go. Sometimes she is close to us – a portrait – and other times she is a small figure in the landscape. This movement between the images – that playful non-conformity to any set of self-imposed rules – adds a cinematic feel to the sequence. Everything feels overcast. The time is always on the verge of twilight. A fire burns on a beach. A fairground ride glows in neon colours. An oil refinery twinkles across the water. These flashes of brightness, of luminosity, suggest a world heading into darkness. And that triggers a protective instinct in us.

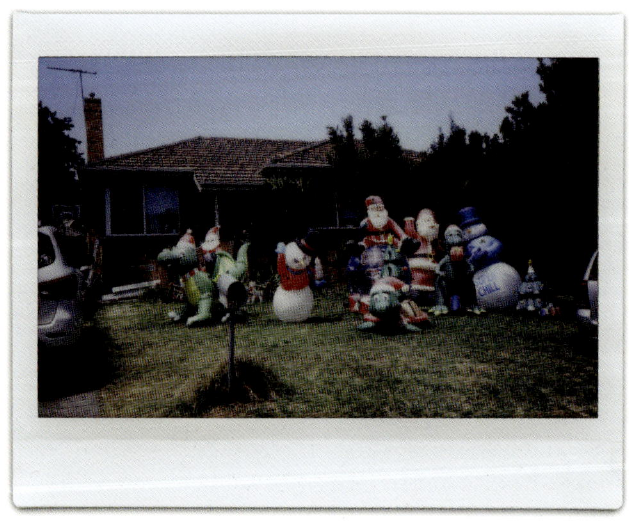

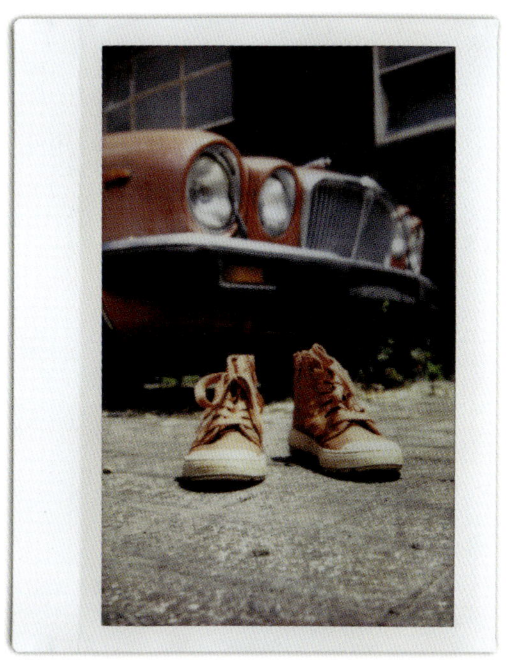

I am a playwright, and my pandemic experience was that of a new father. My days were spent caring for a son for whom the future seemed so uncertain, trying to write scripts that required theatres to be full of people again. Hope was a scarce resource. Imagination was an essential life skill. During this time of heightened worry, exasperation and grief, we all had to dig deep and cling to beauty, laughter, love and care – even in the smallest amounts. Like the proverbial boiling frog, we are mostly immune to how much the world has changed in the past five years, and there will no doubt be years of unpacking and repair ahead of us as we make sense of that peculiar time. How much it has damaged us and how much we have normalised it will probably not be fully apparent for quite some time.

What we have are contemporaneous artefacts such as this – art that captured not only a specific set of circumstances, but also the ways in which we as parents, friends and partners tried to hold each other through the dark times.

I was delighted when Andrew allowed me to use one of his images (The Reception) for the cover of my first collection of plays. To return the favour, I'm honoured to write this foreword. What follows are beautiful images, full of wonder, innocence and fragile beauty. There is sadness here, but sadness also signifies the existence of hope. My hope is that you take from this book a sense of the curiosity that the Rocketgirl embodies.

Tom Morton-Smith
November 2025

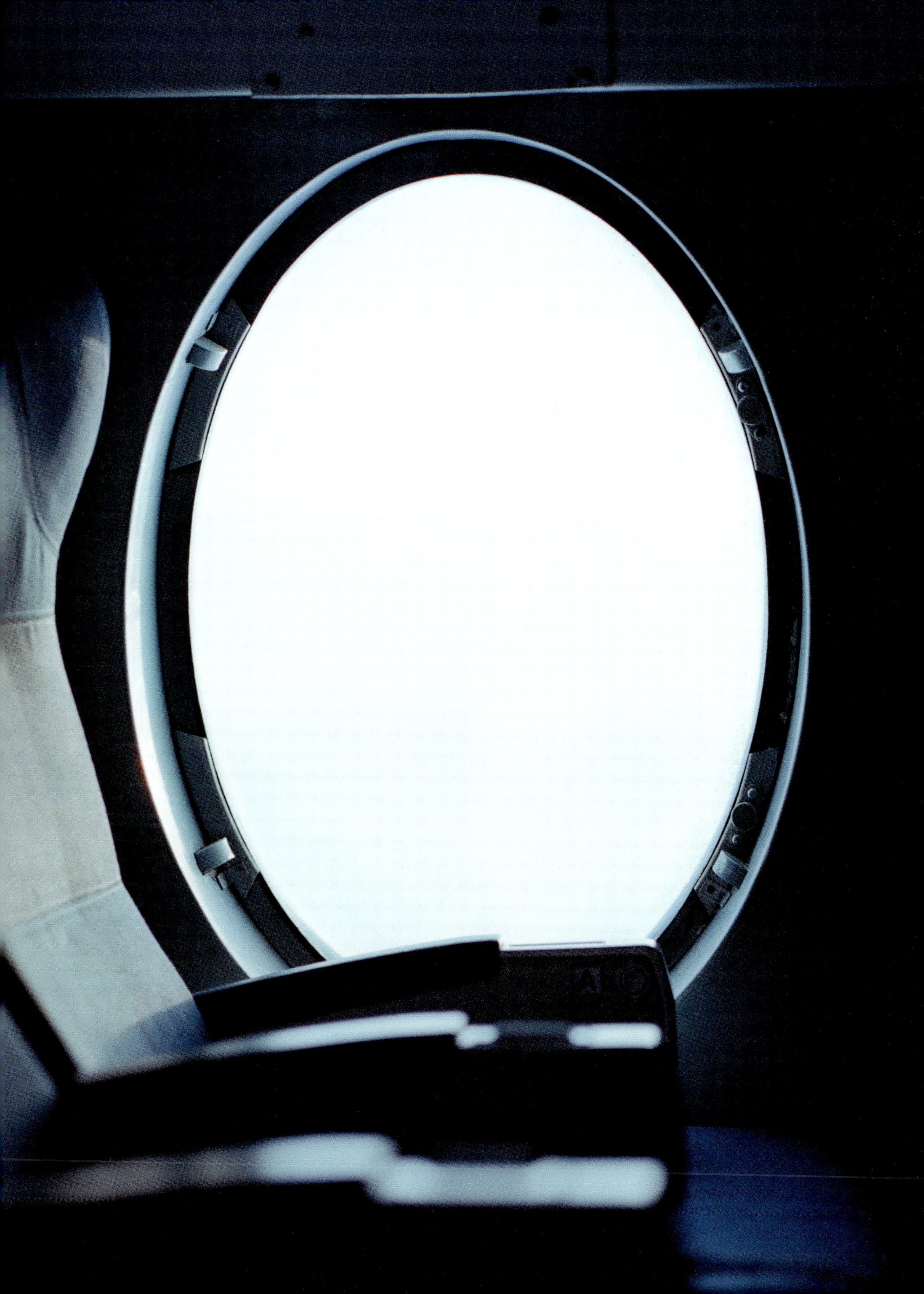

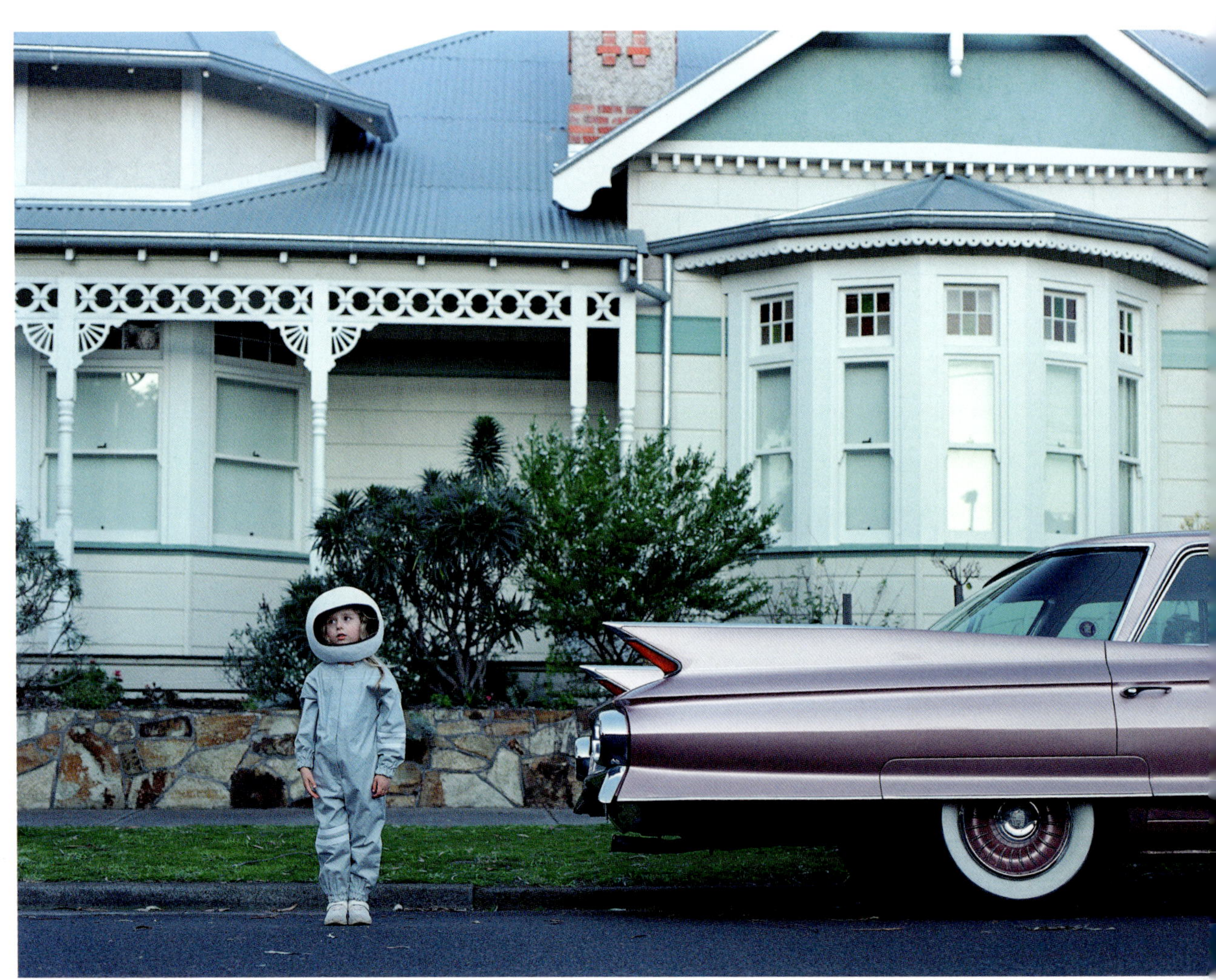

Homecoming

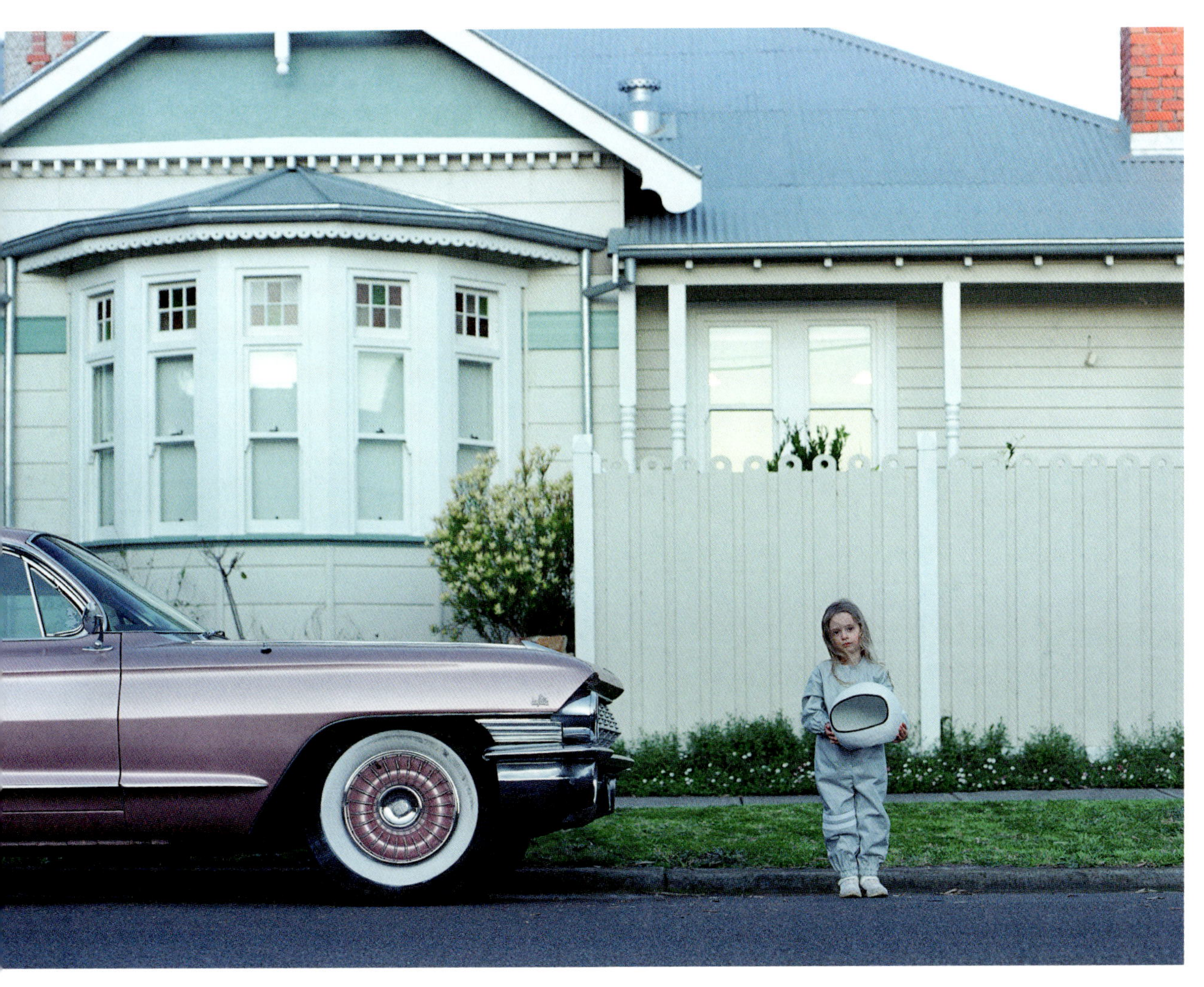

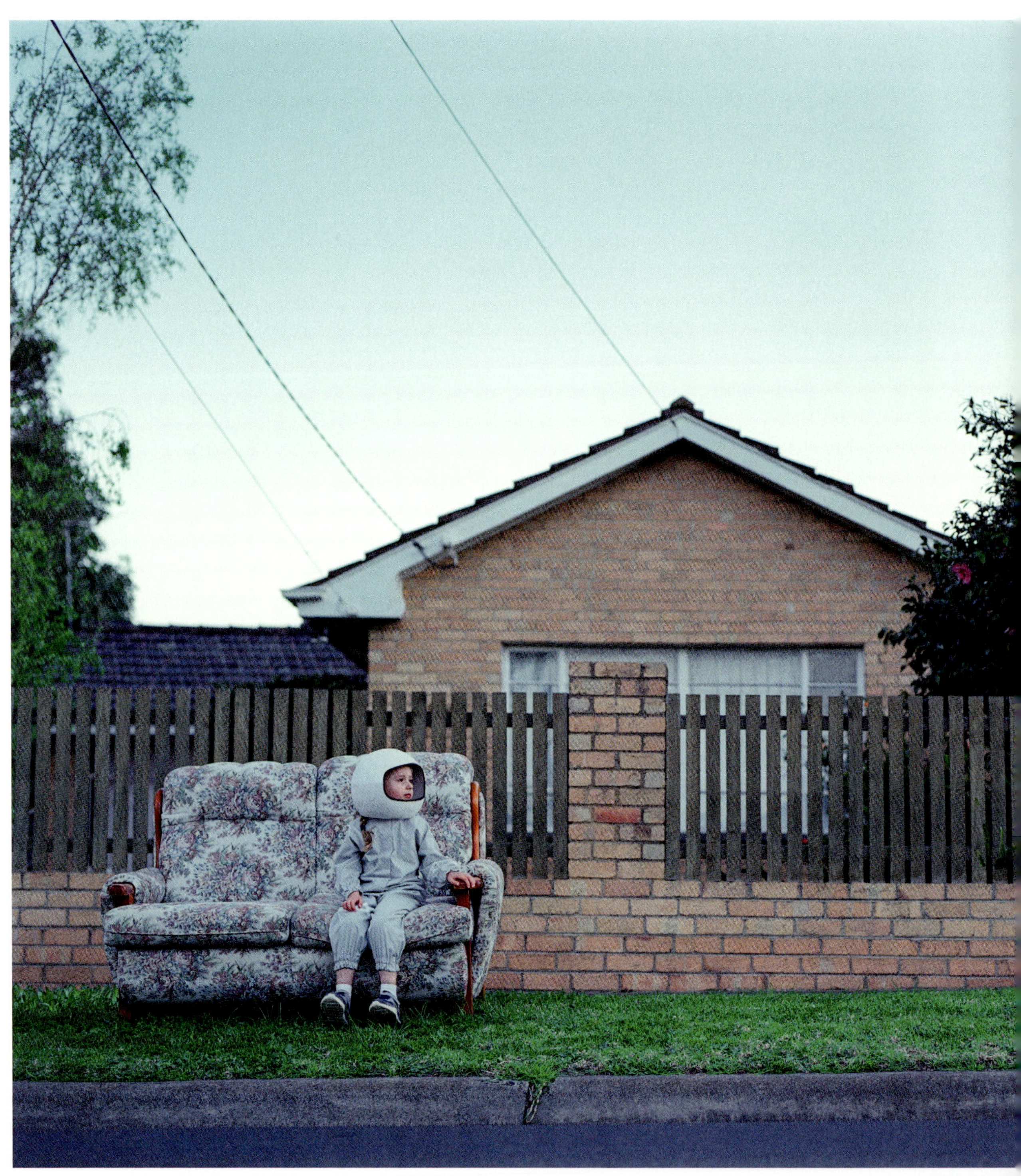

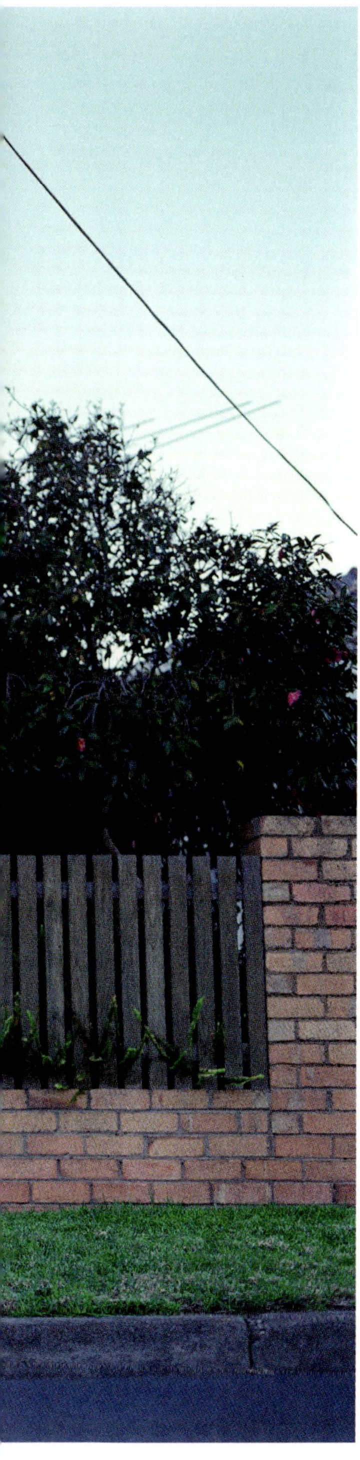

So Near, Sofa

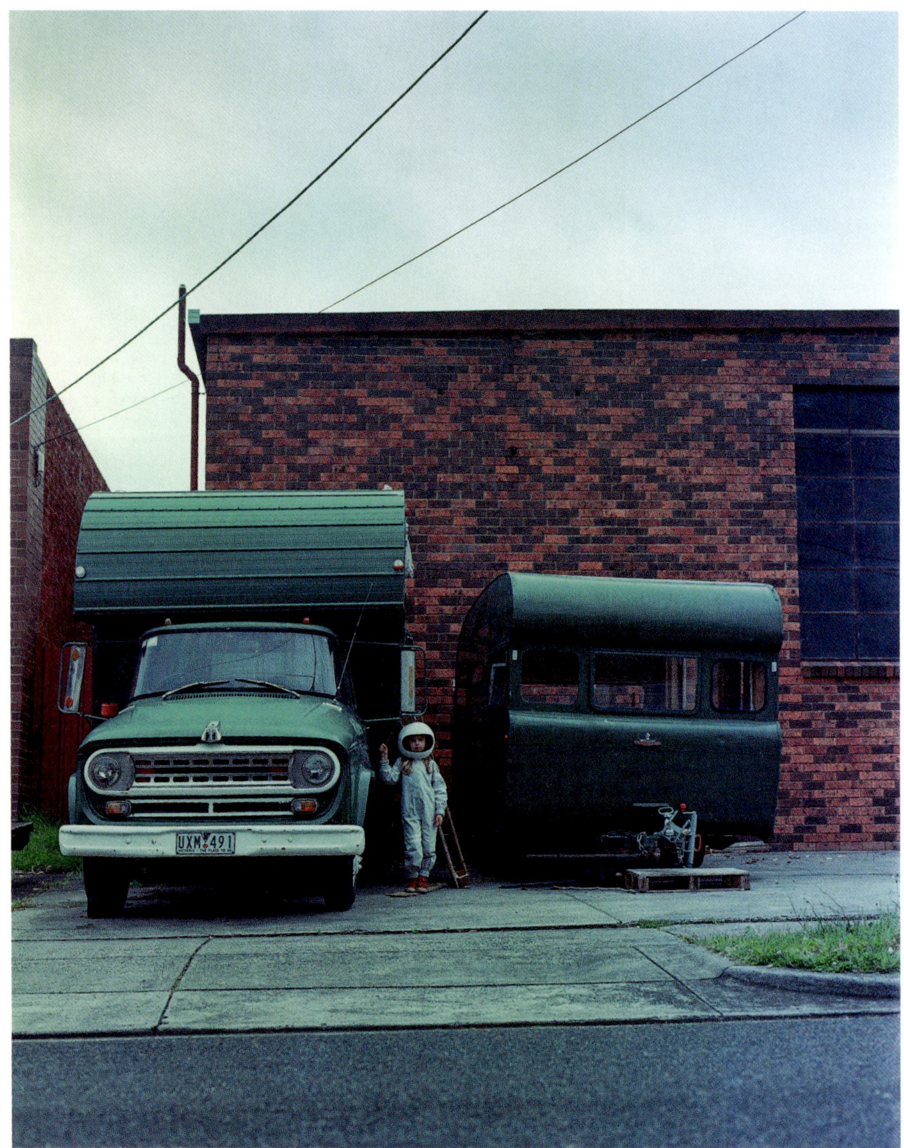

The Wayfarer

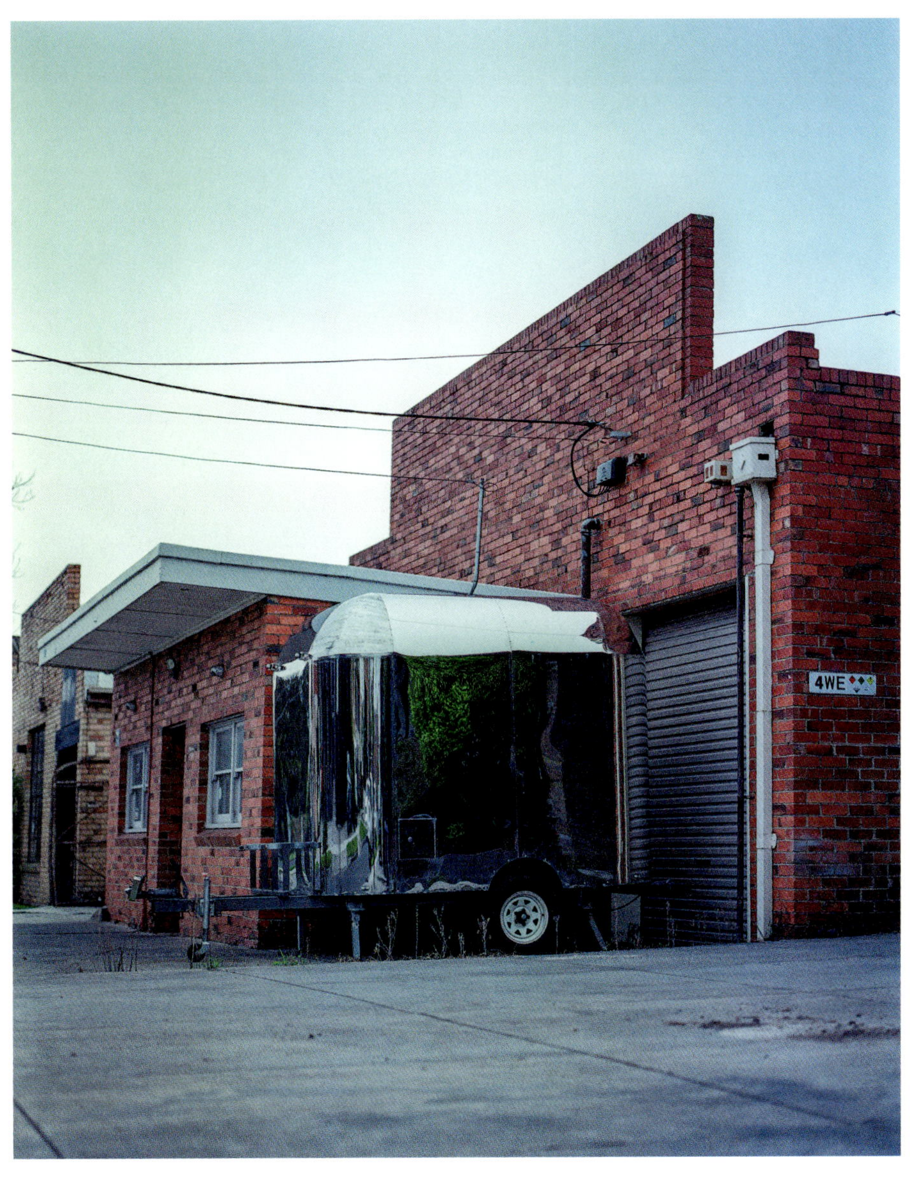
4WE

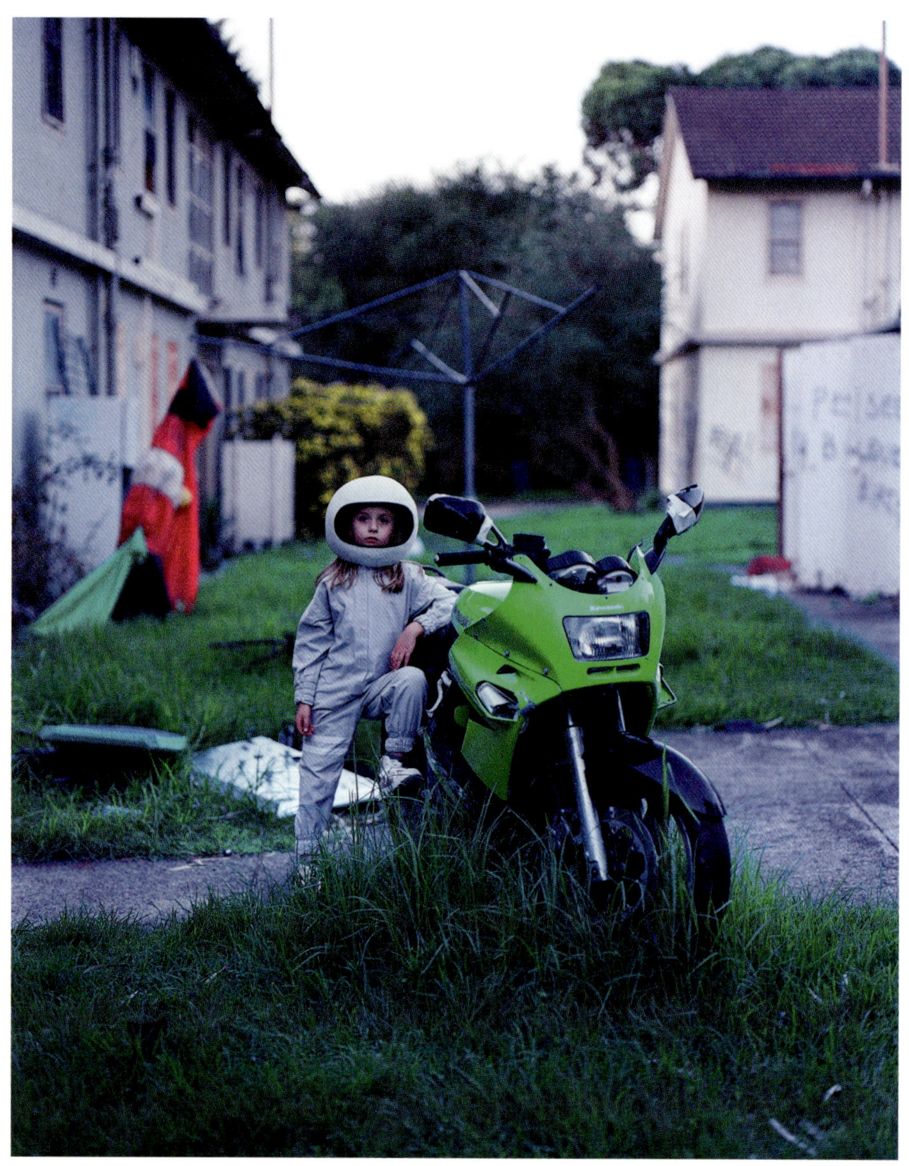

> The Antenna

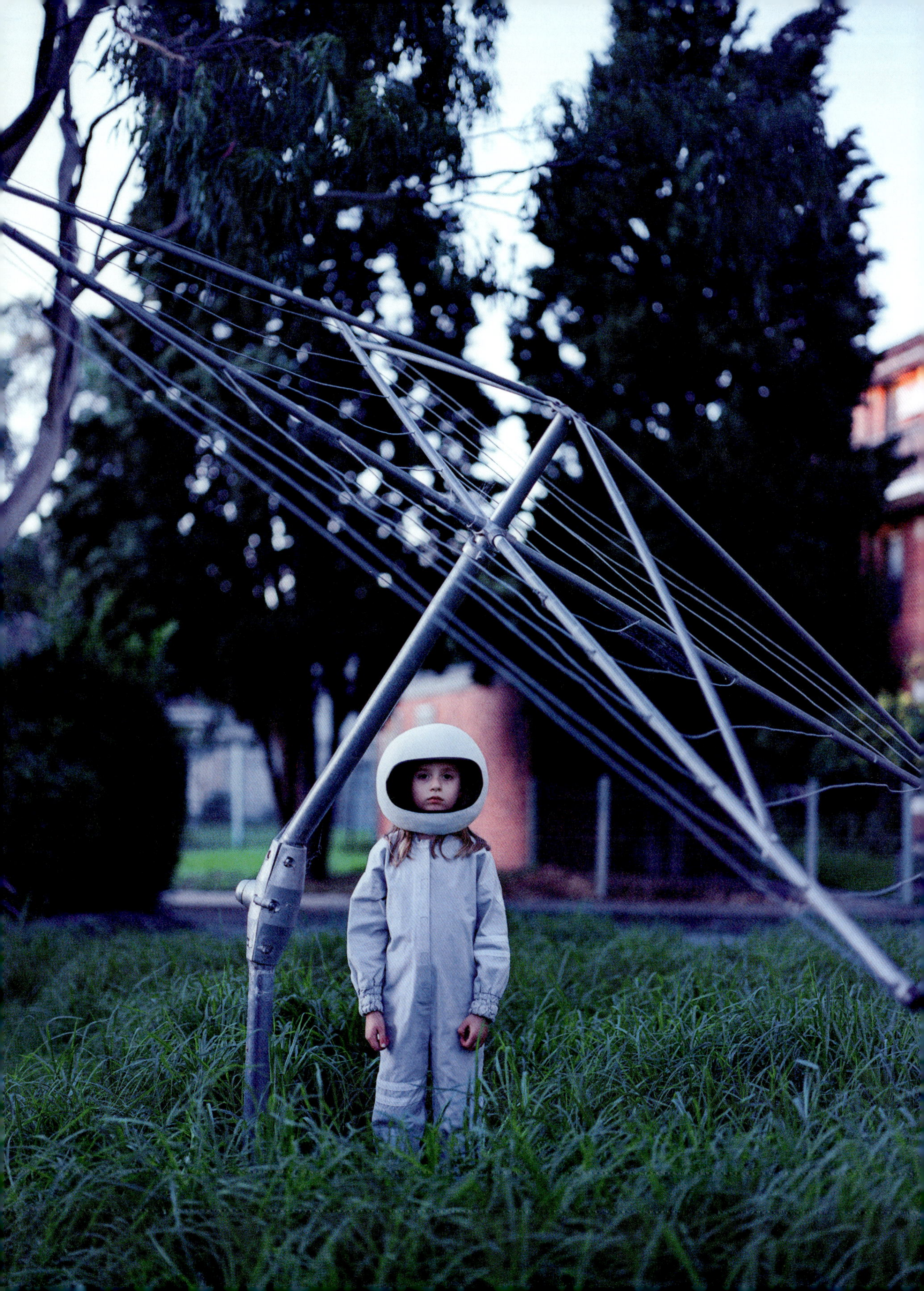

Stop No. 1

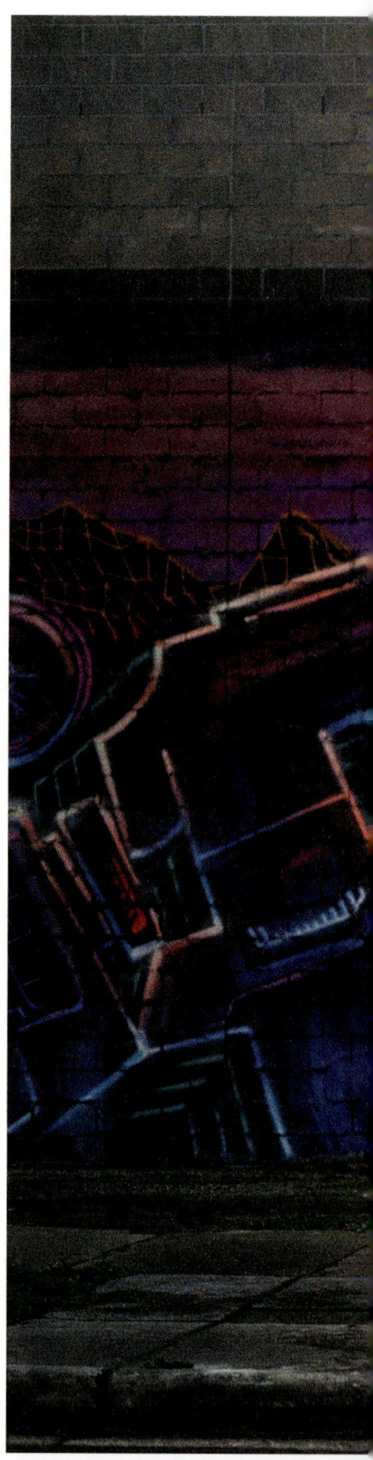

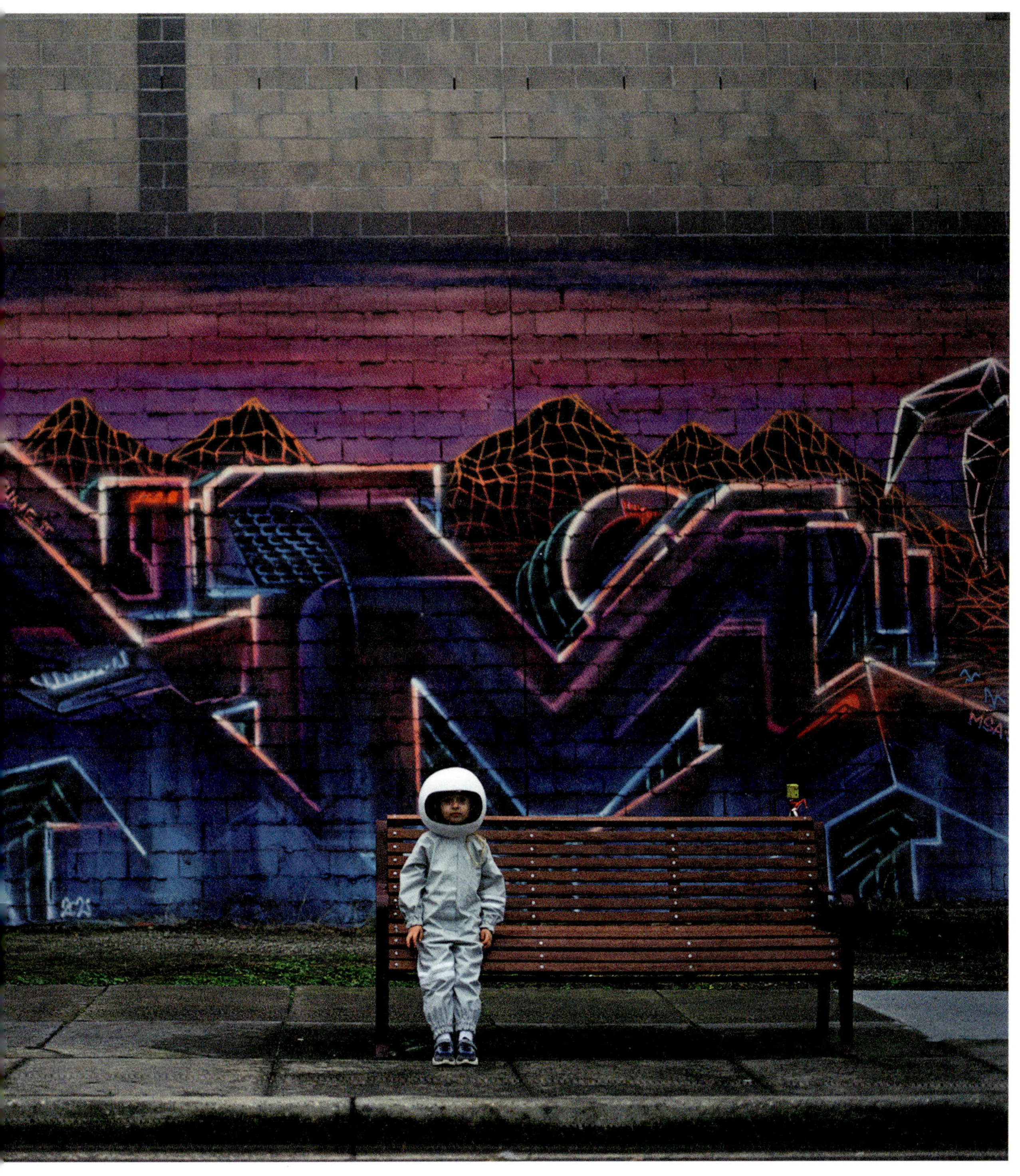

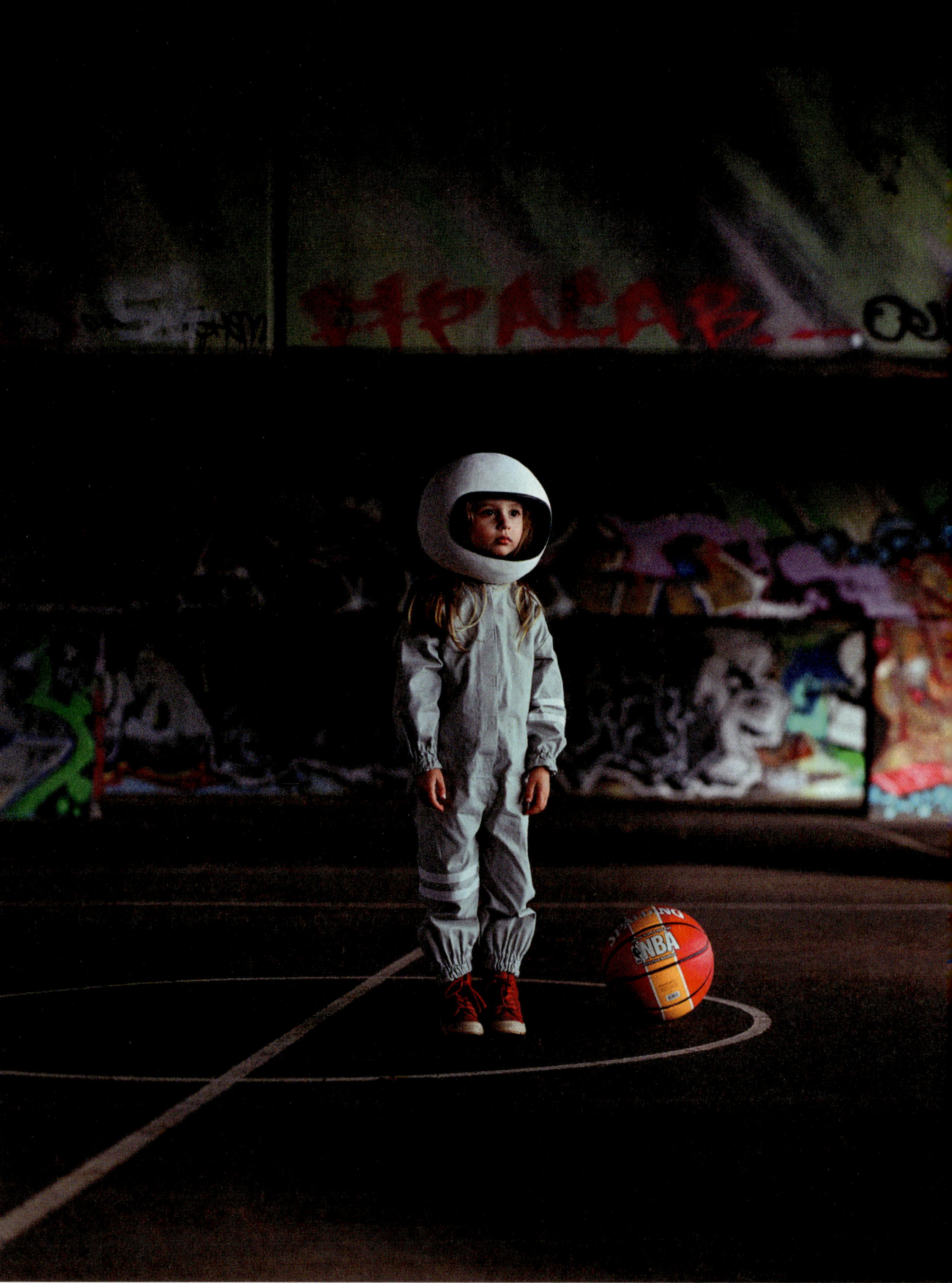
NBA

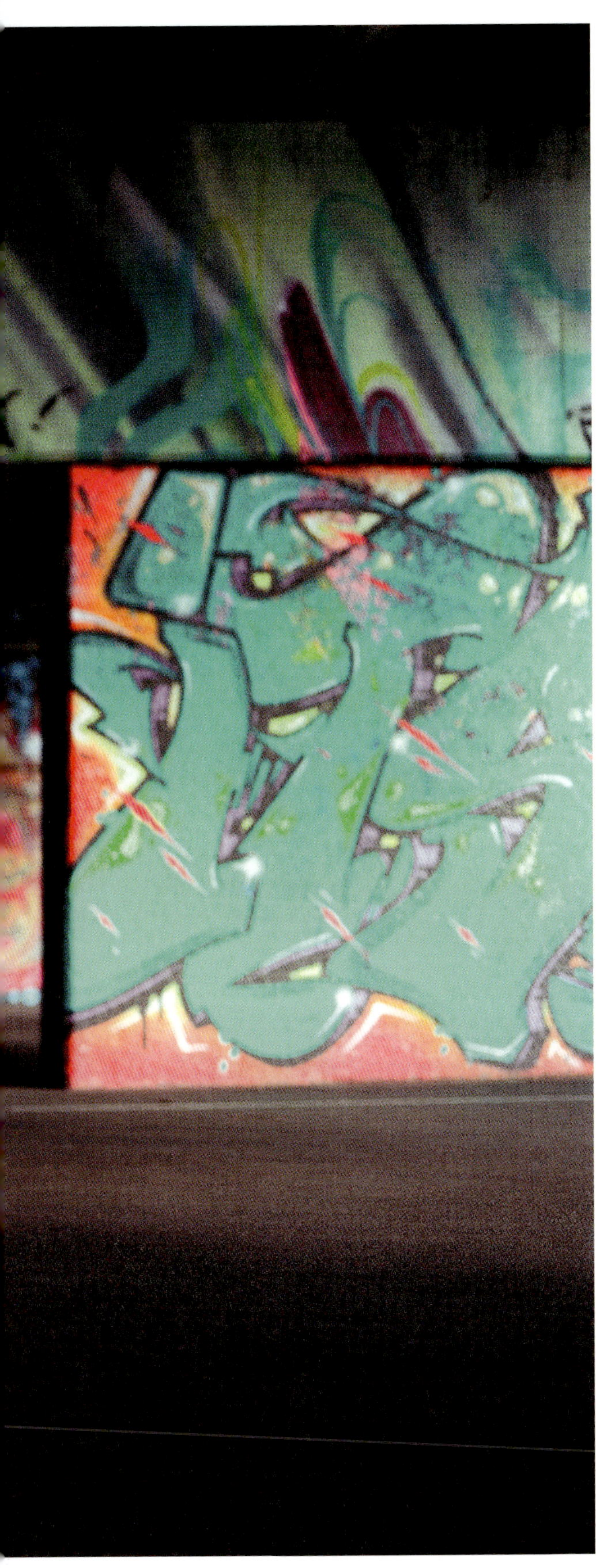

Hope was a scarce resource.
Imagination was
an essential life skill.

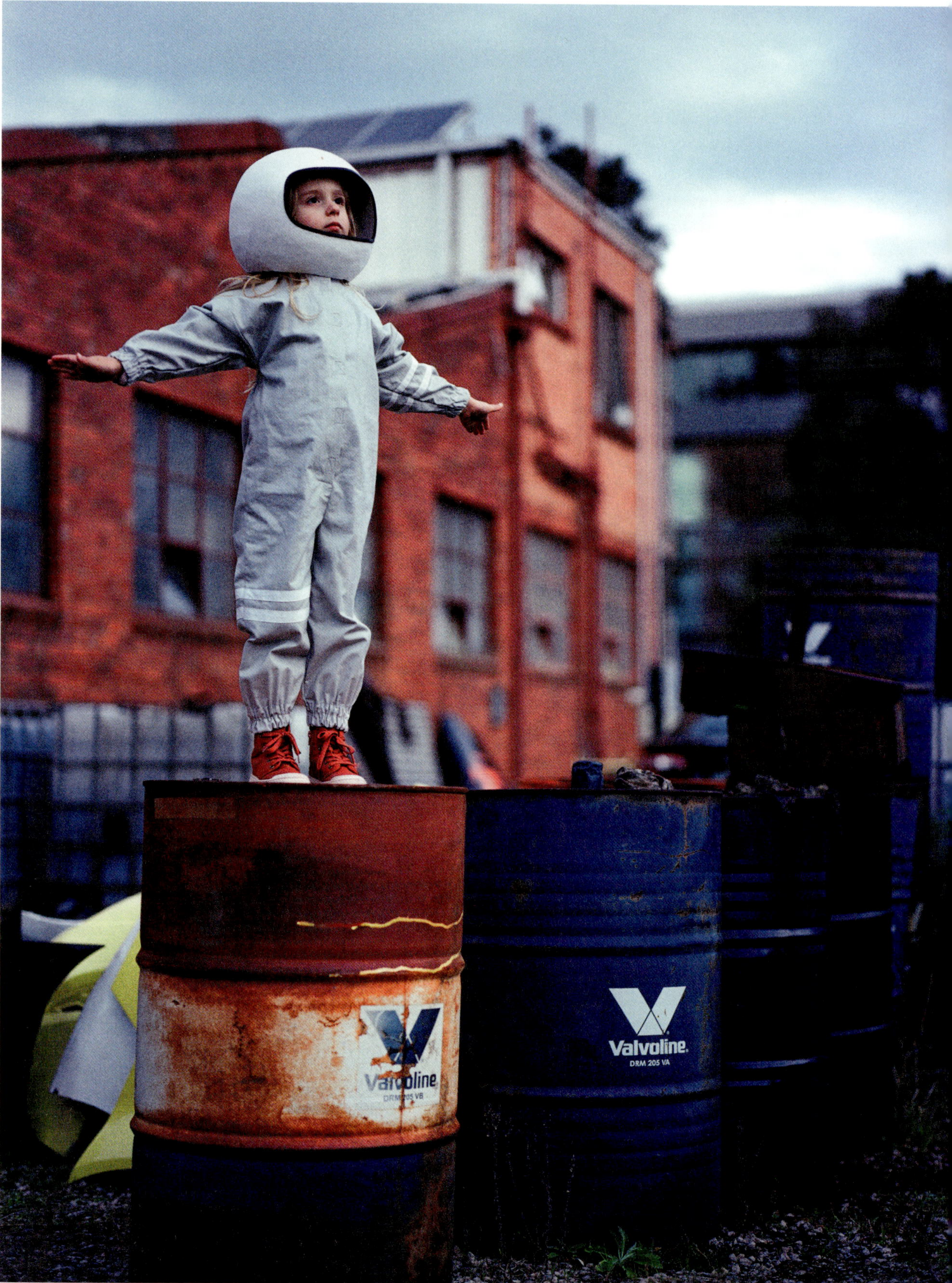
Valvoline
DRM 205 VA

> No Man's Land

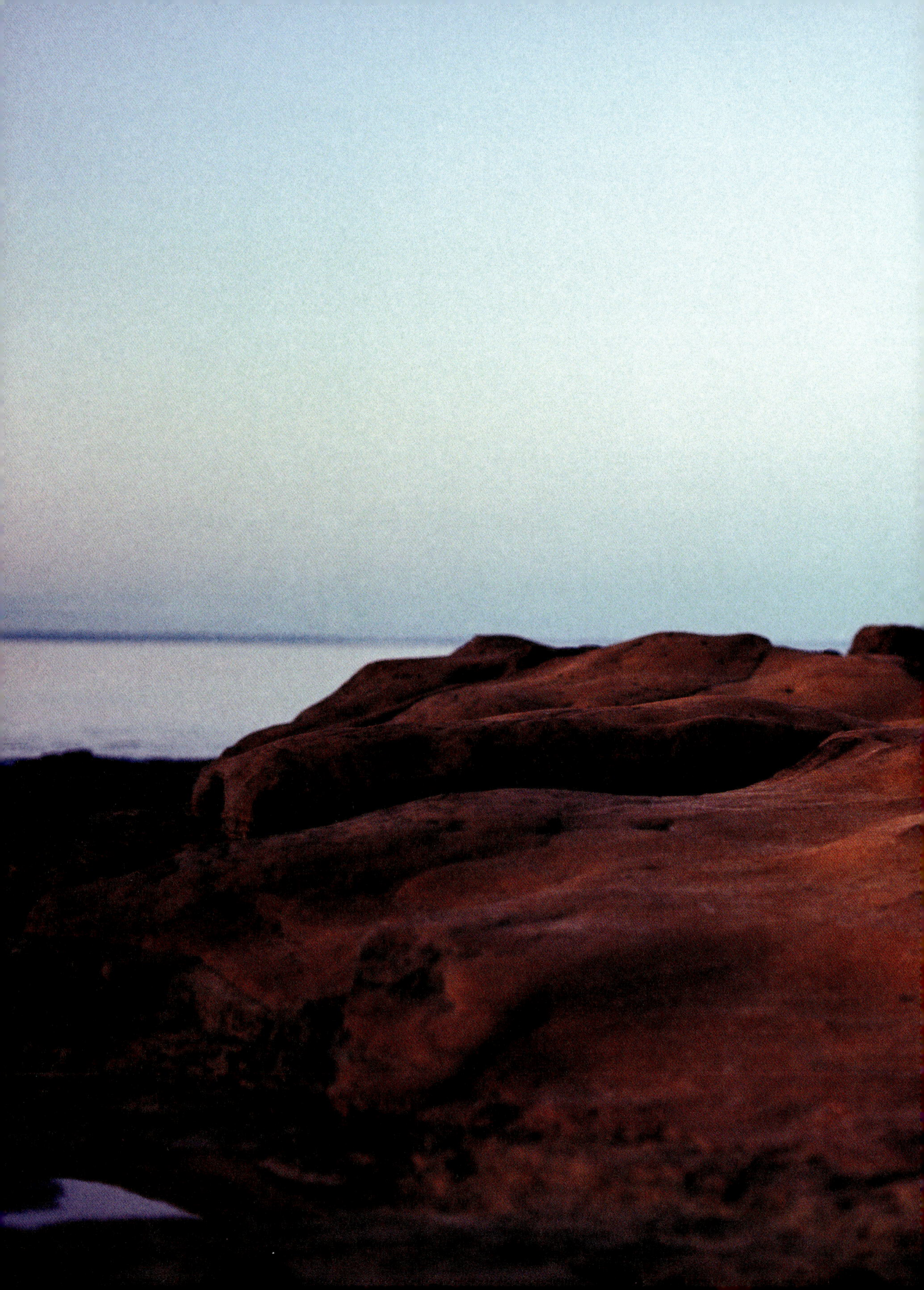

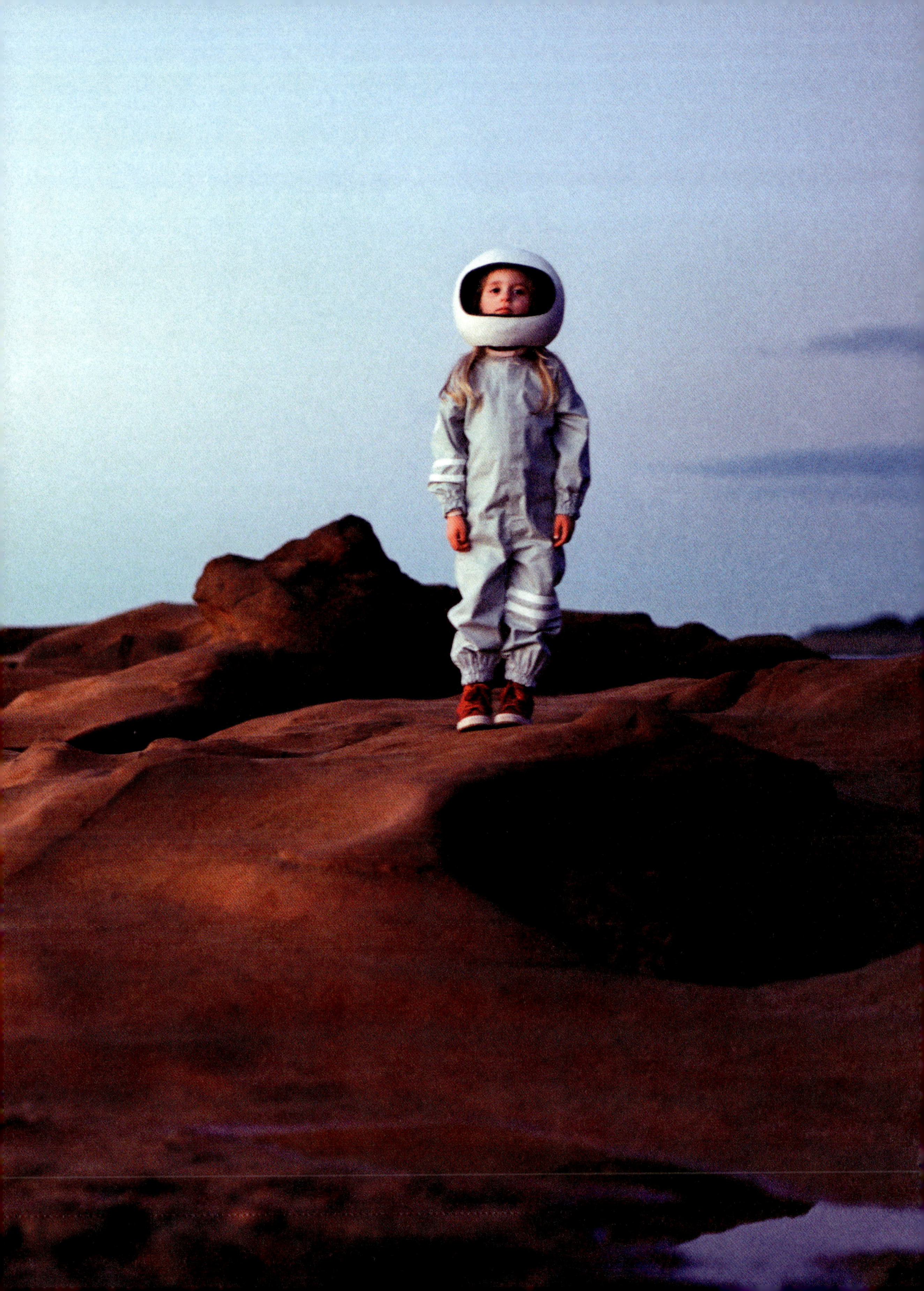

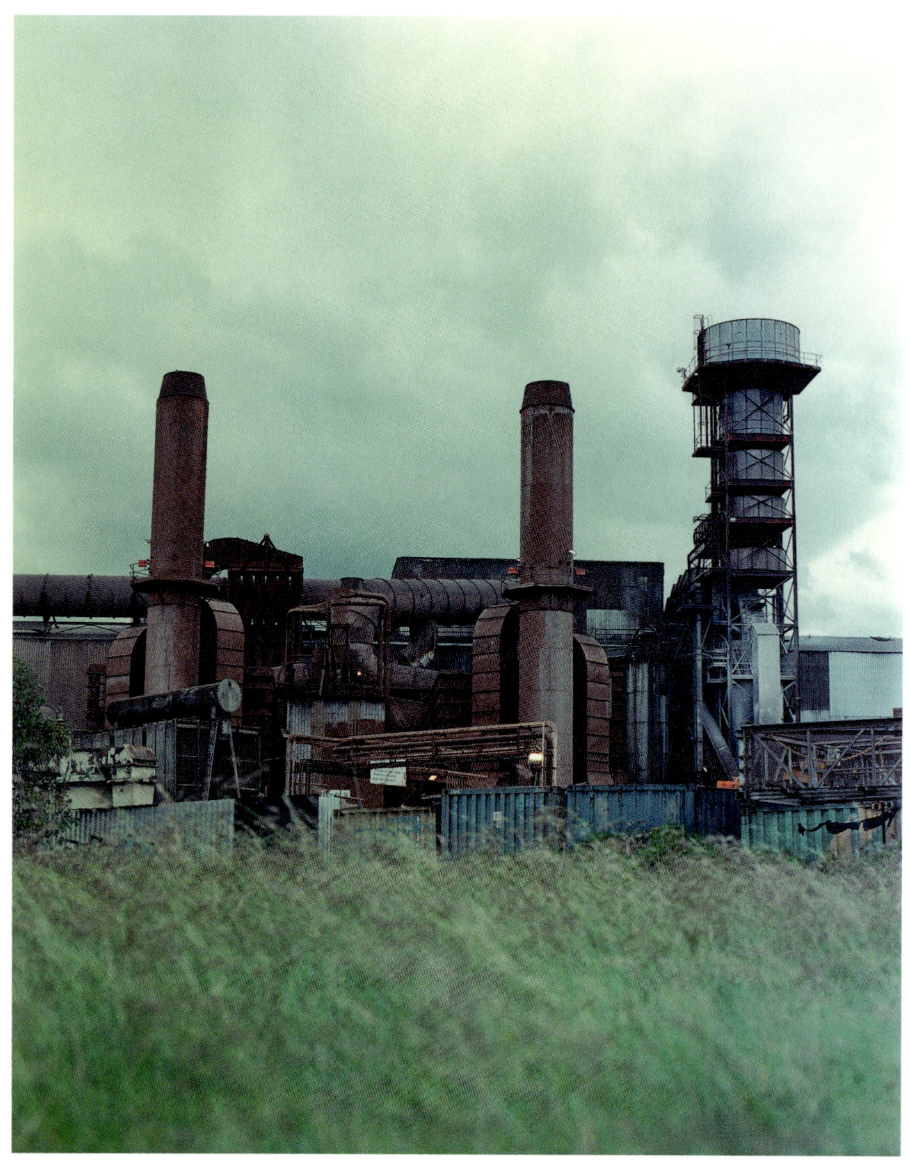

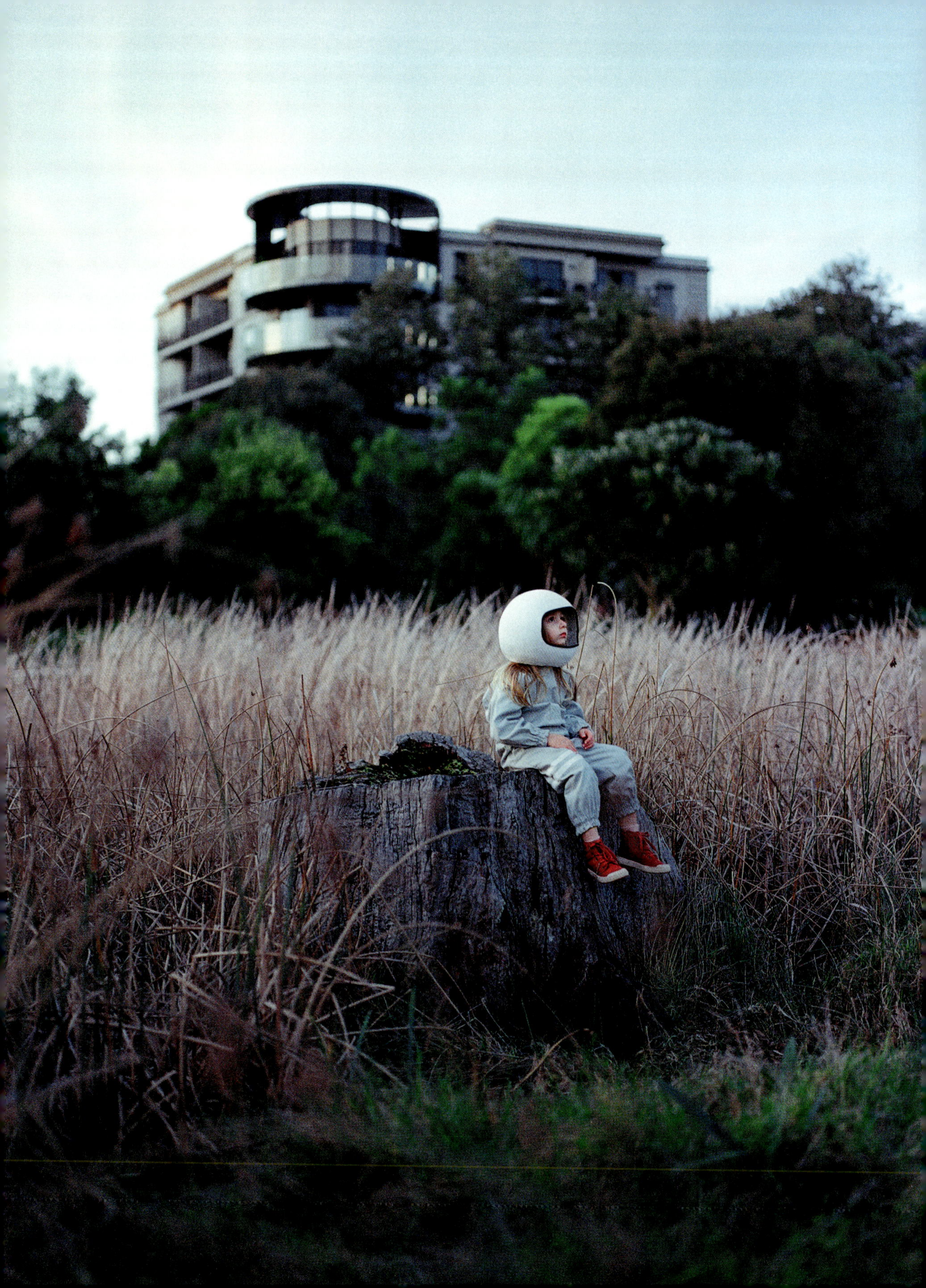

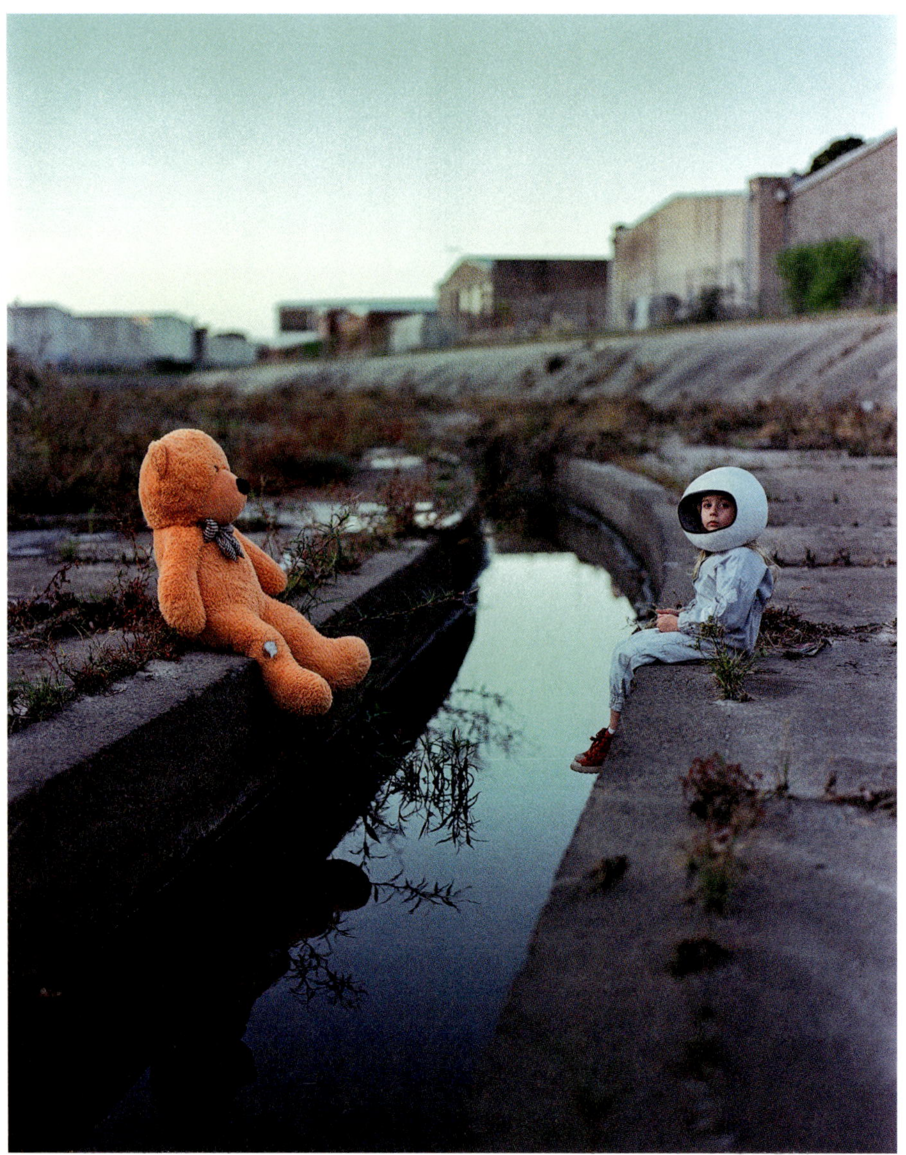

The Encounter

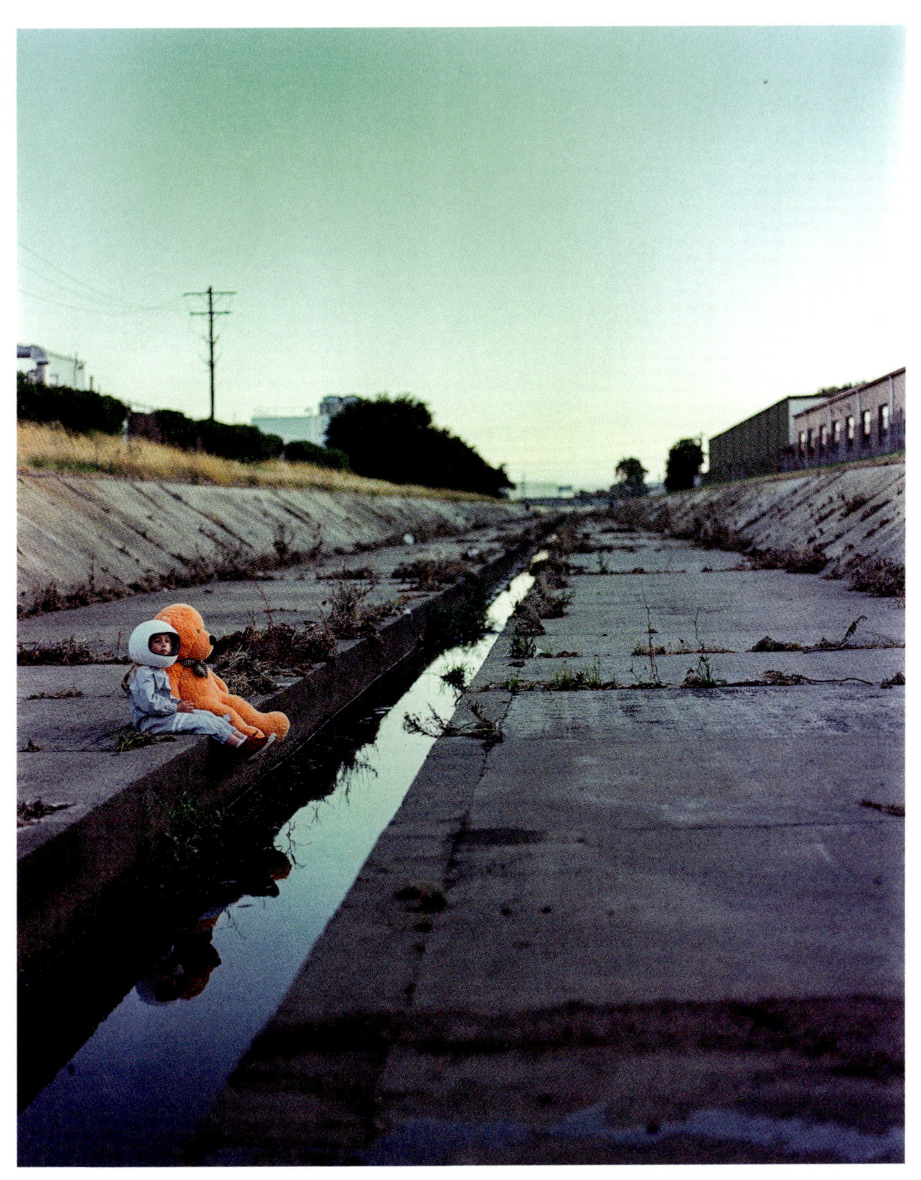

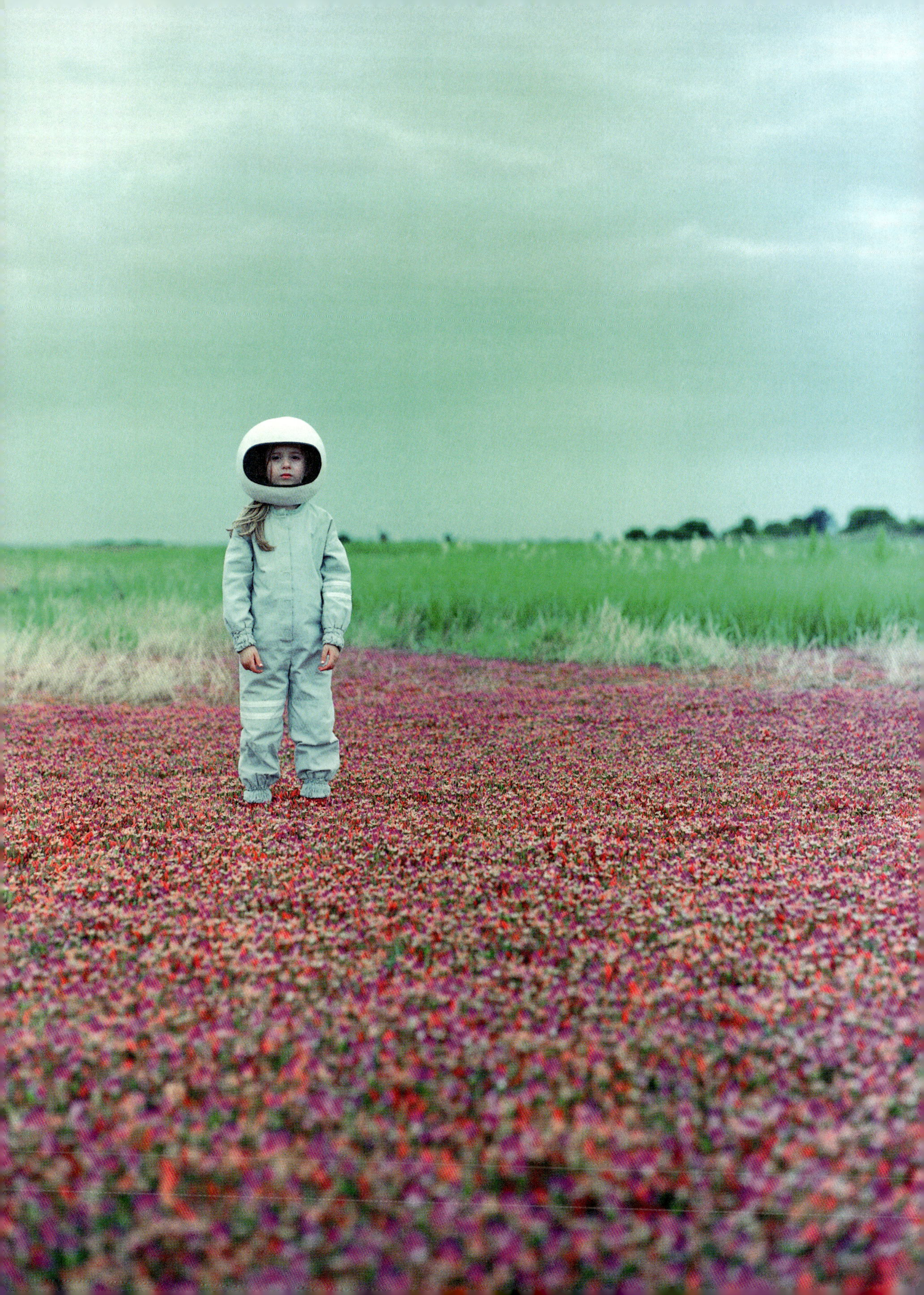

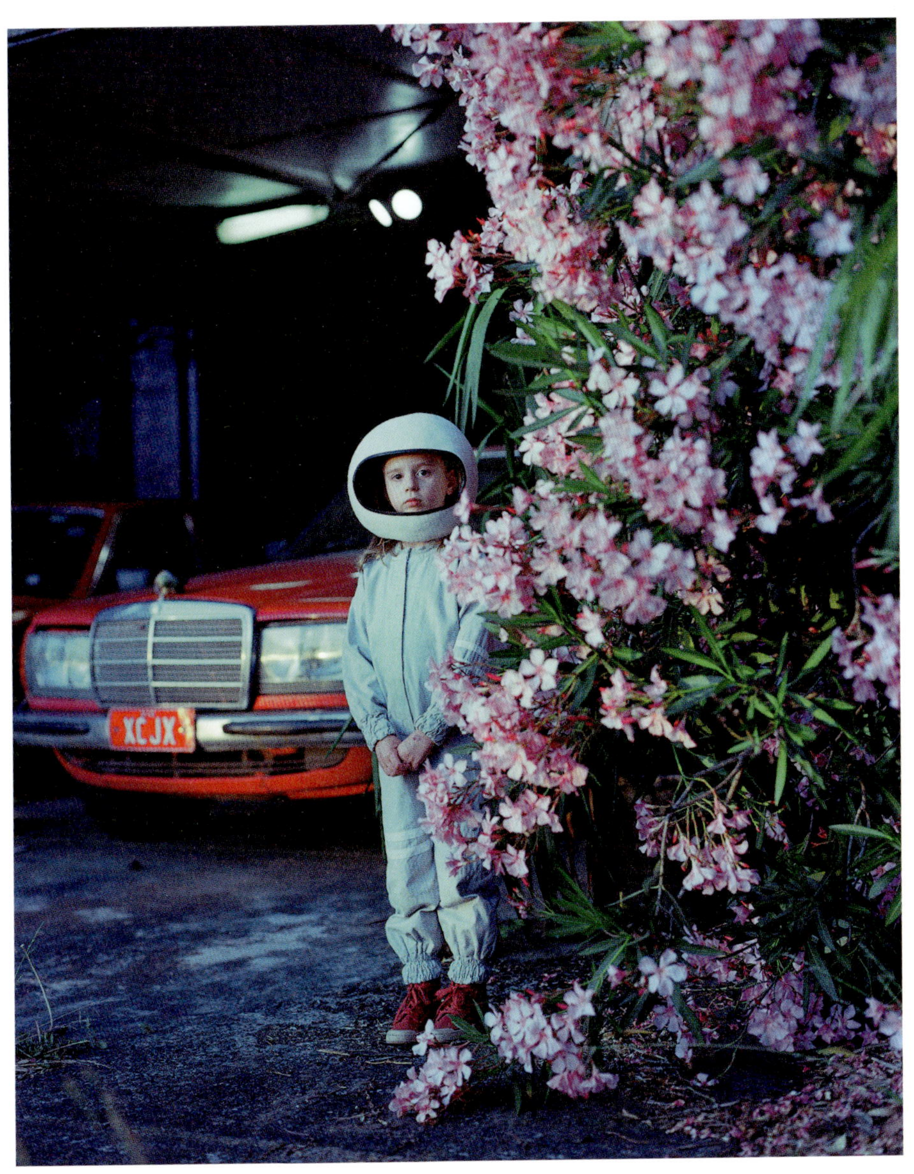
XCJX

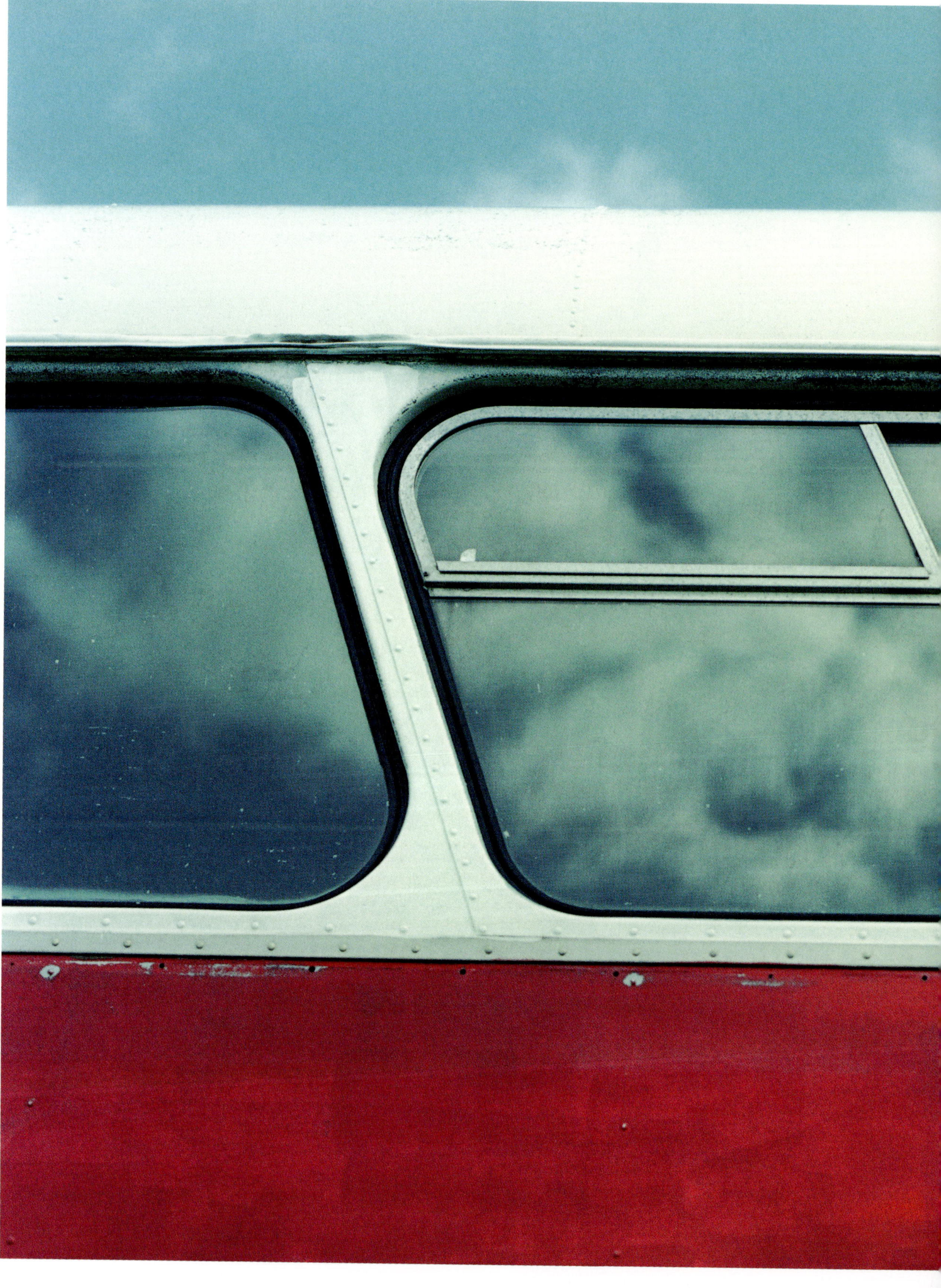

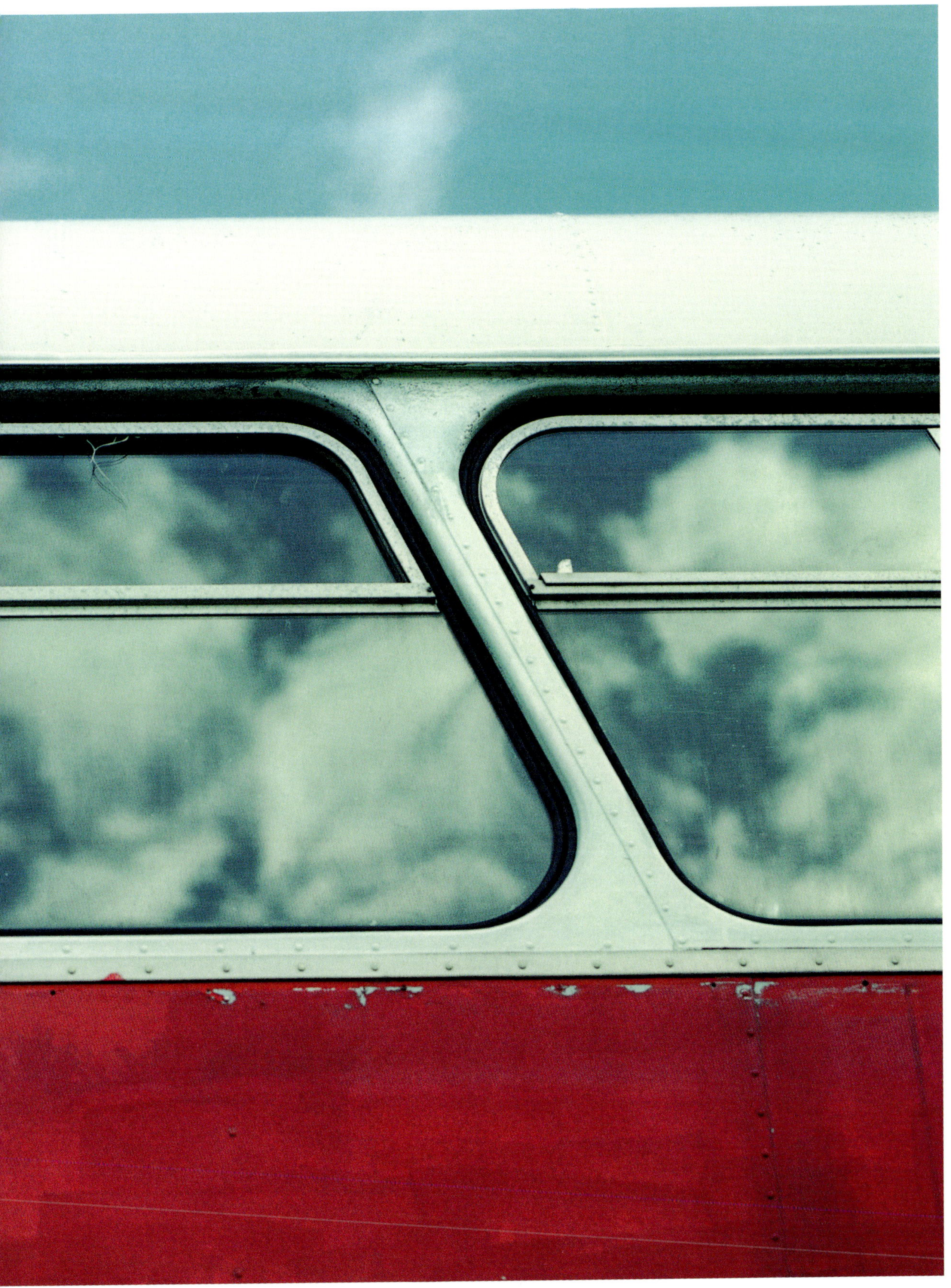

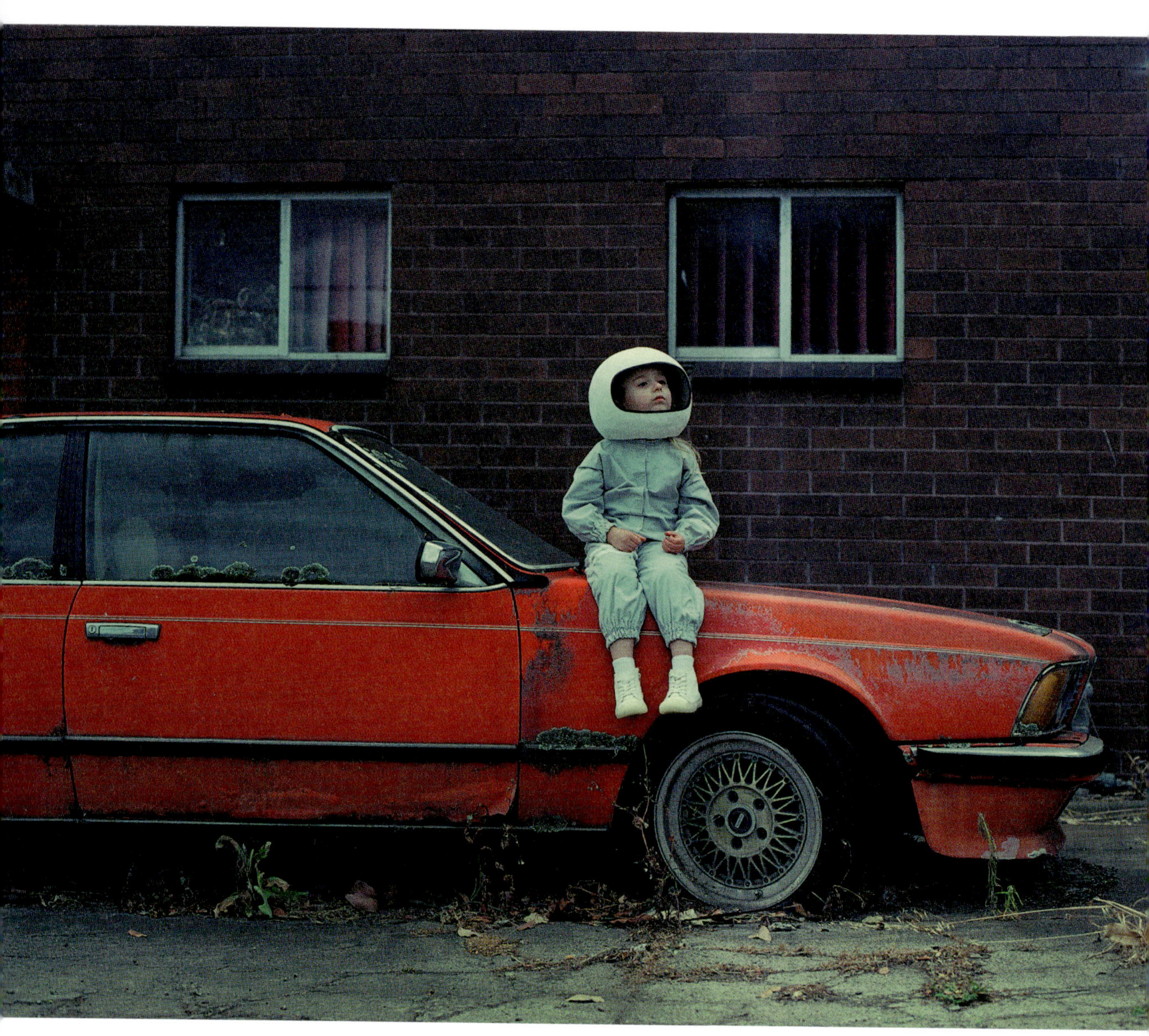

Beneath Maroon Window

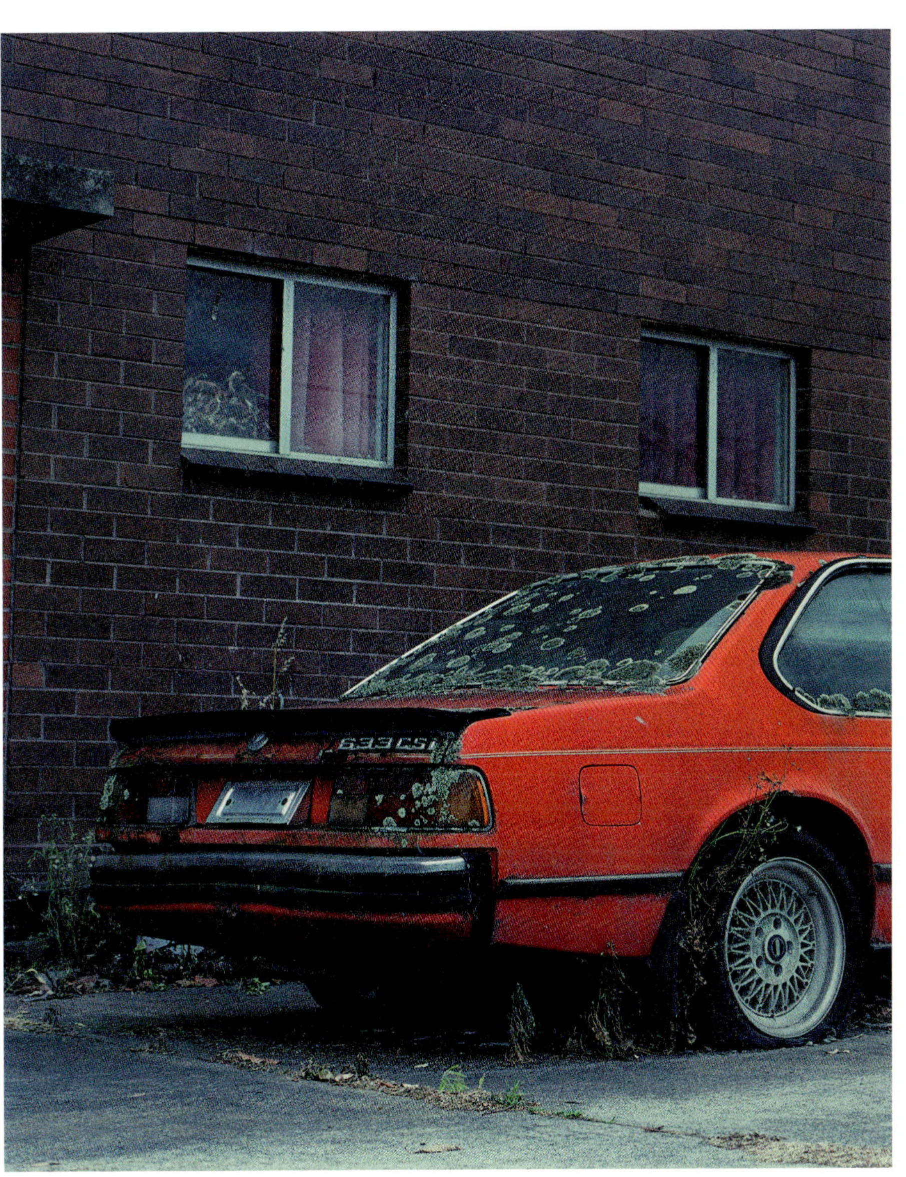
633 CSi

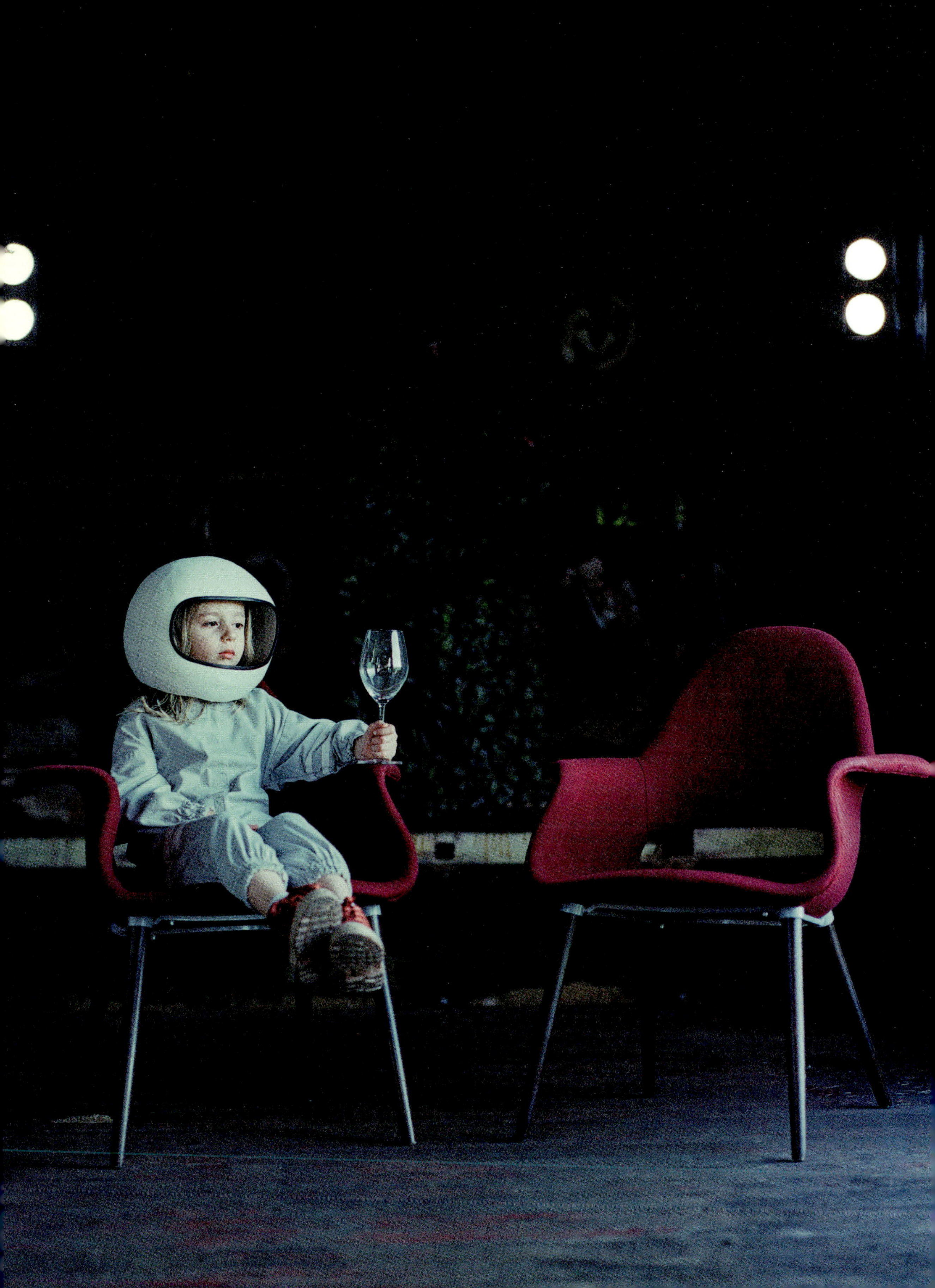

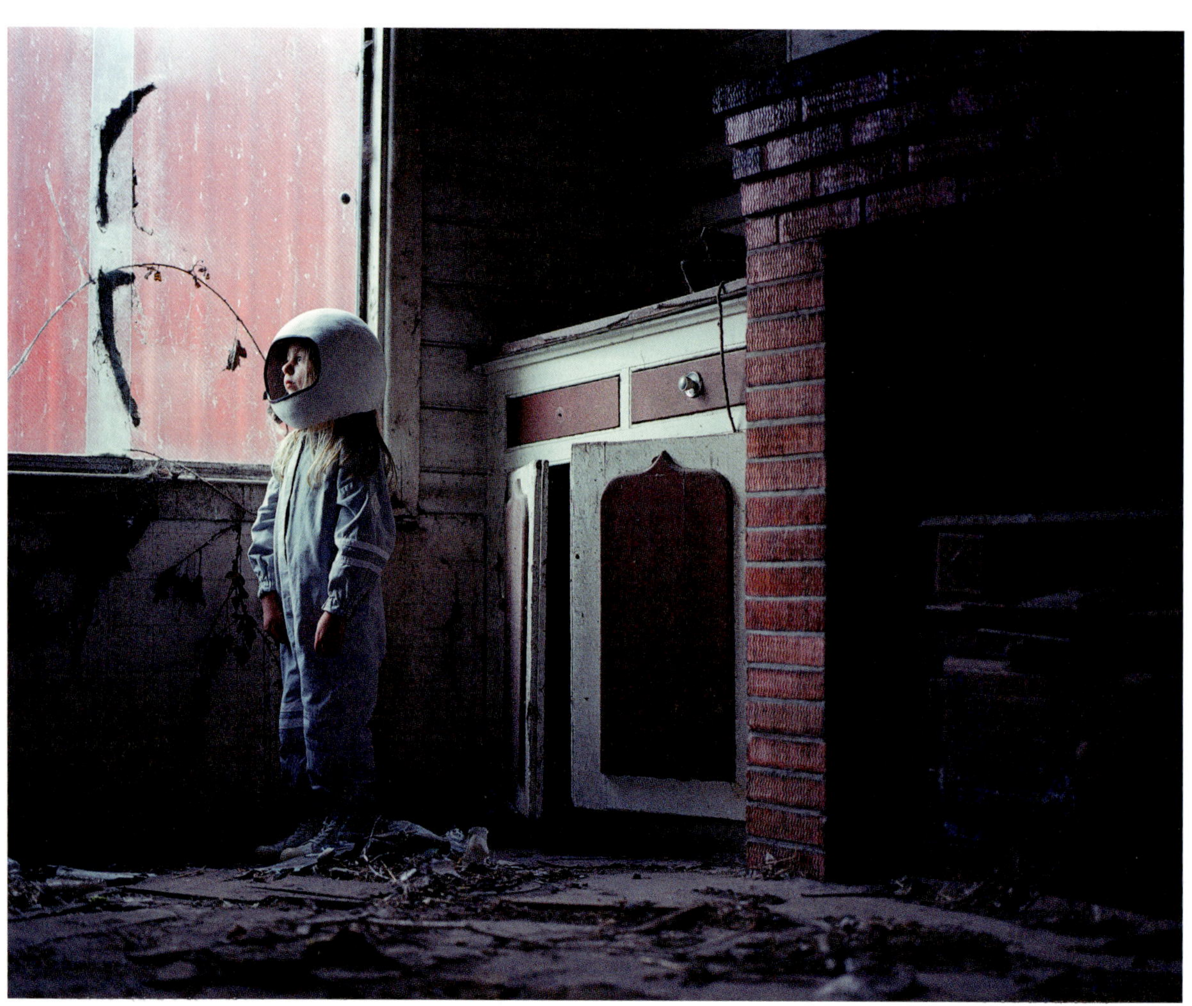

The Heritage

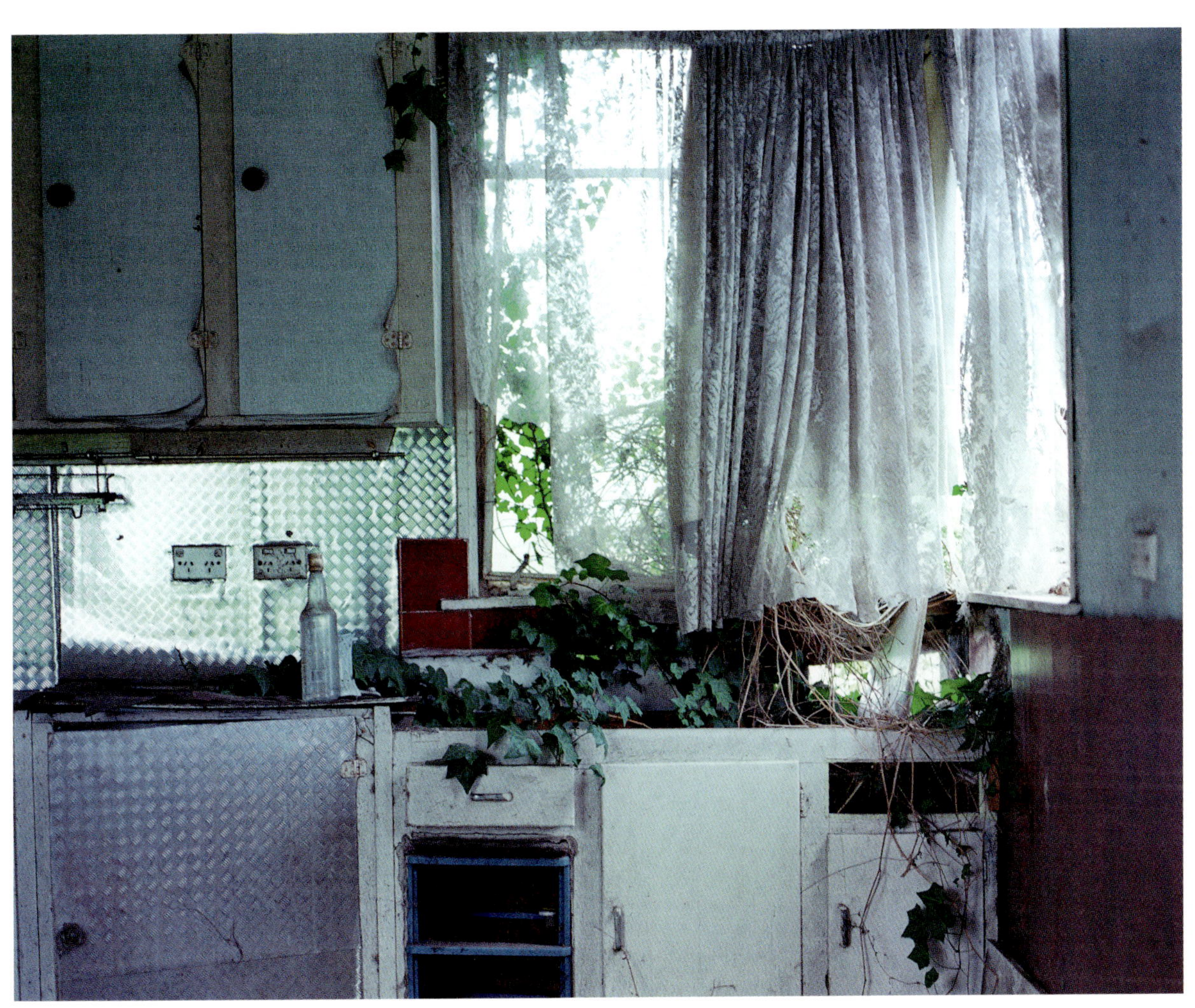

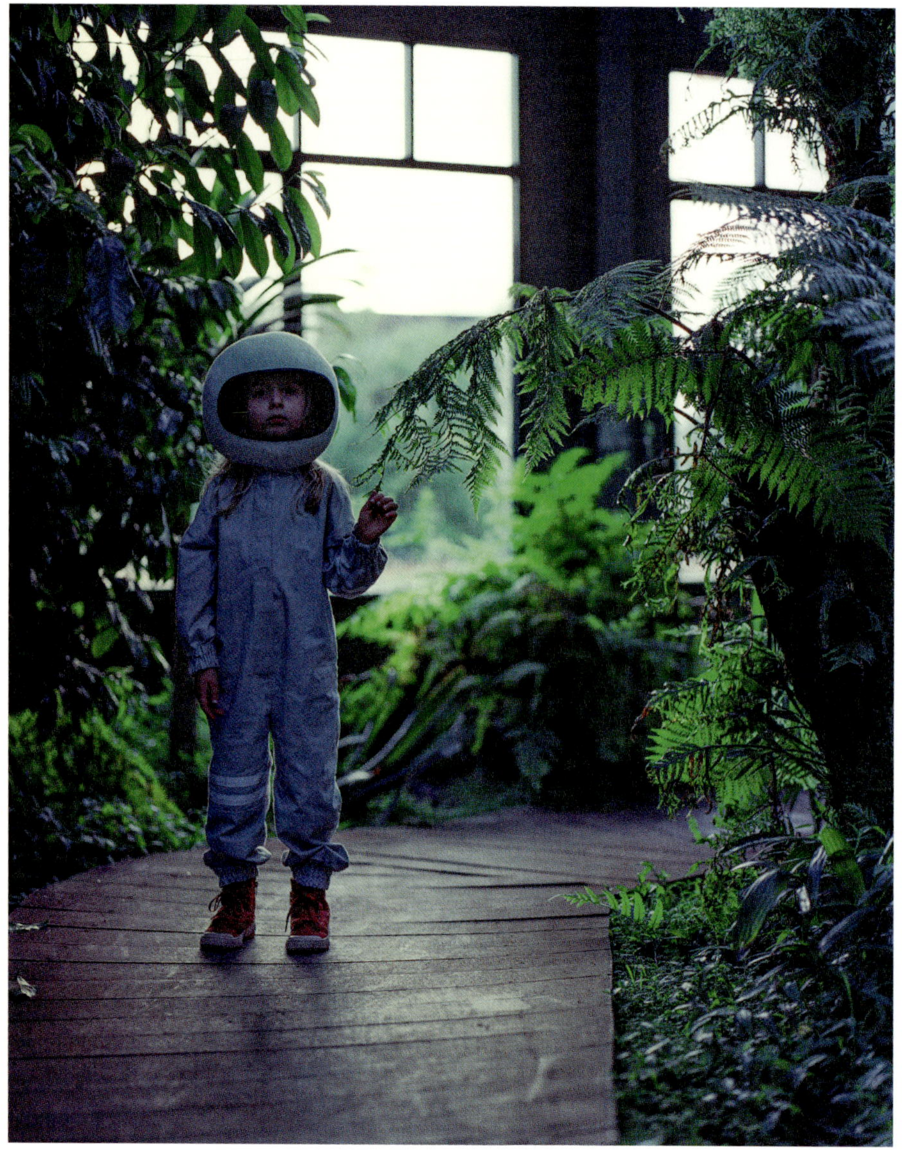

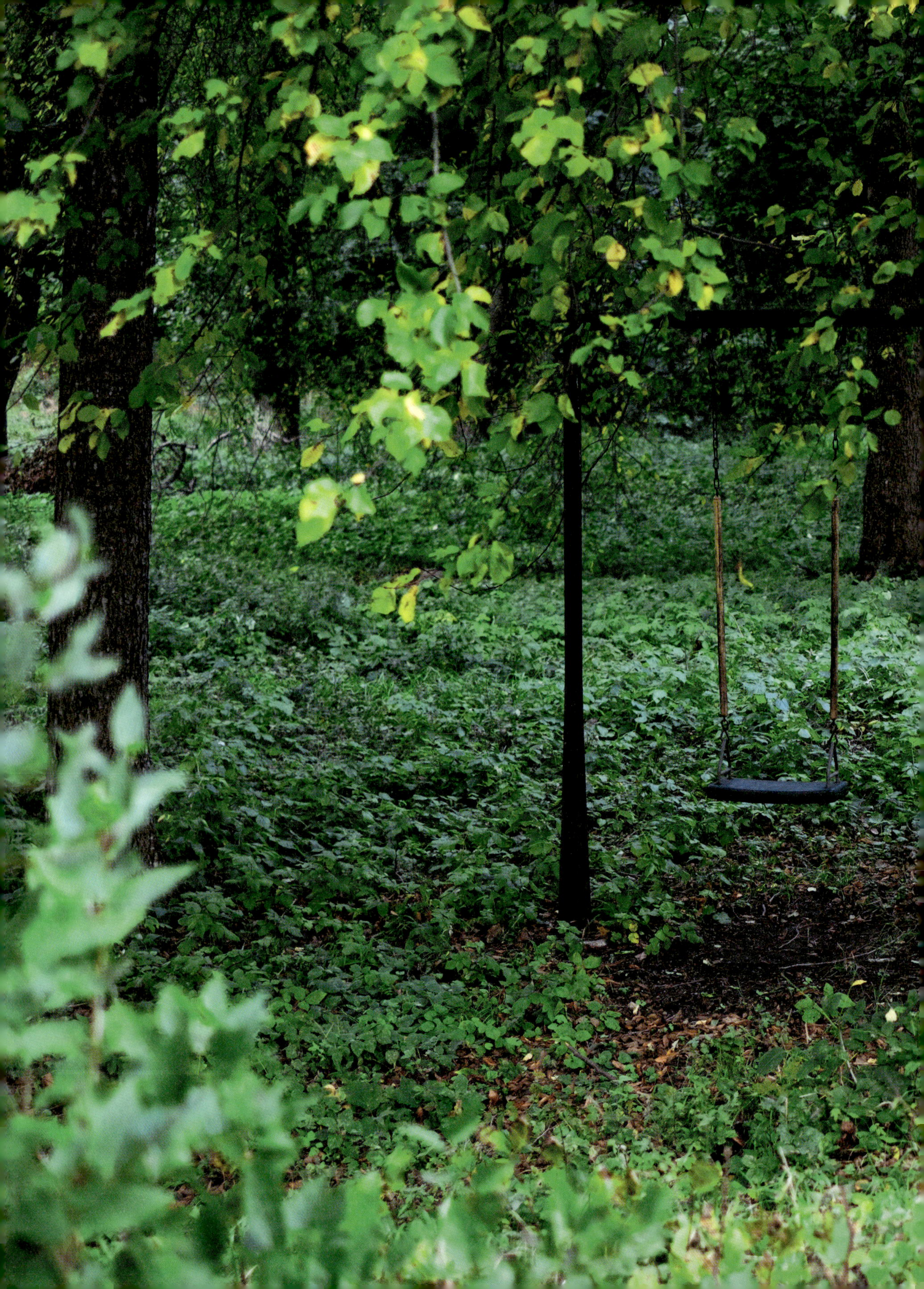

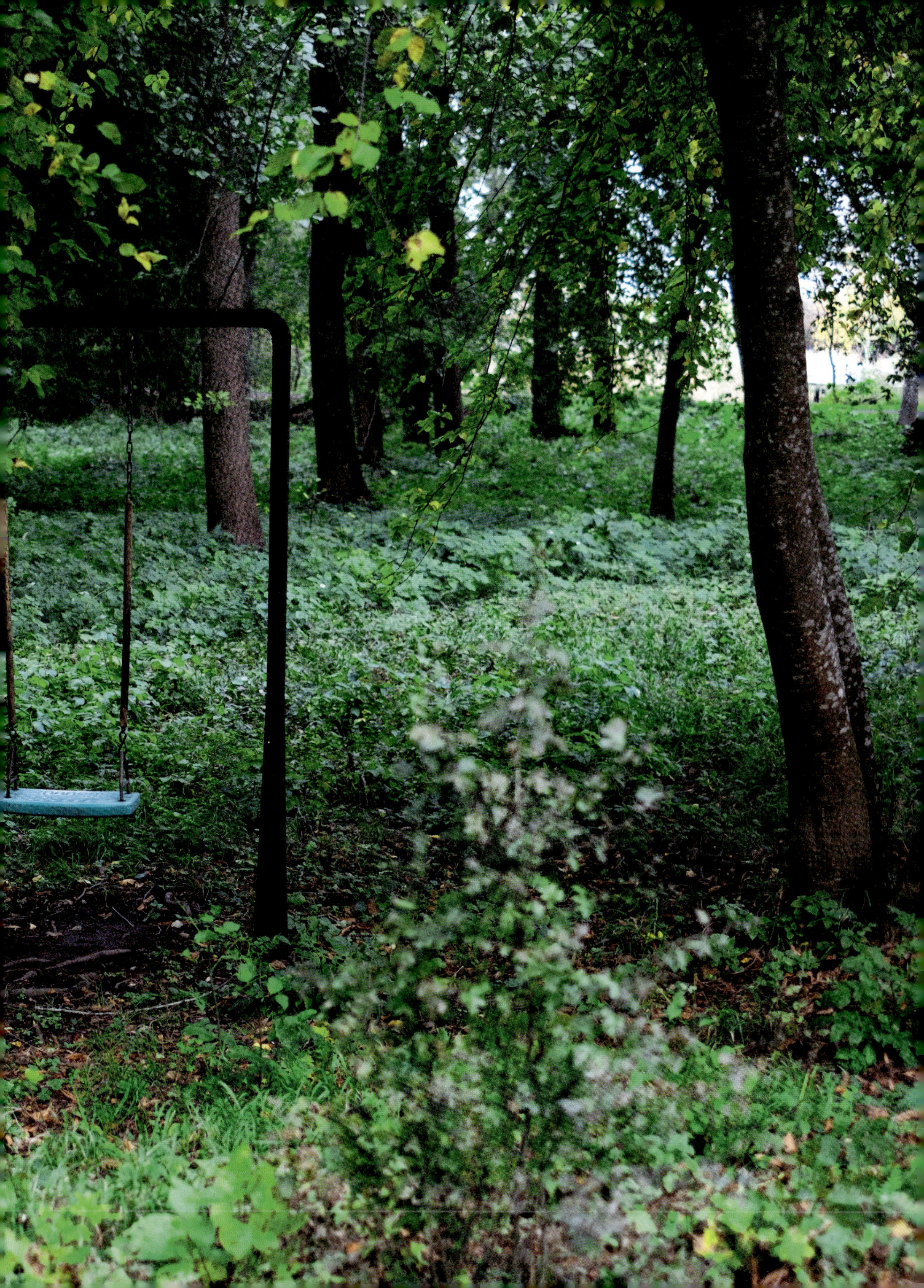

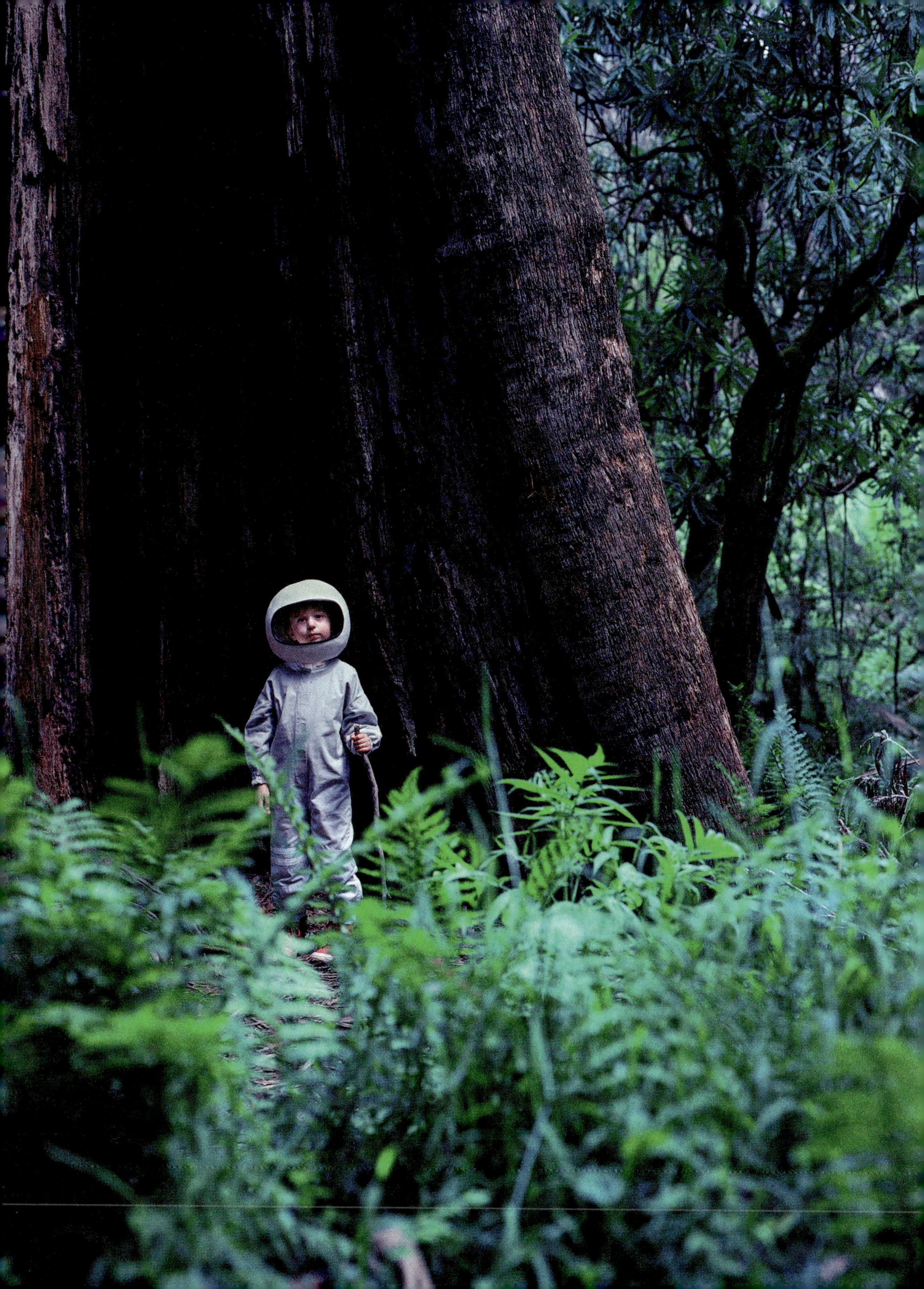

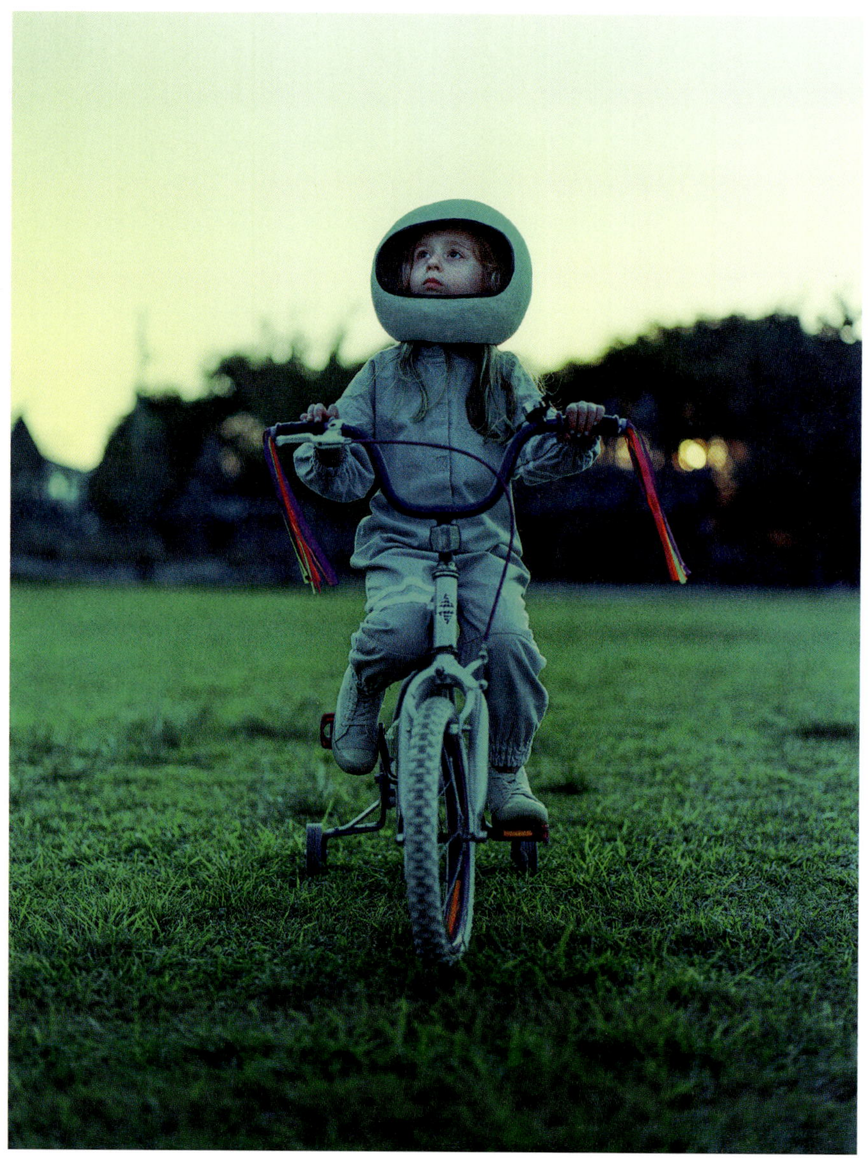

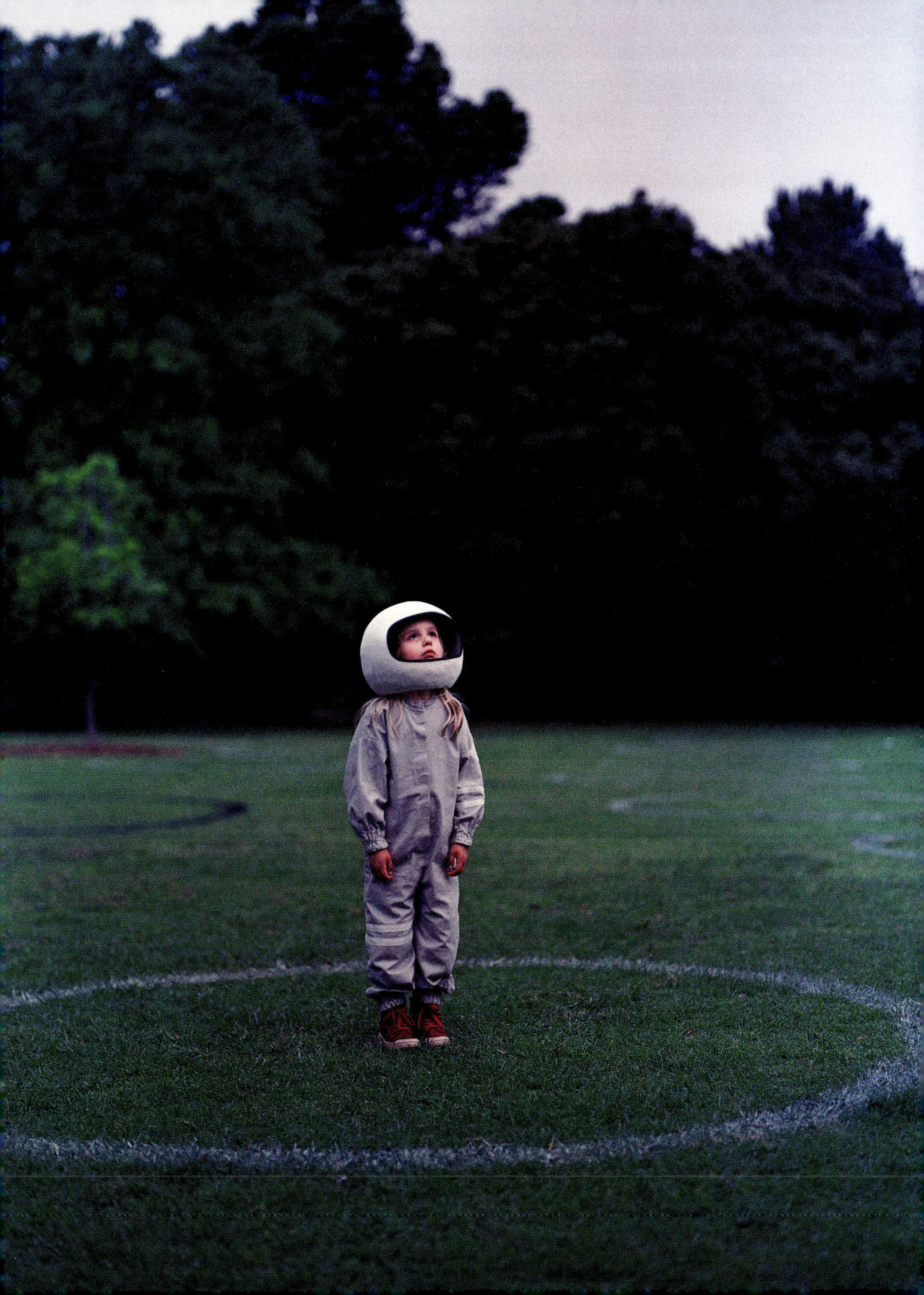

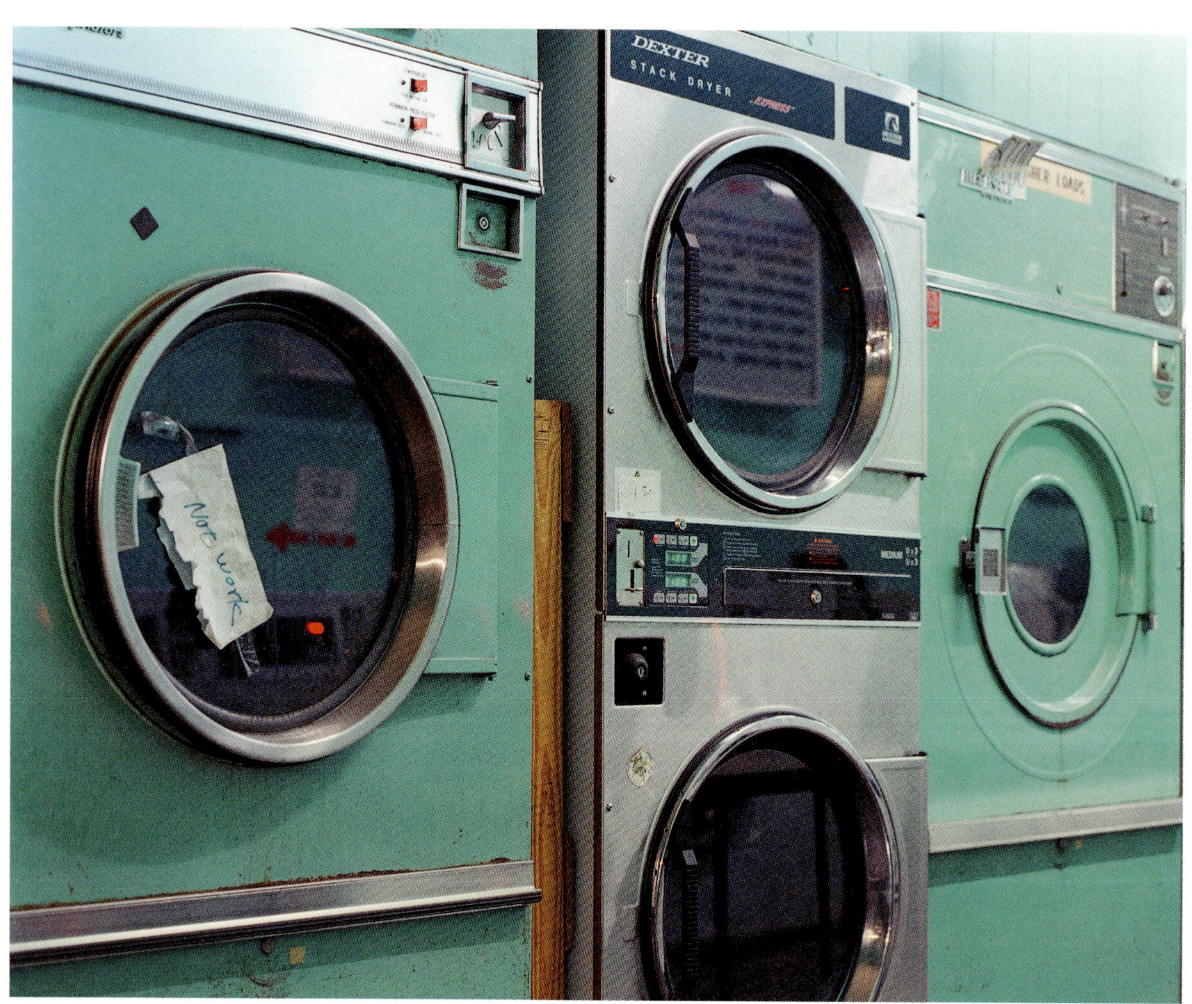

Washing Night

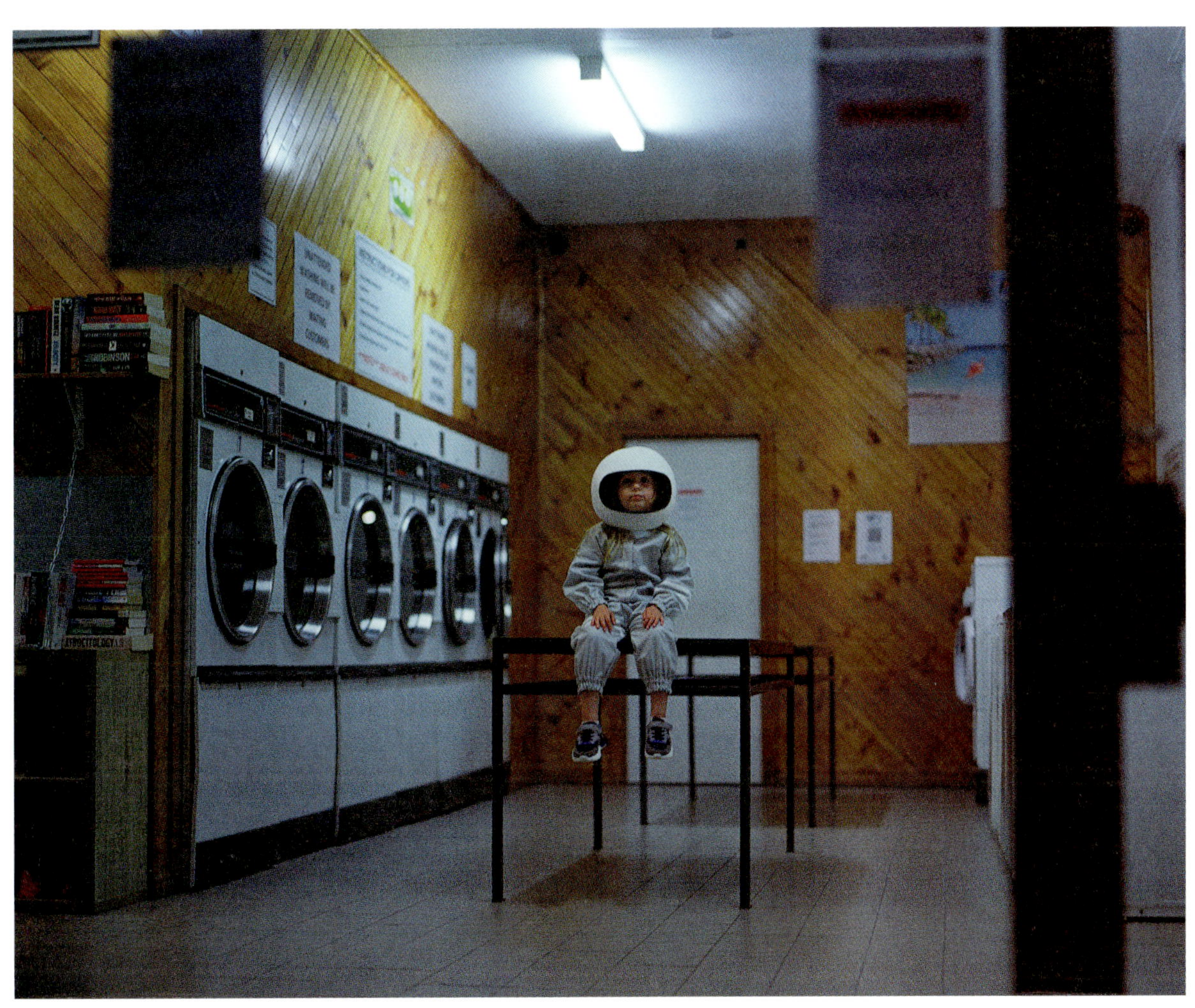
ROBINSON

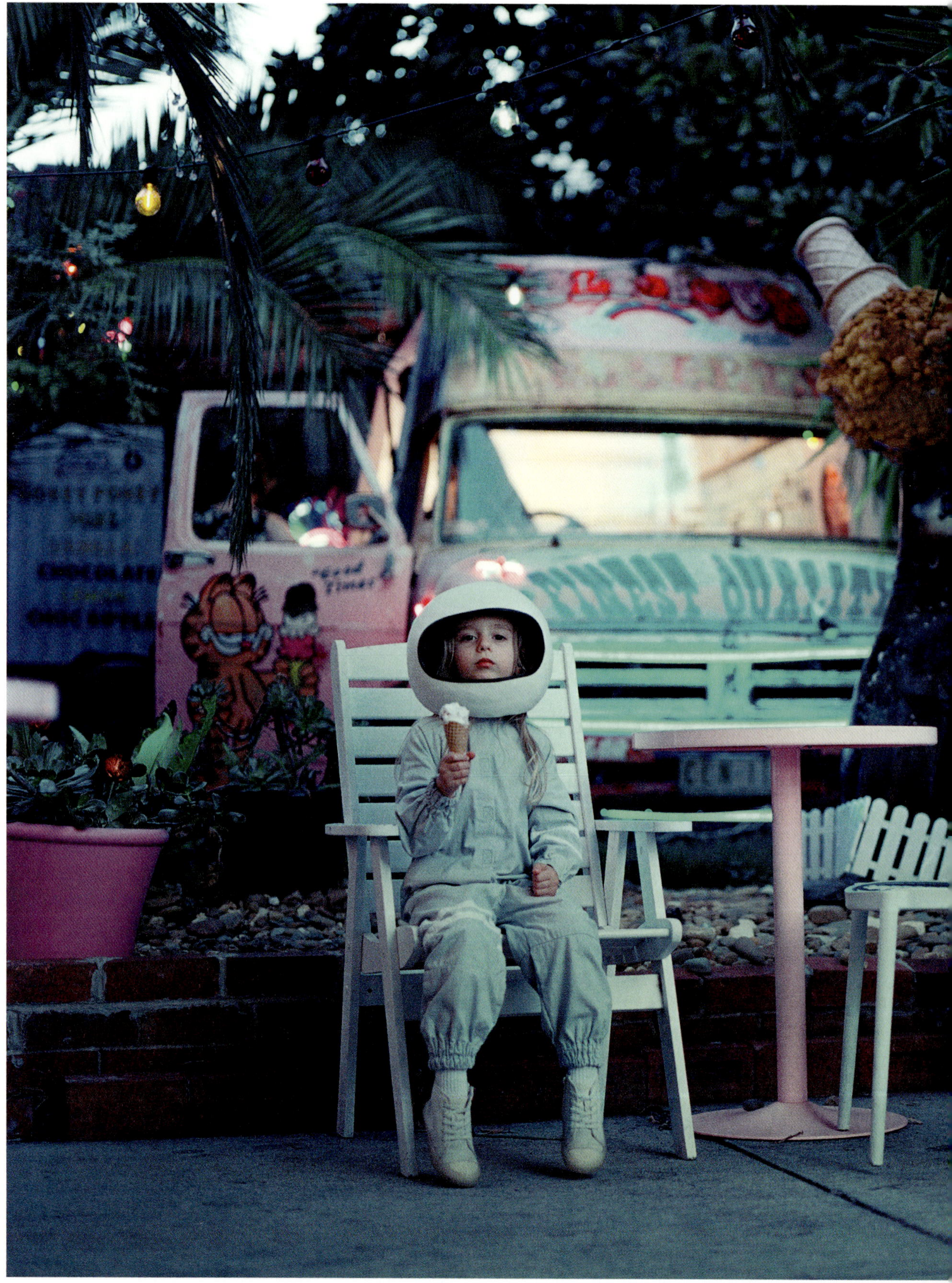

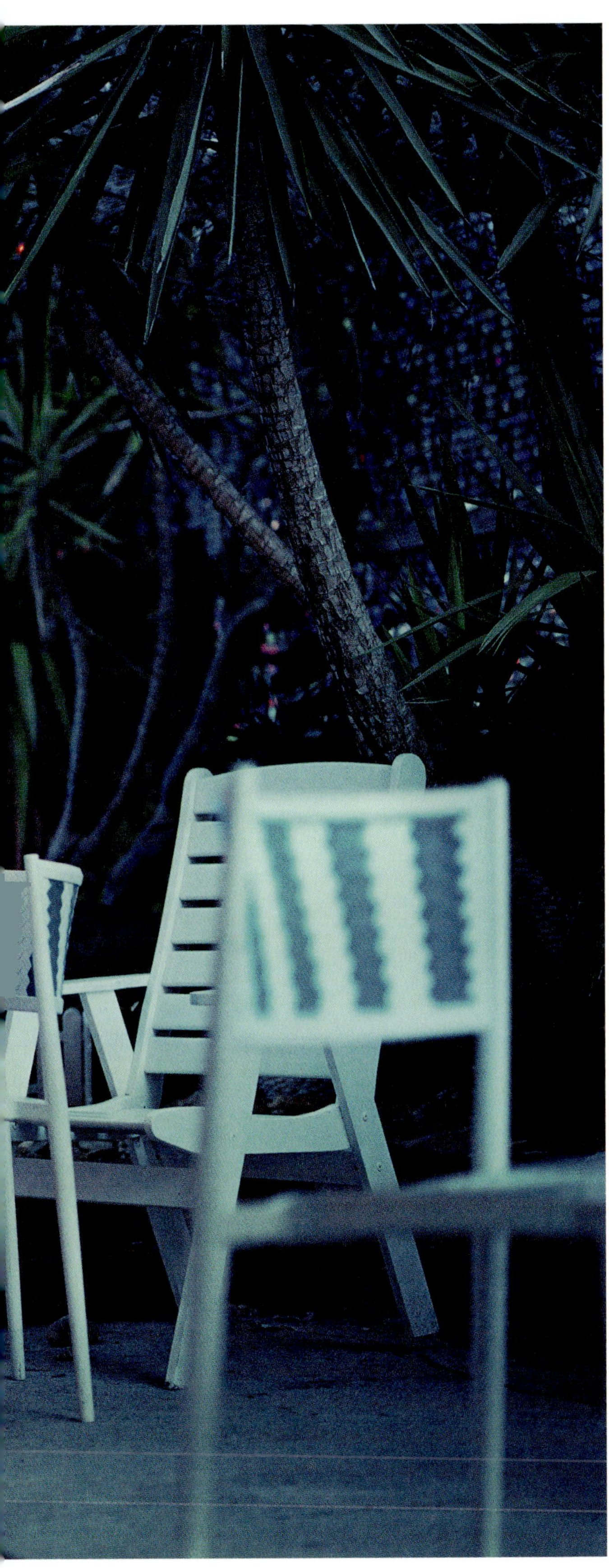

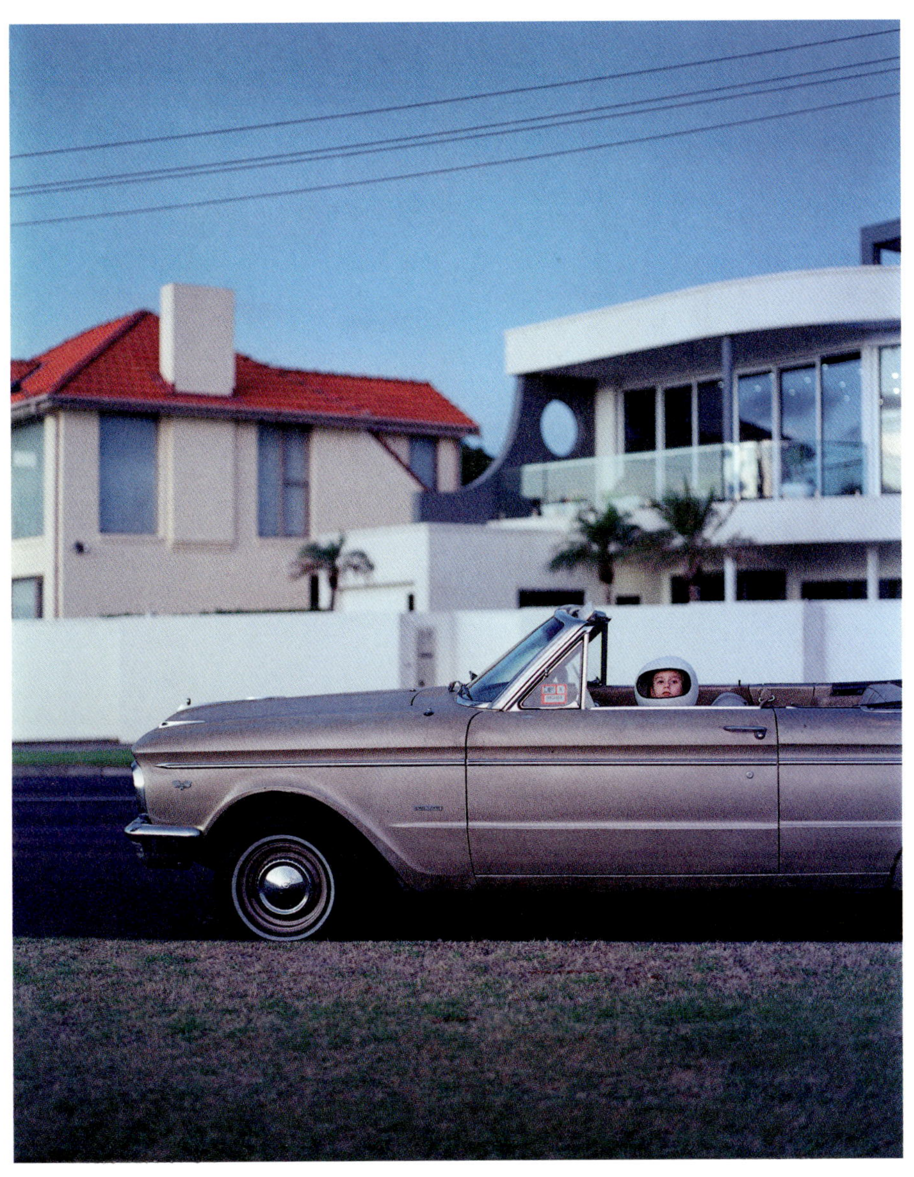

Millenium Falcon

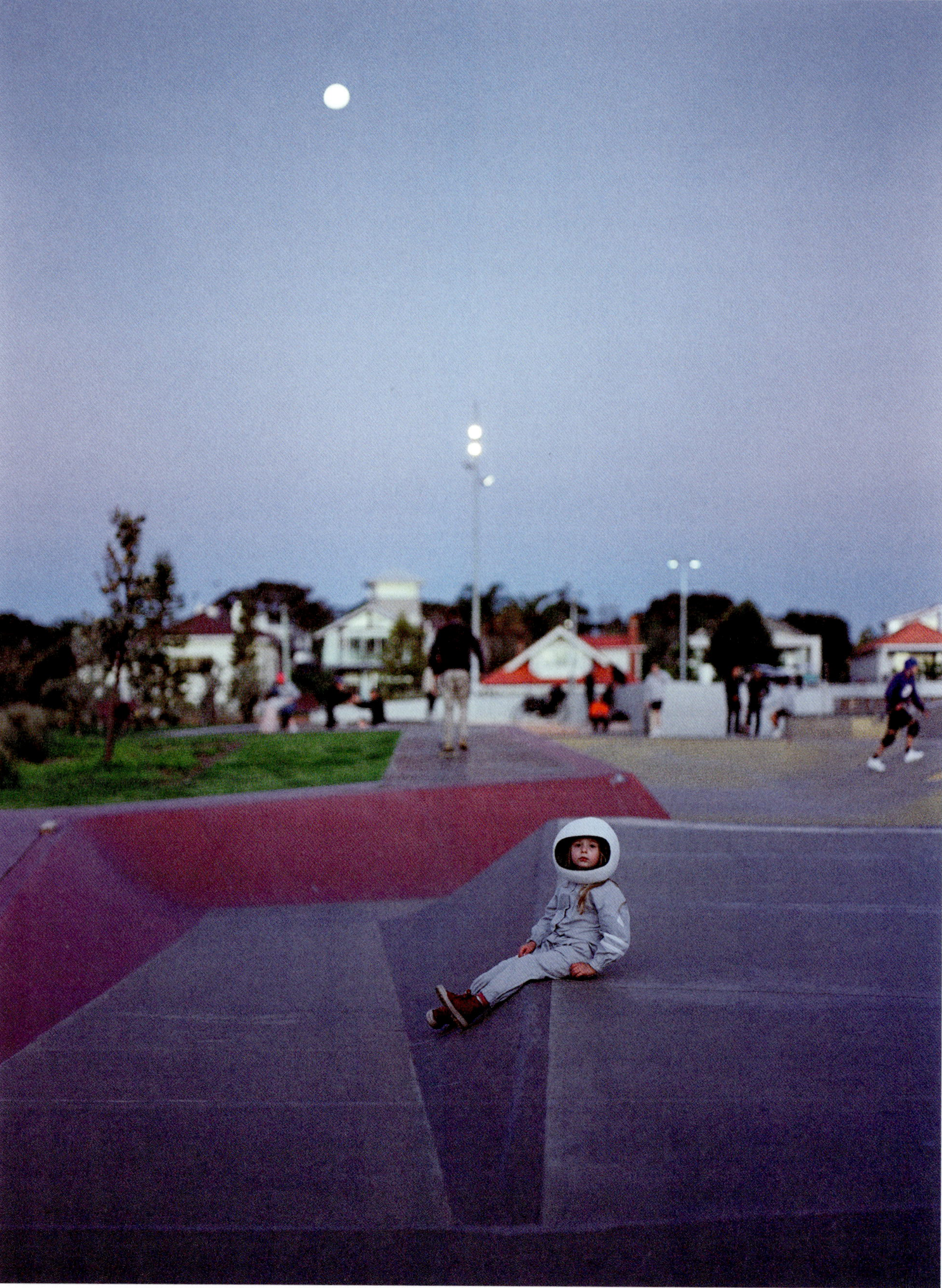

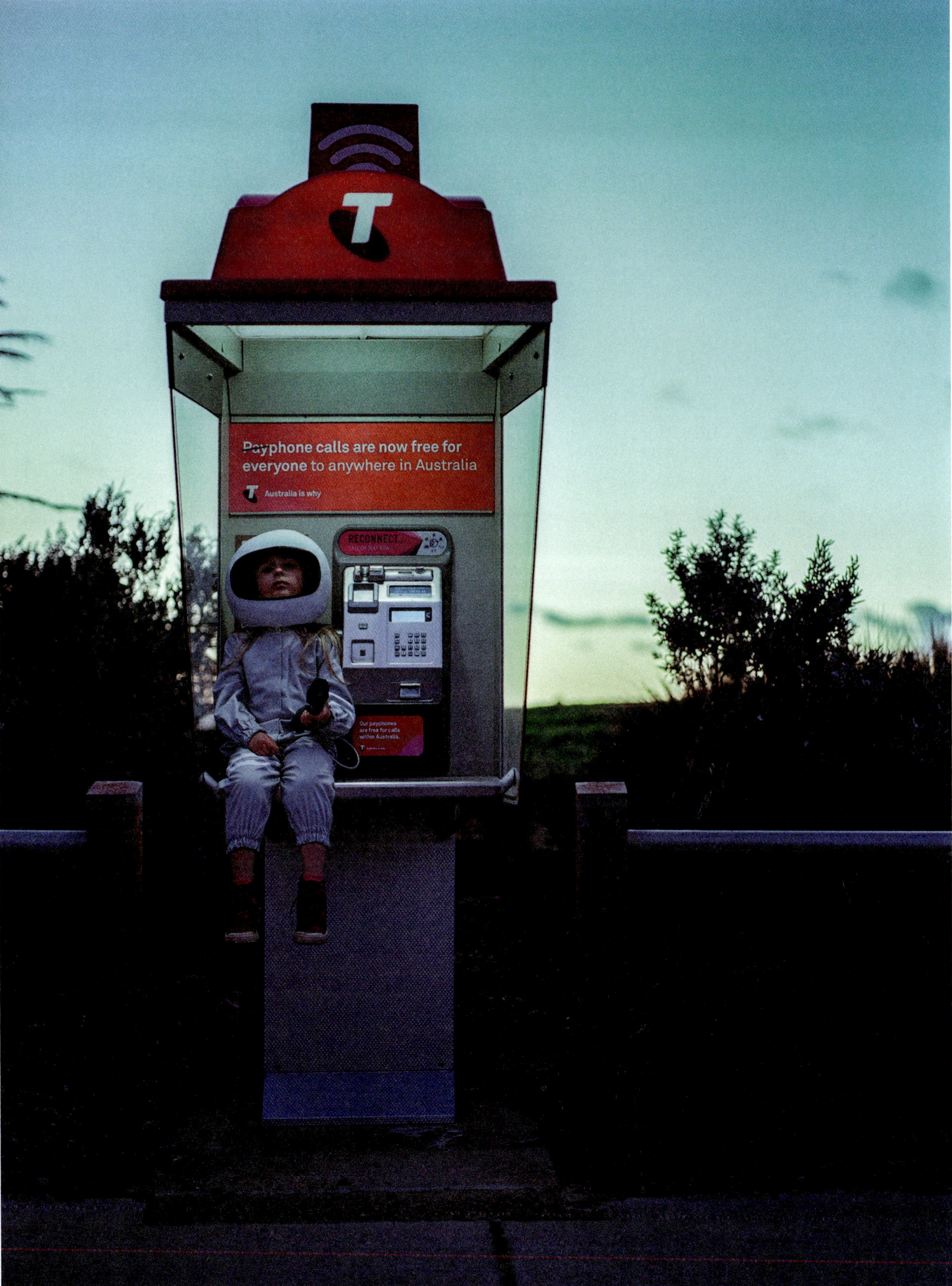
Payphone calls are now free for
everyone to anywhere in Australia
Australia is why
RECONNECT.
Our payphones
are free for calls
within Australia.

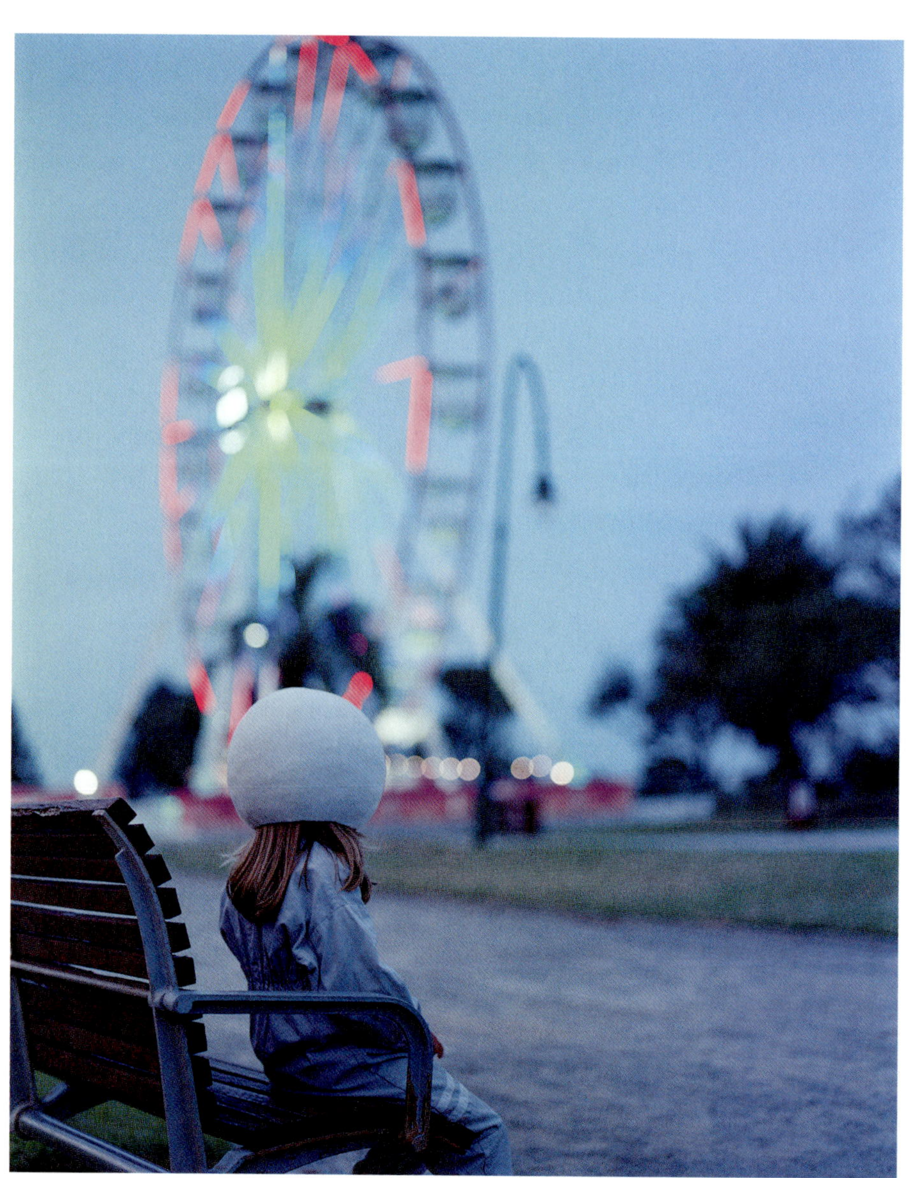

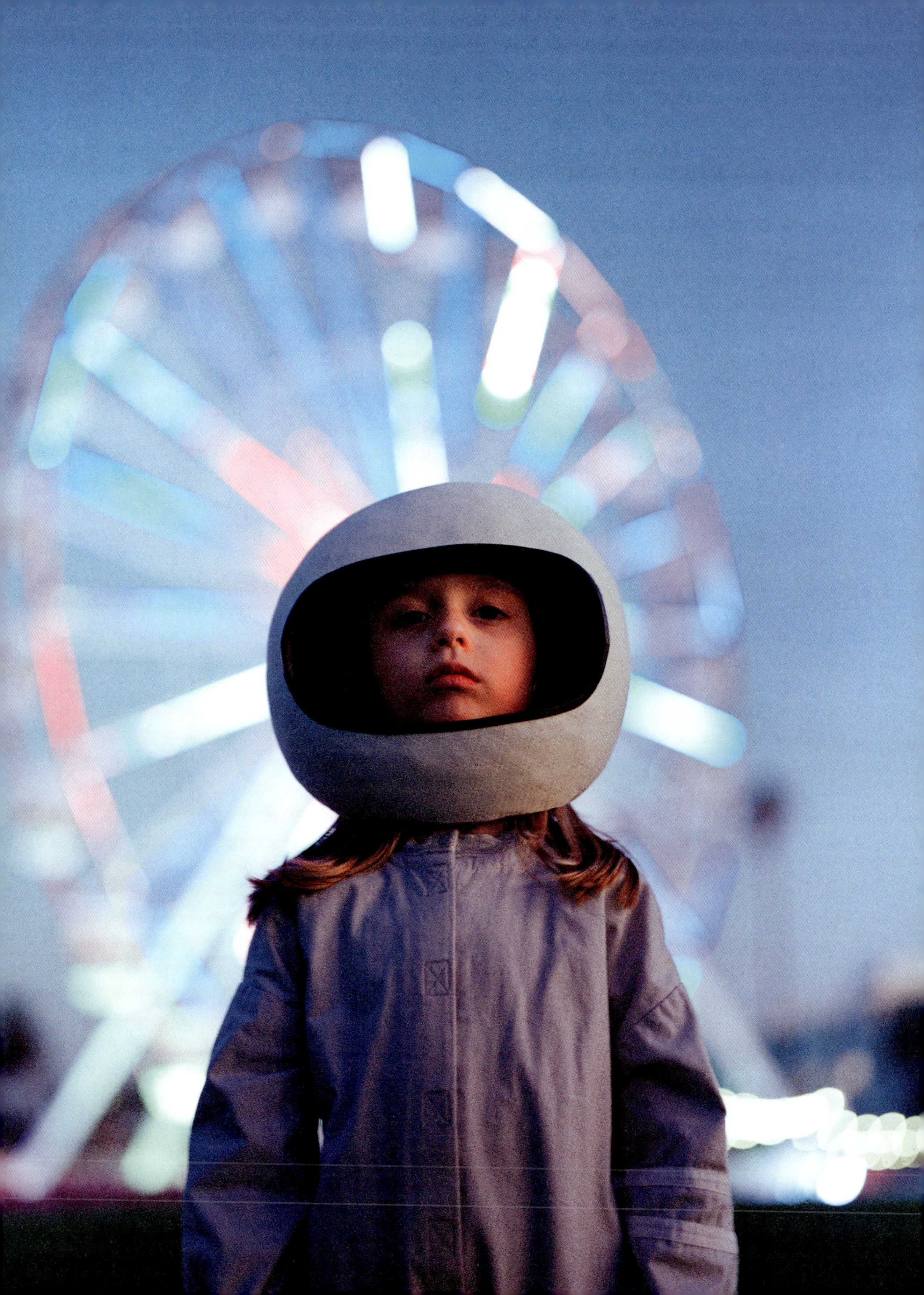

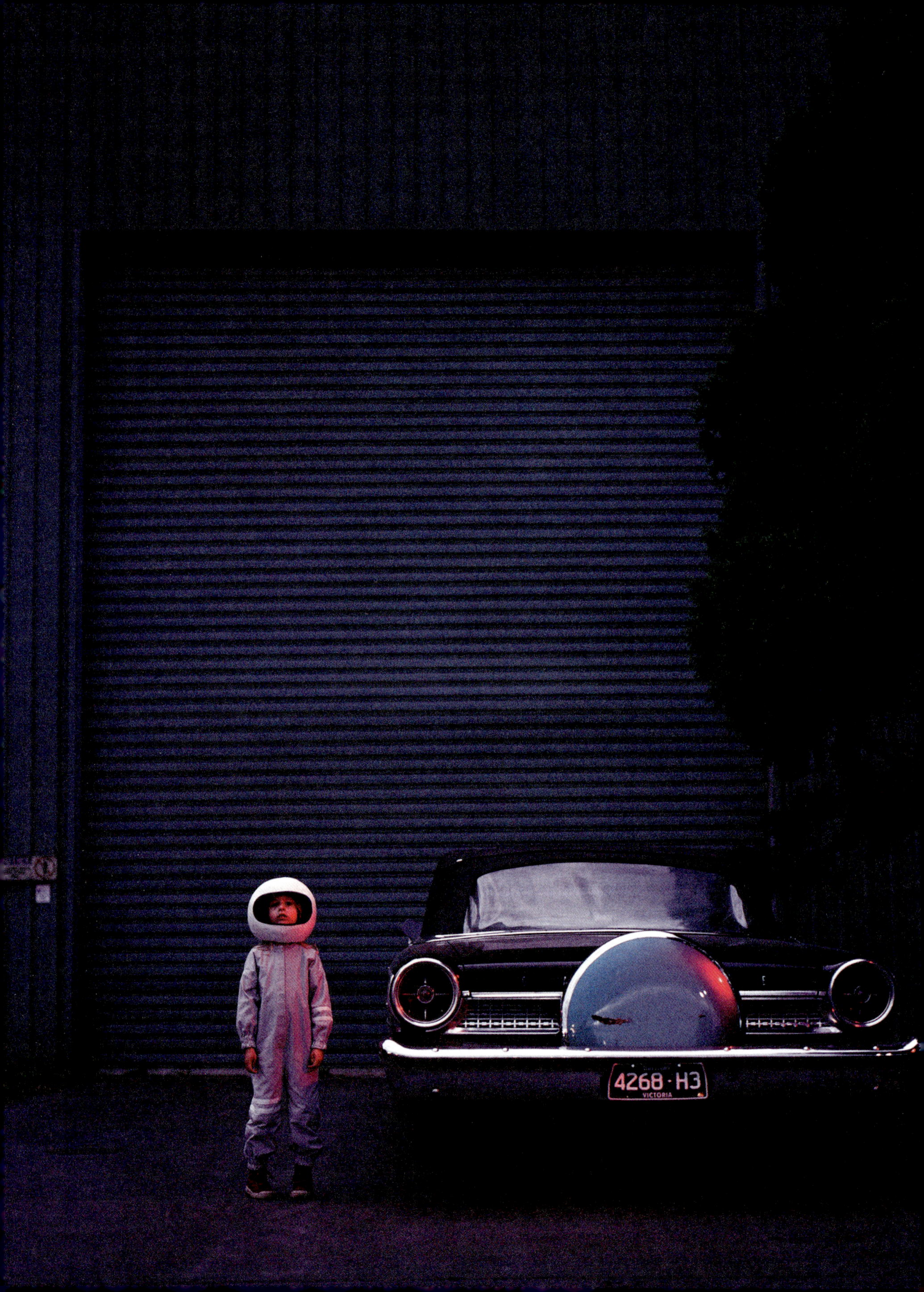

4268·H3
VICTORIA

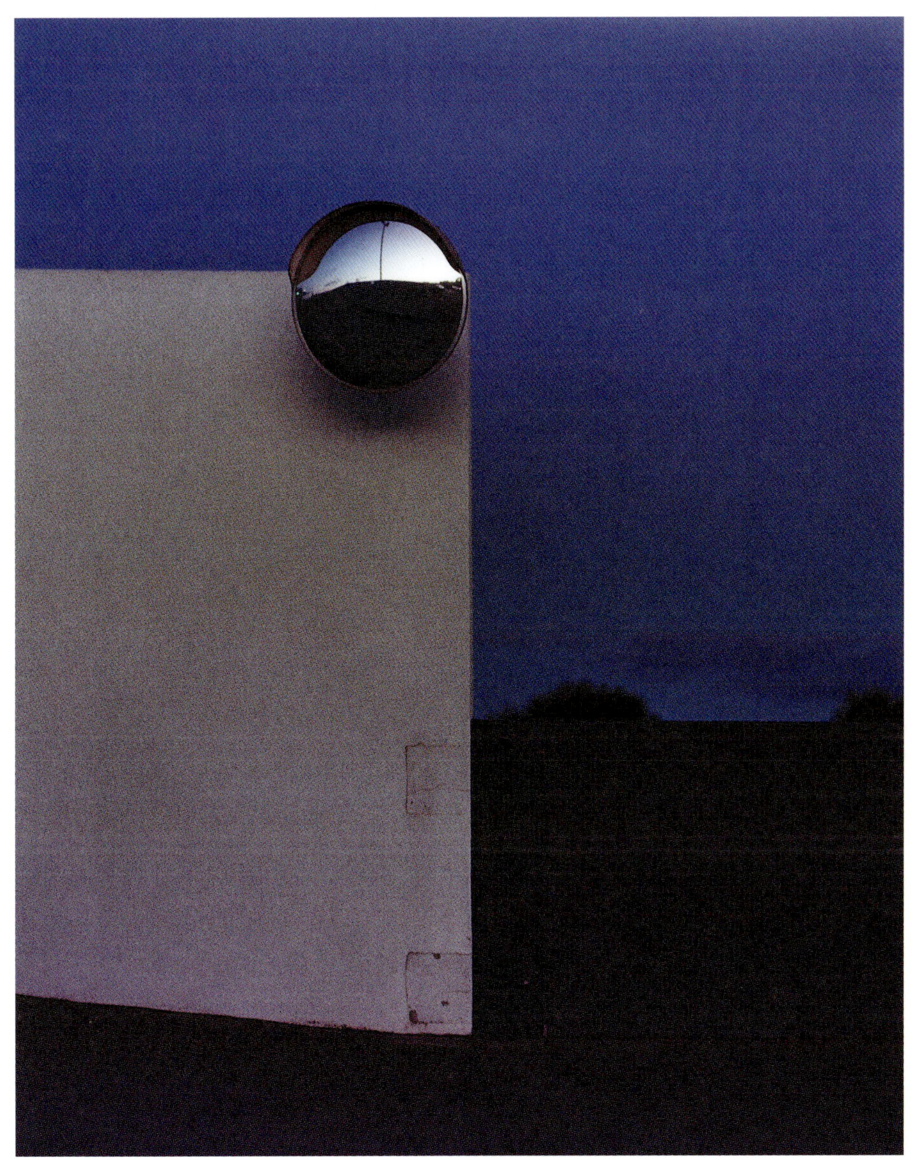

The Eye

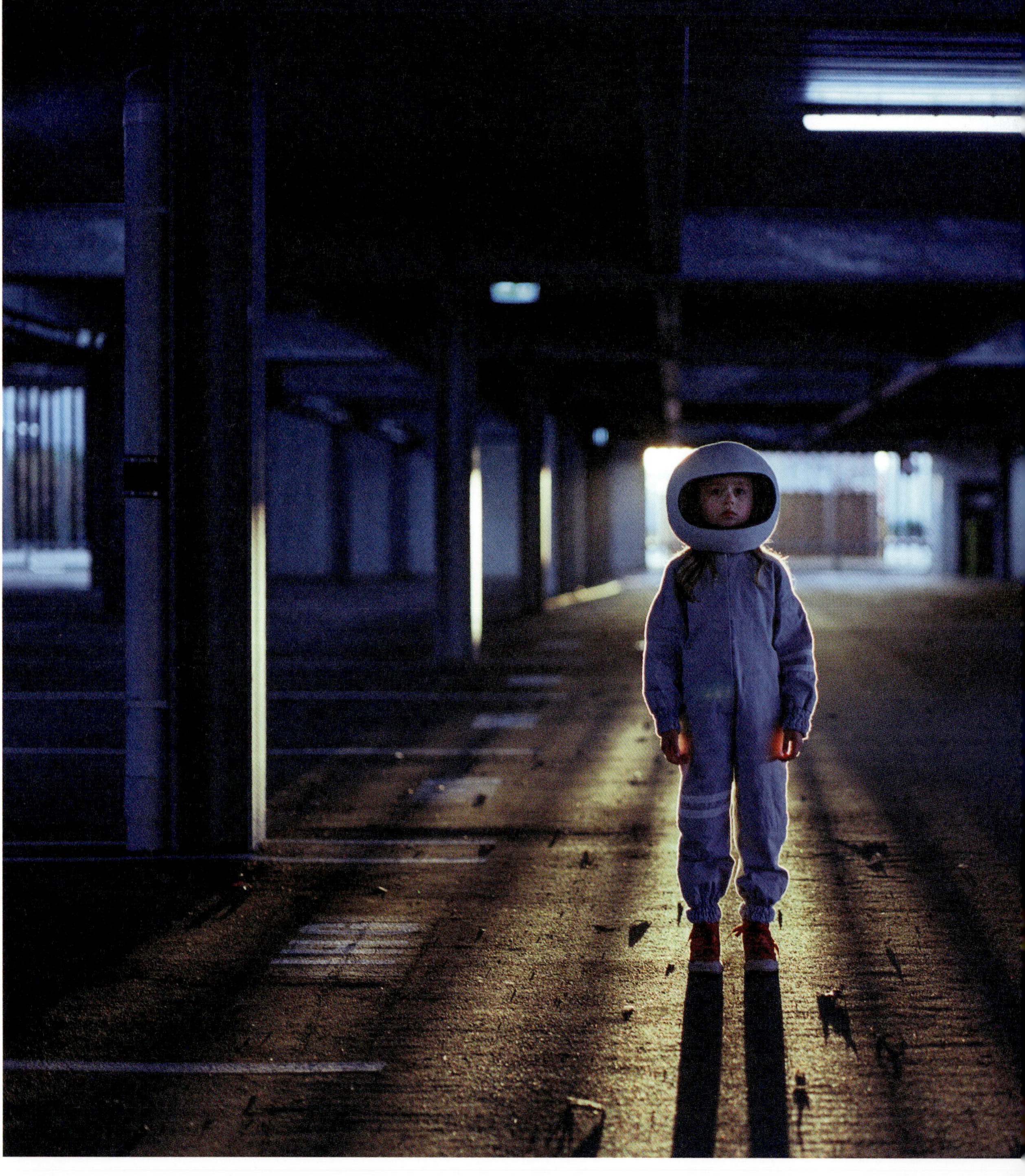

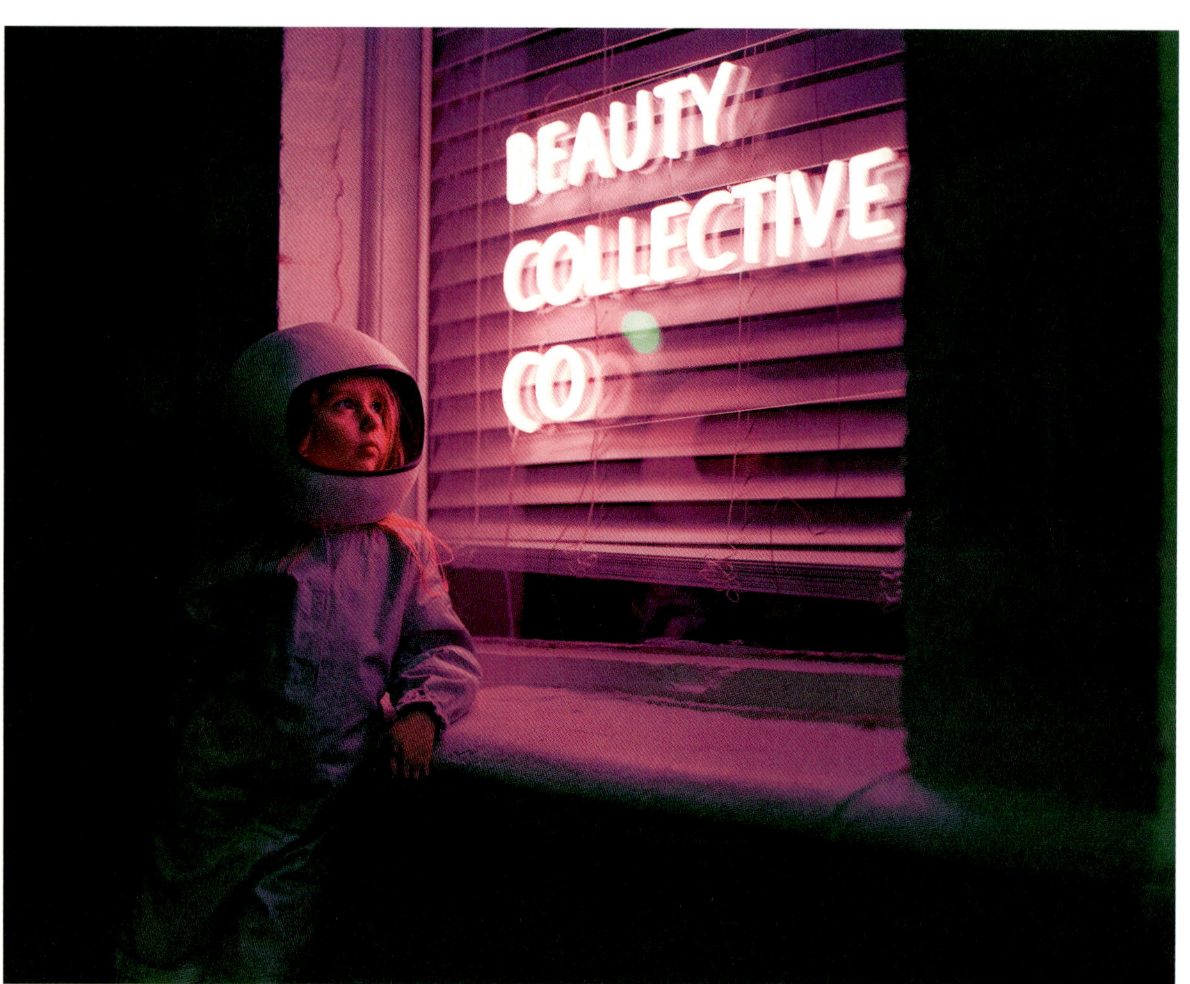
BEAUTY
COLLECTIVE
CO

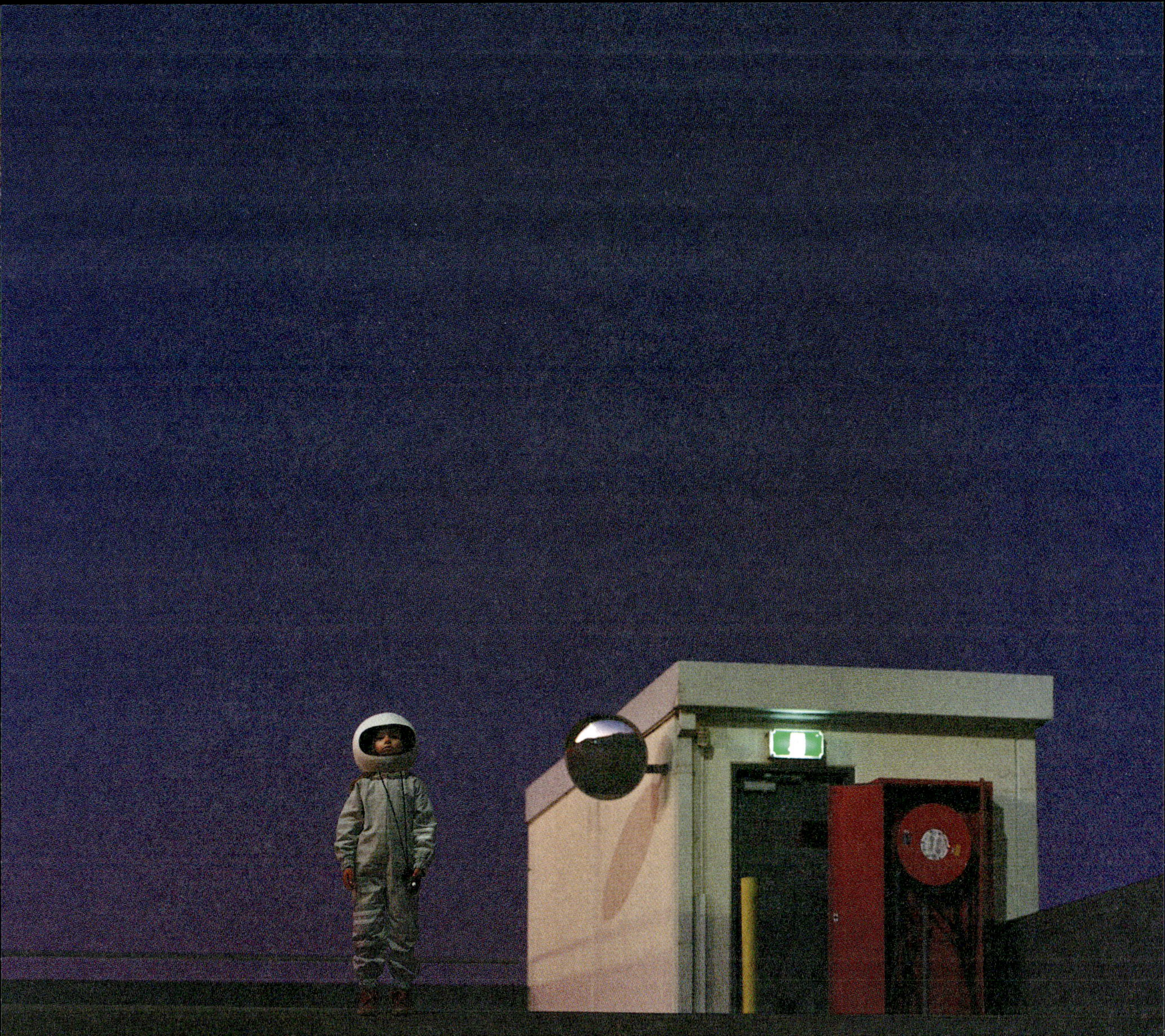

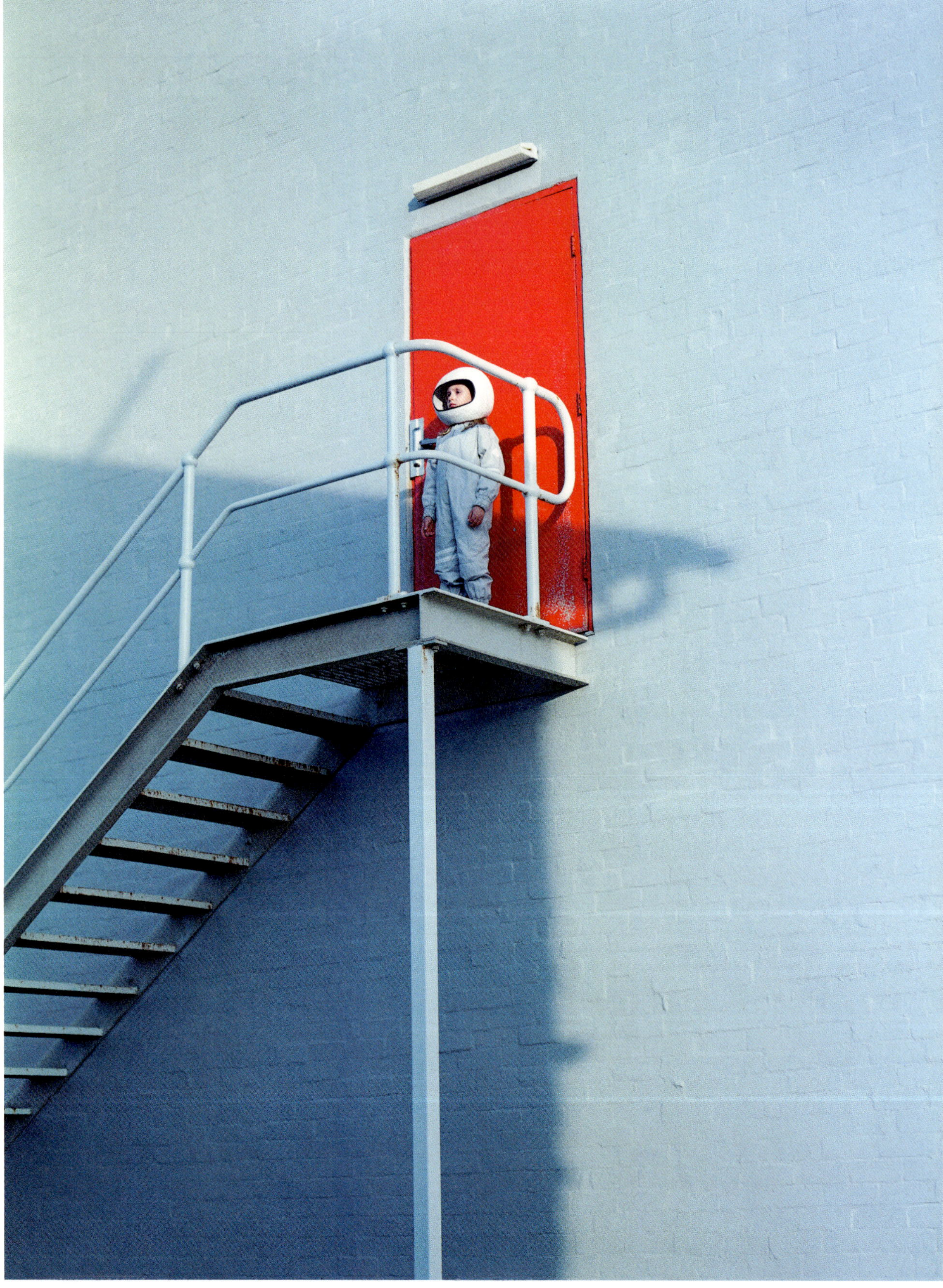

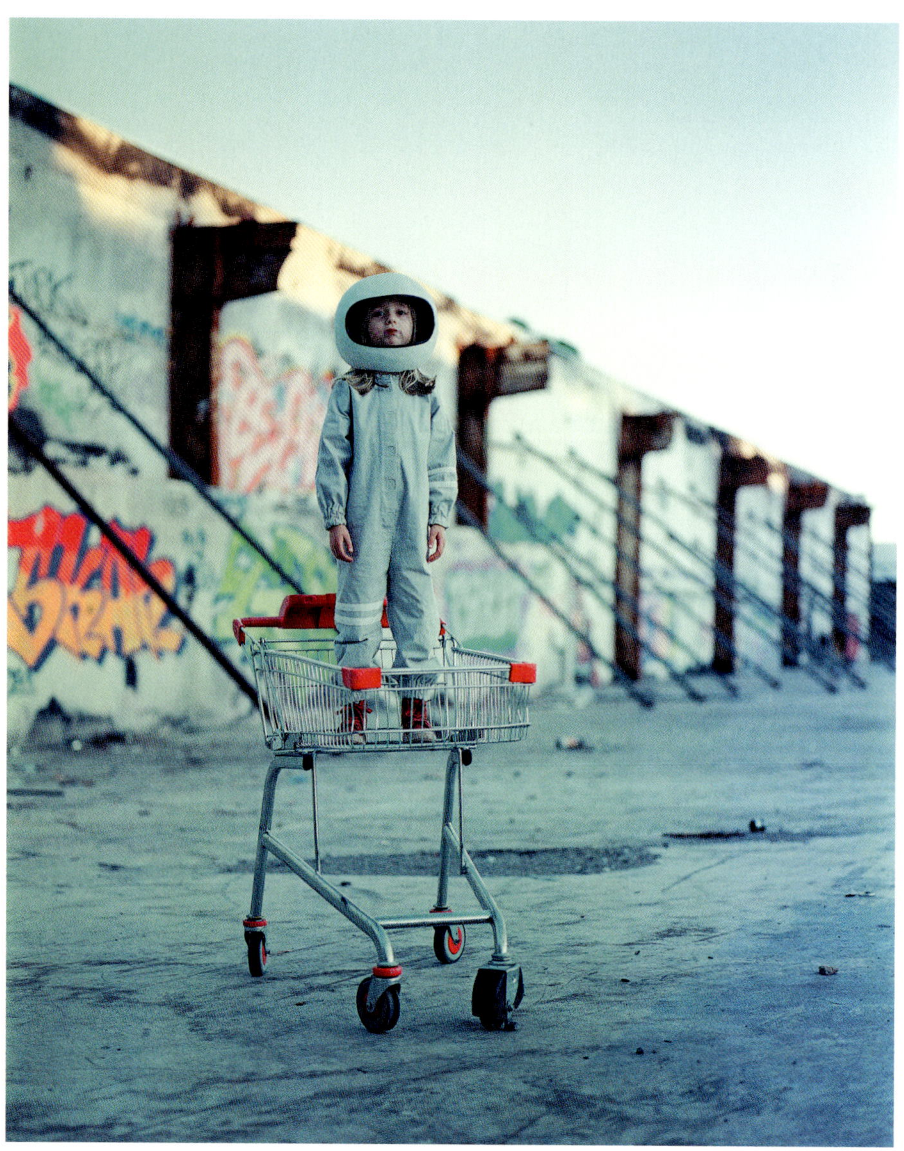

The Yard

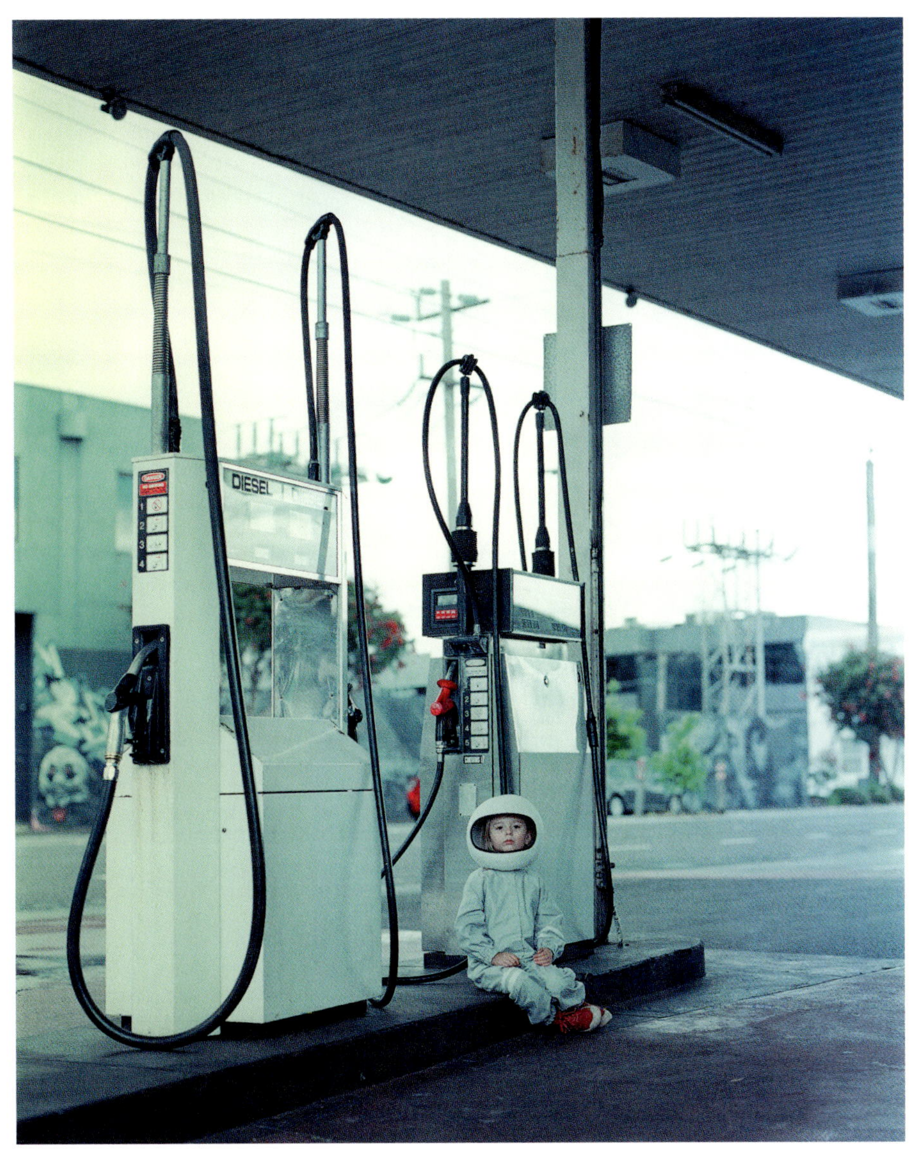
DIESEL

What was once futuristic is now old.
And they were old long before this
young humanoid was born.

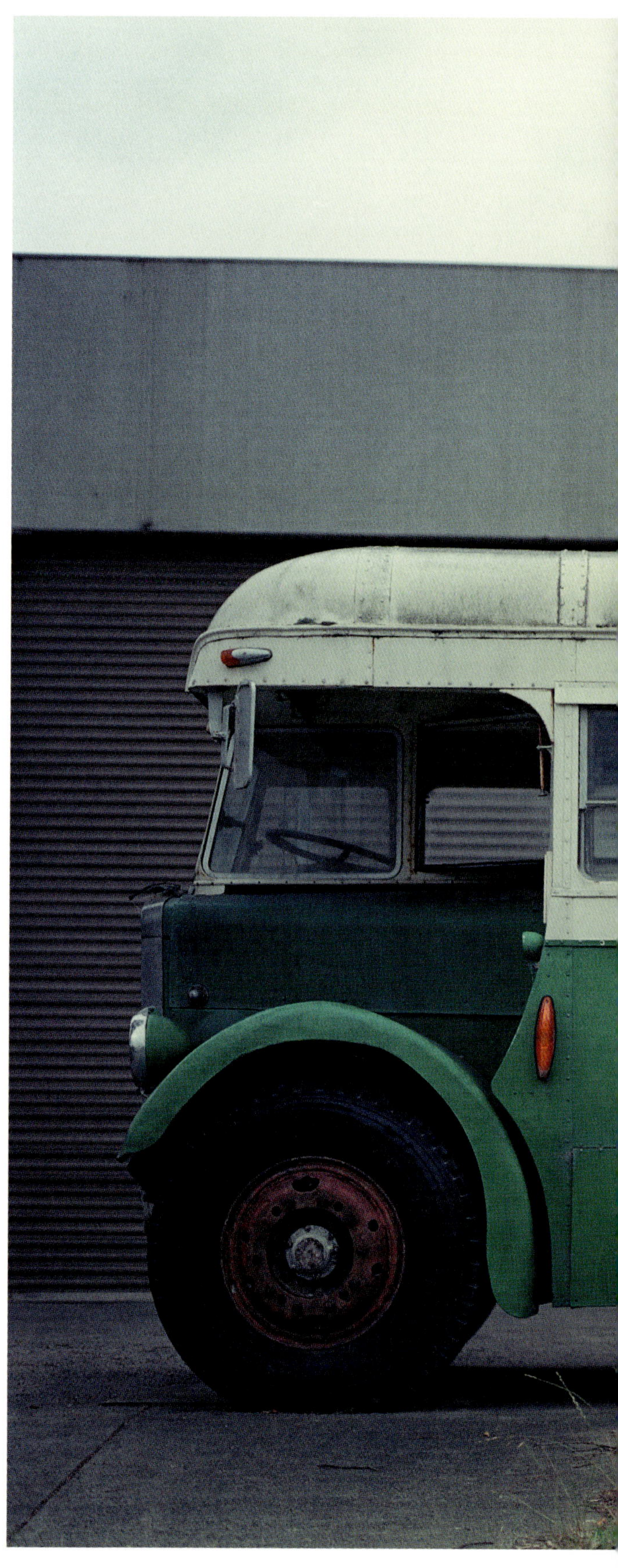

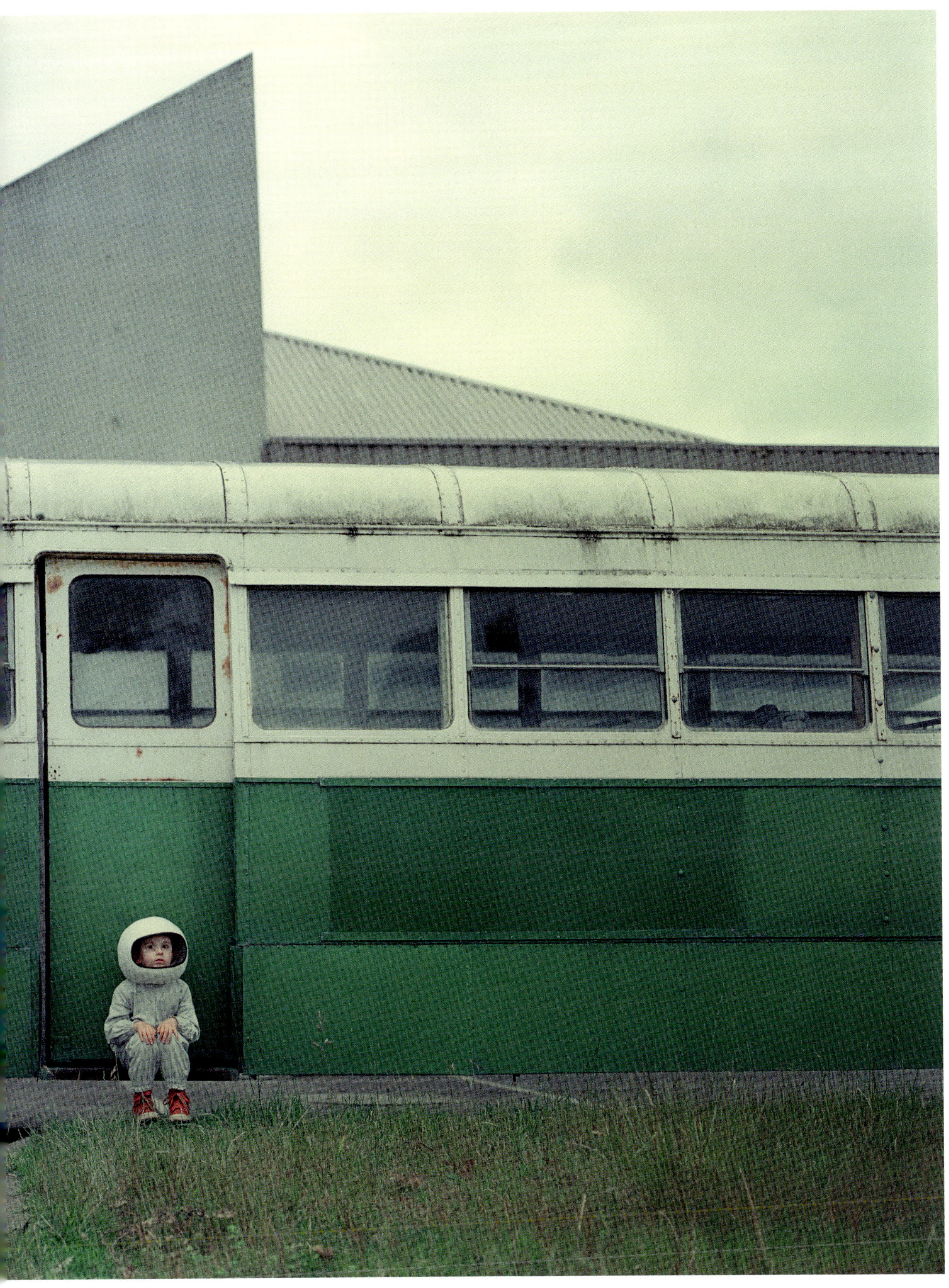

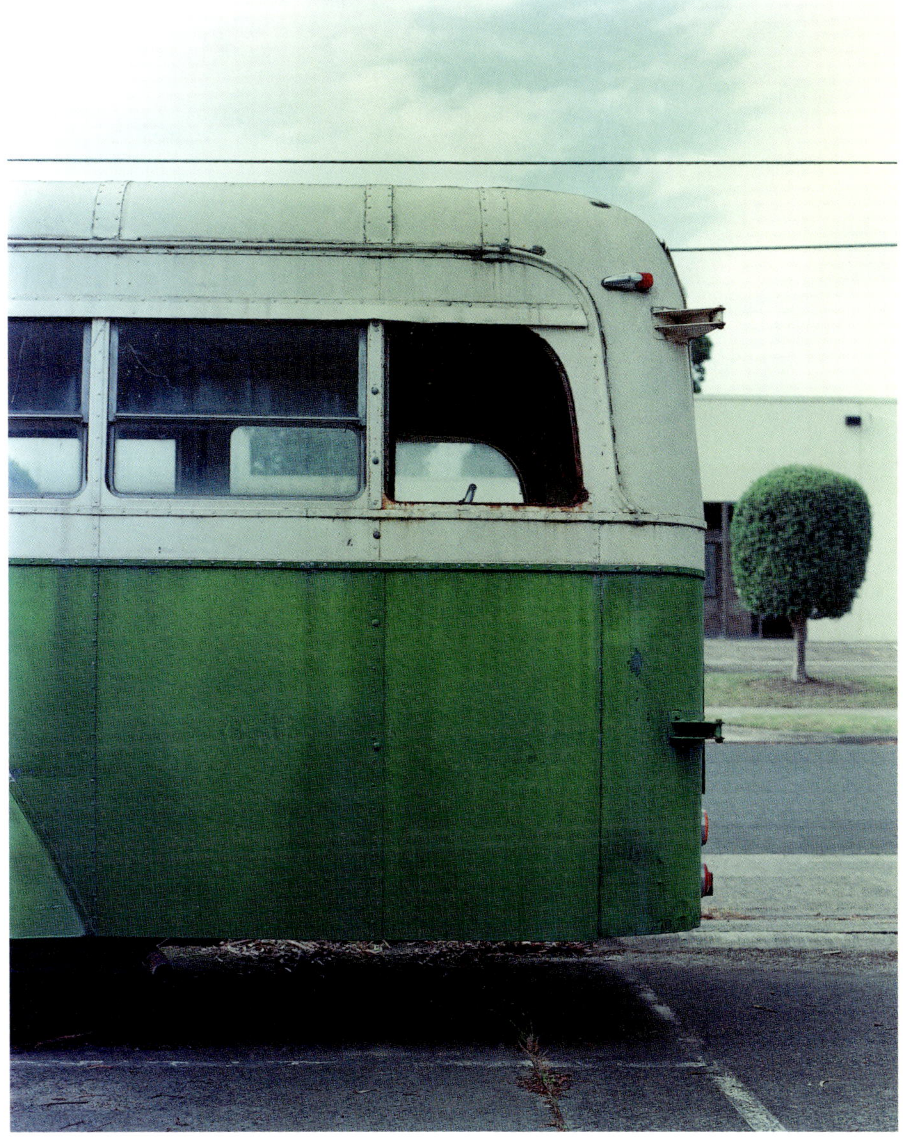

The Tail

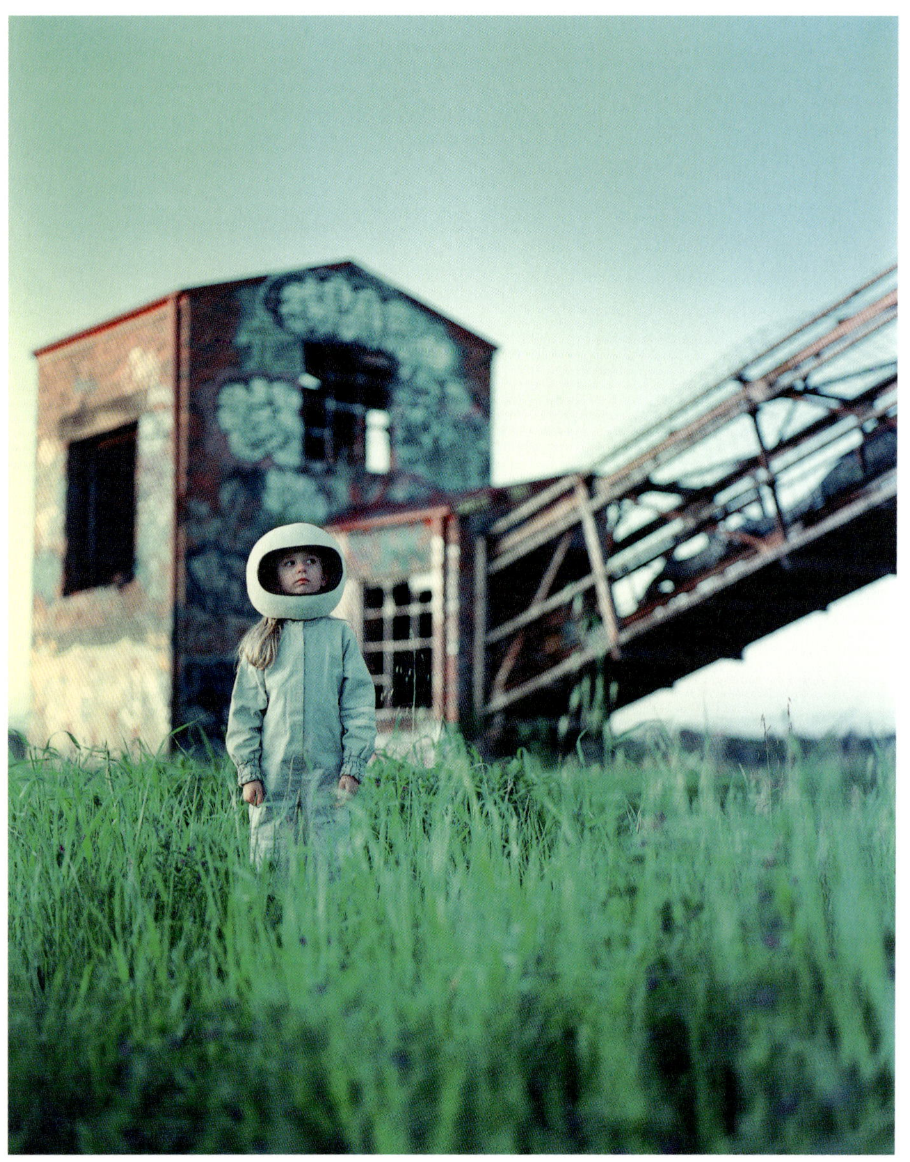

Up!

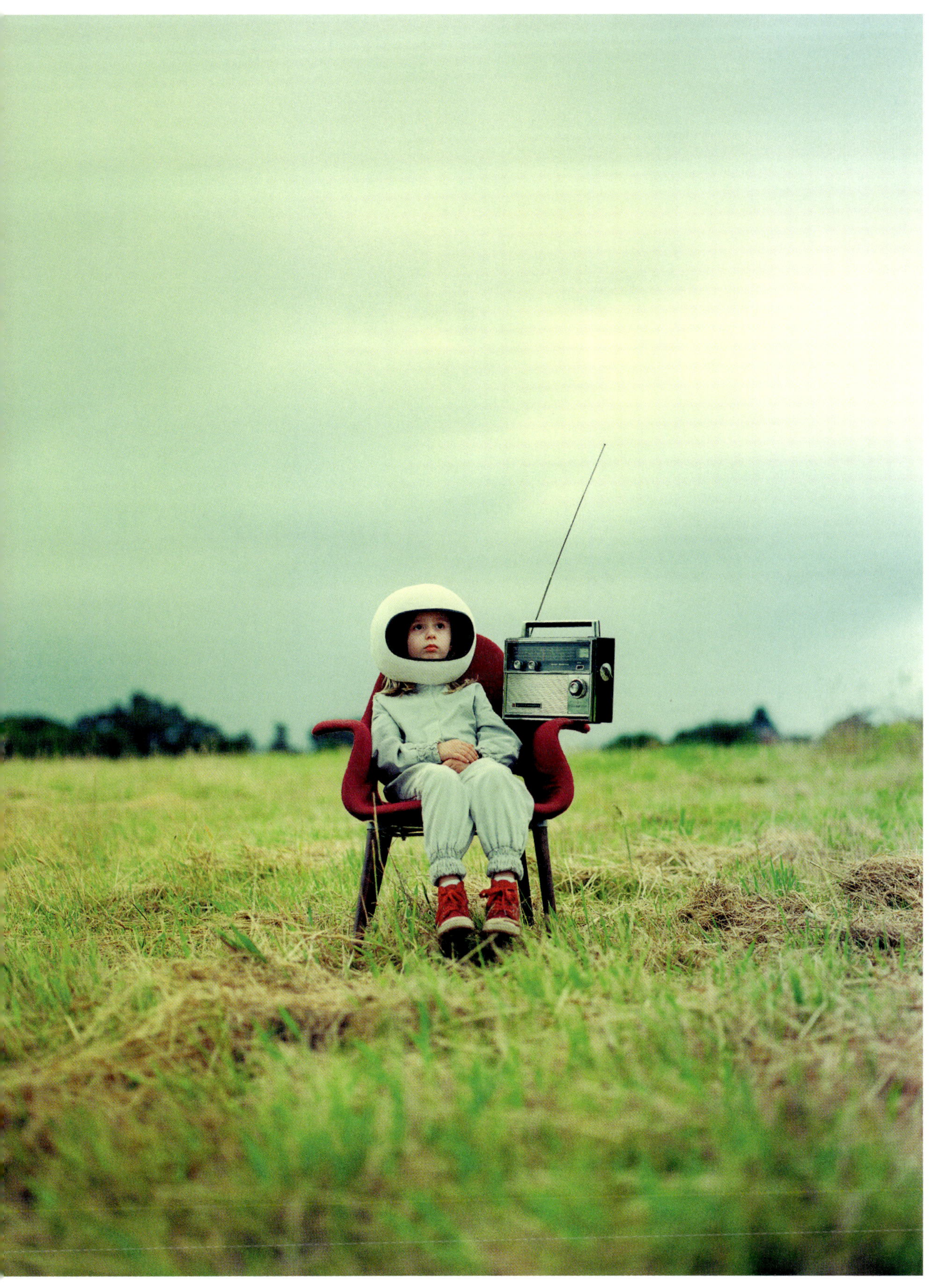

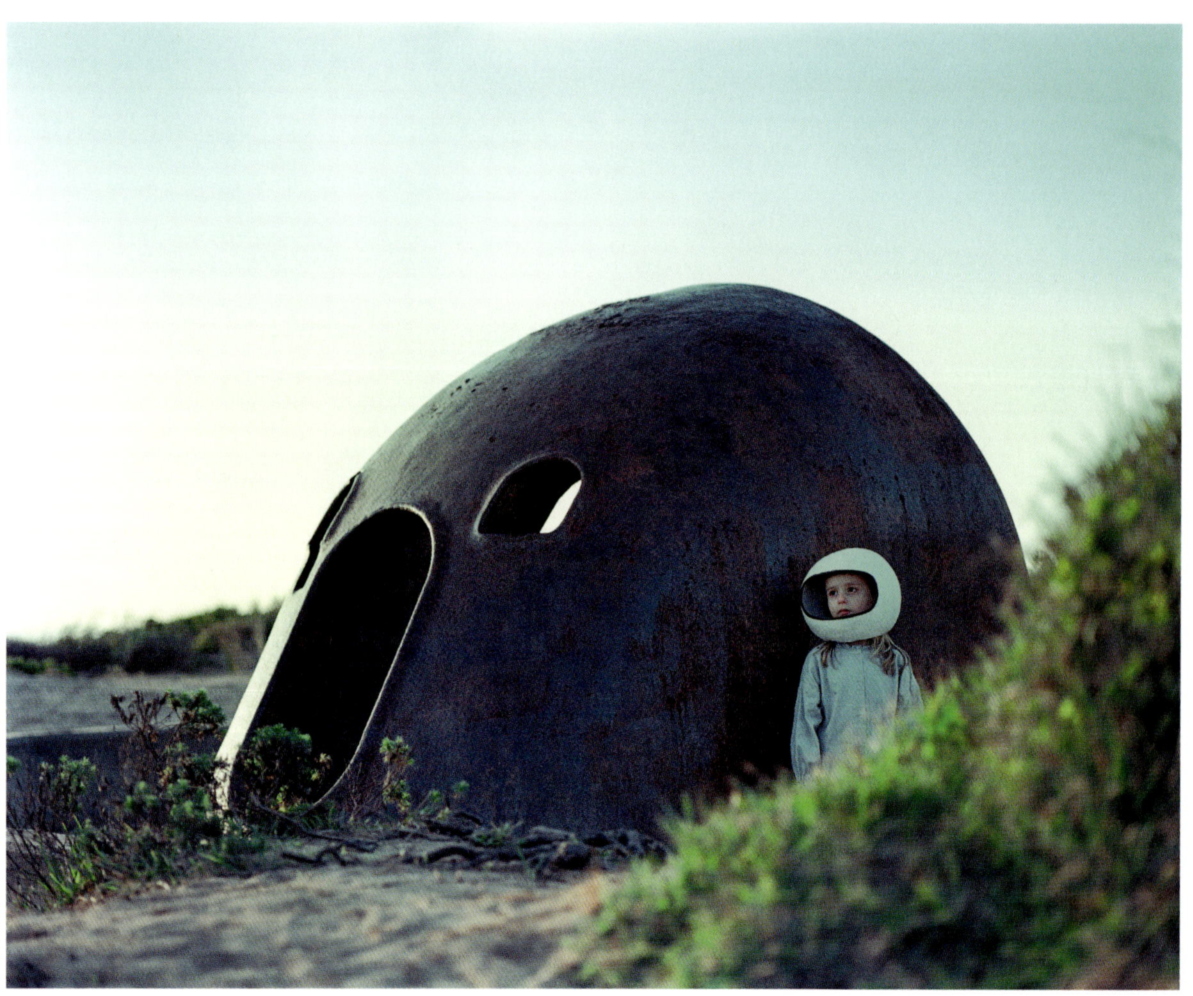

The Face

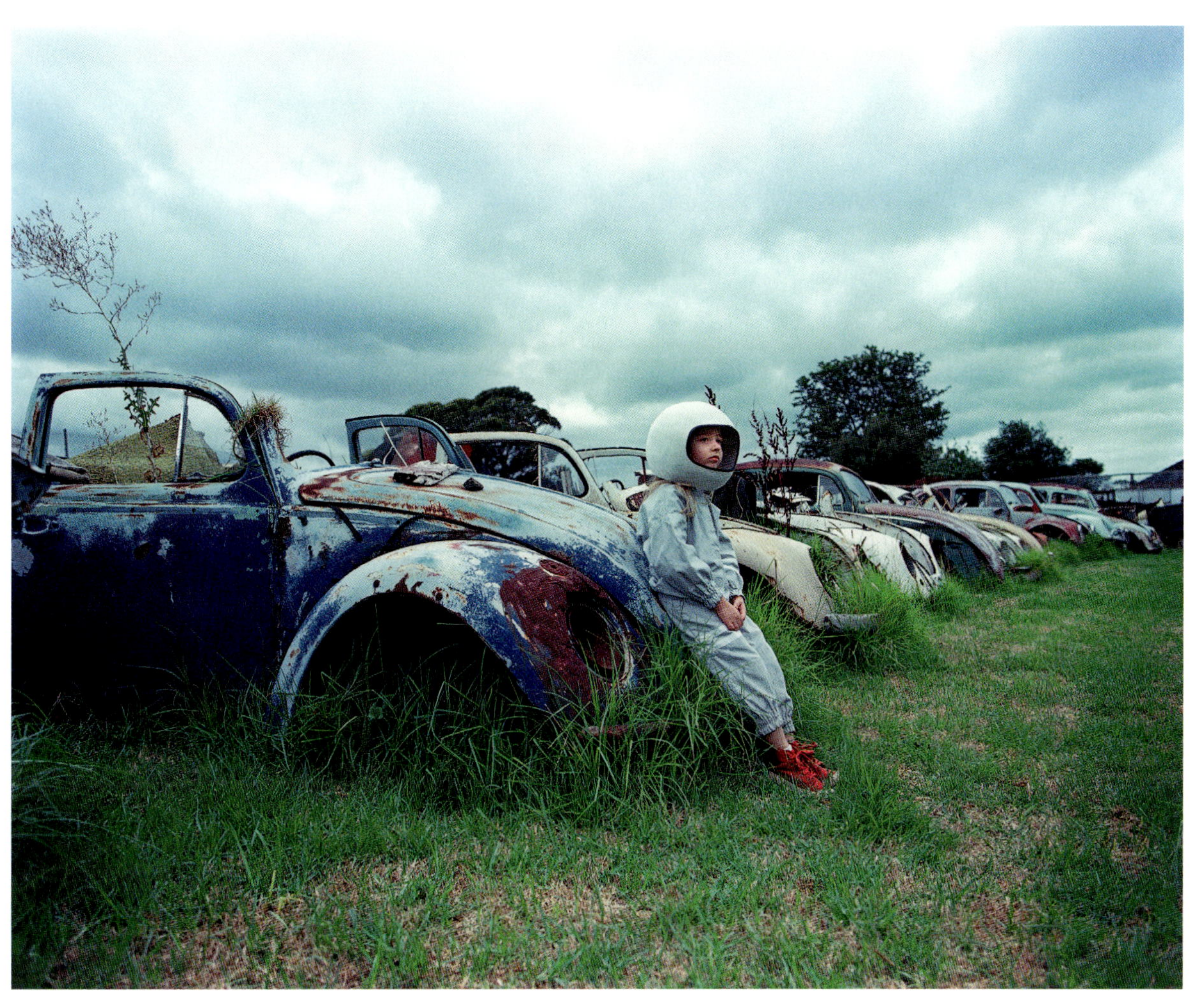

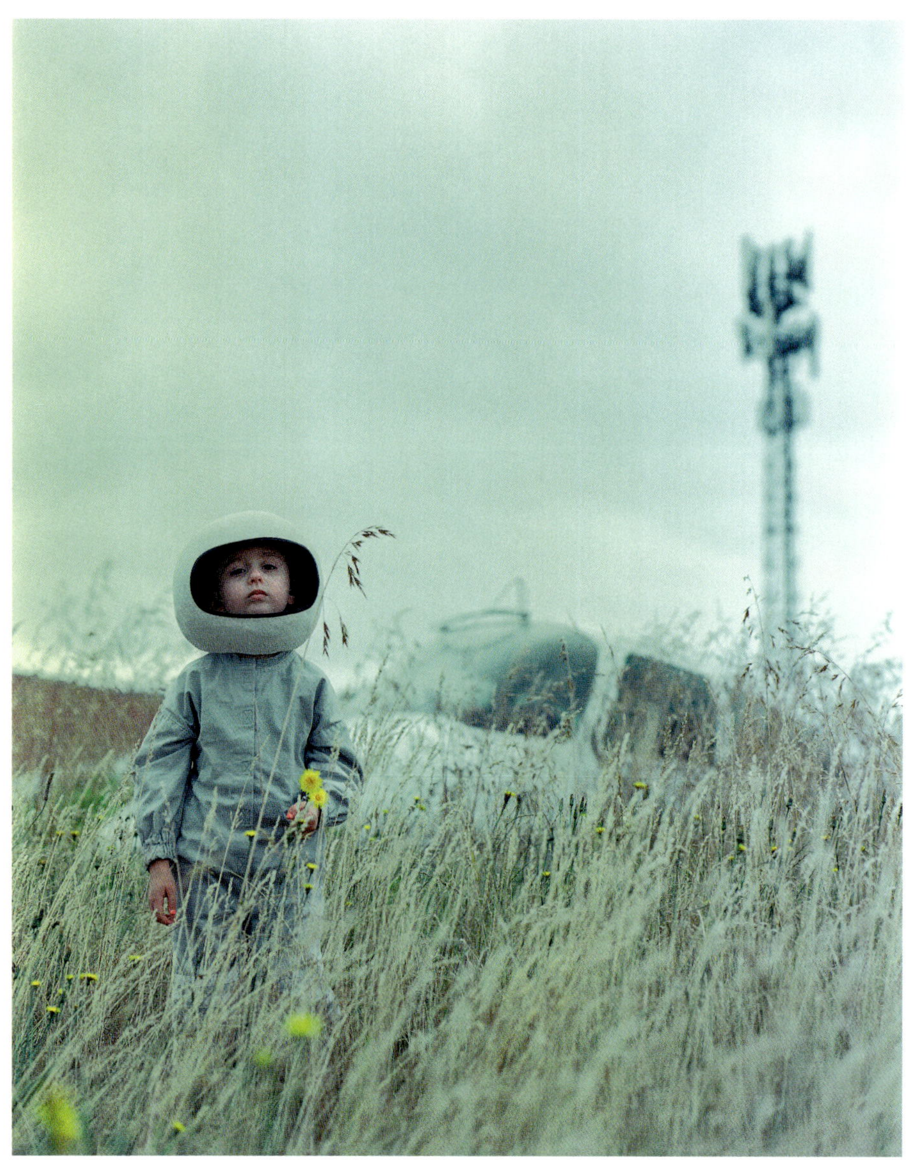

Wildflowers

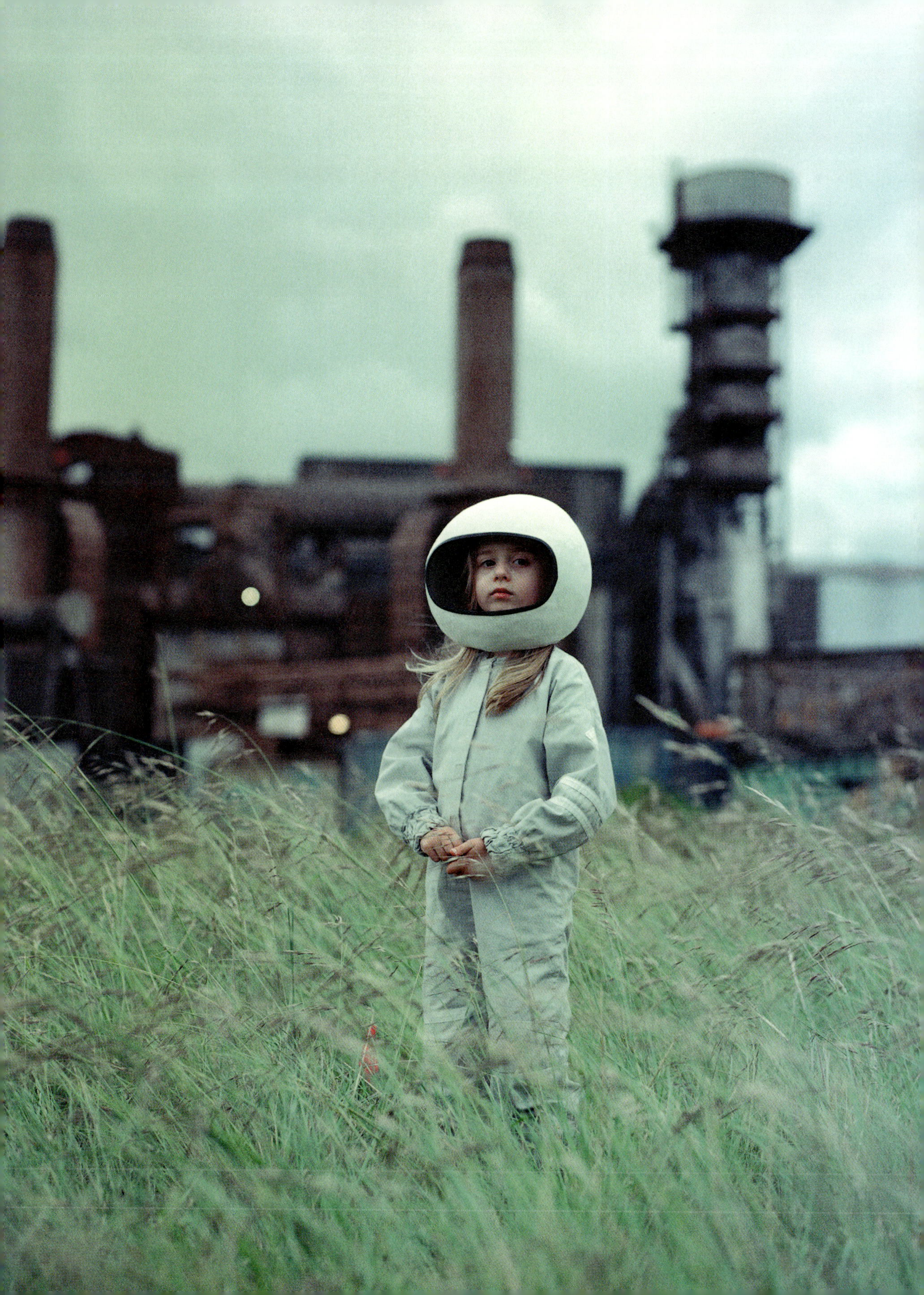

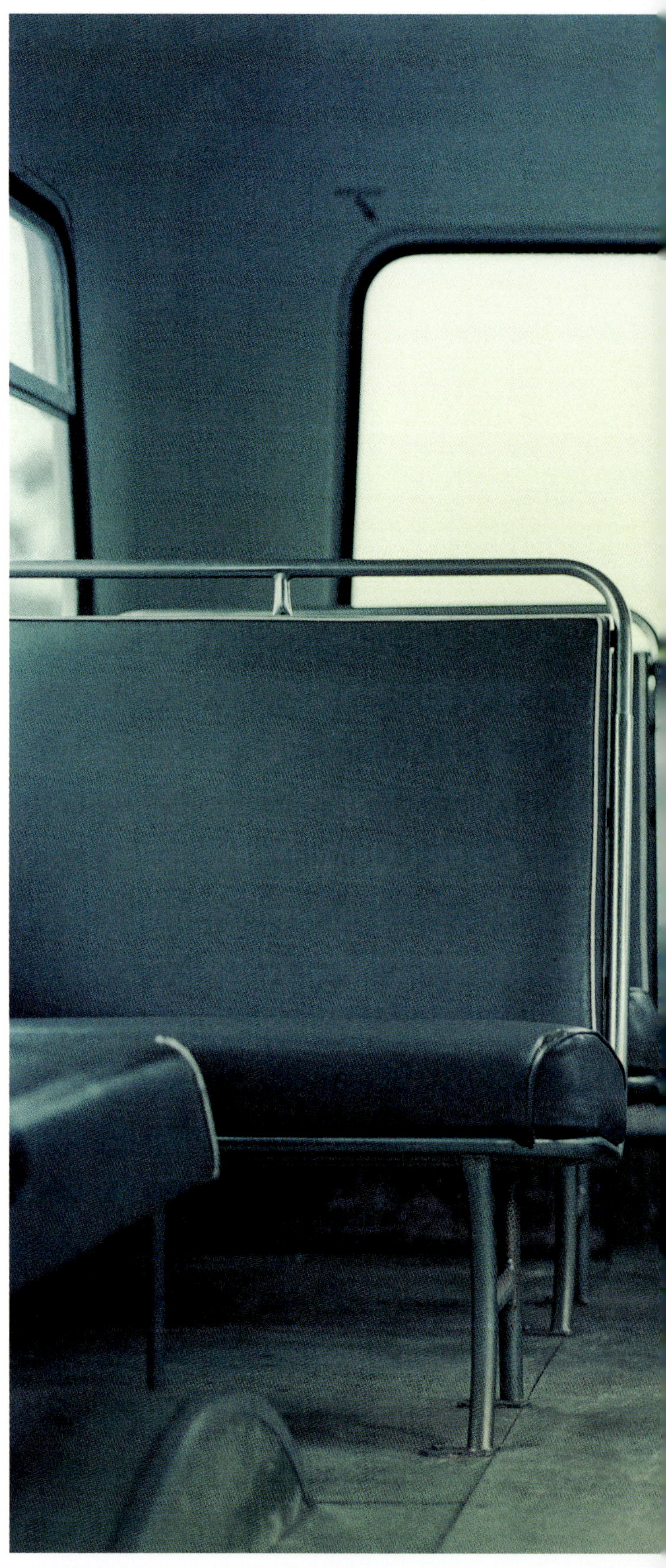

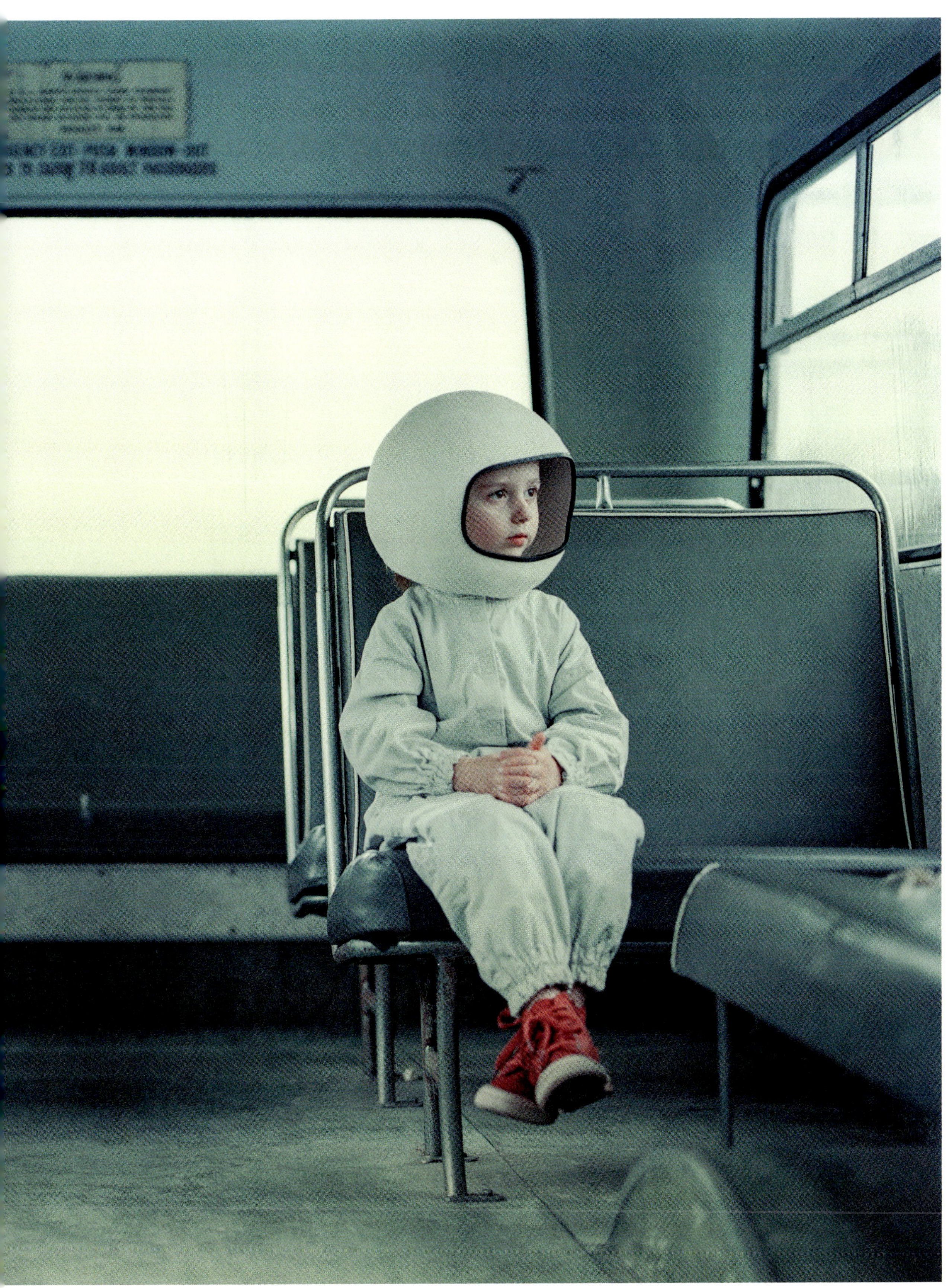

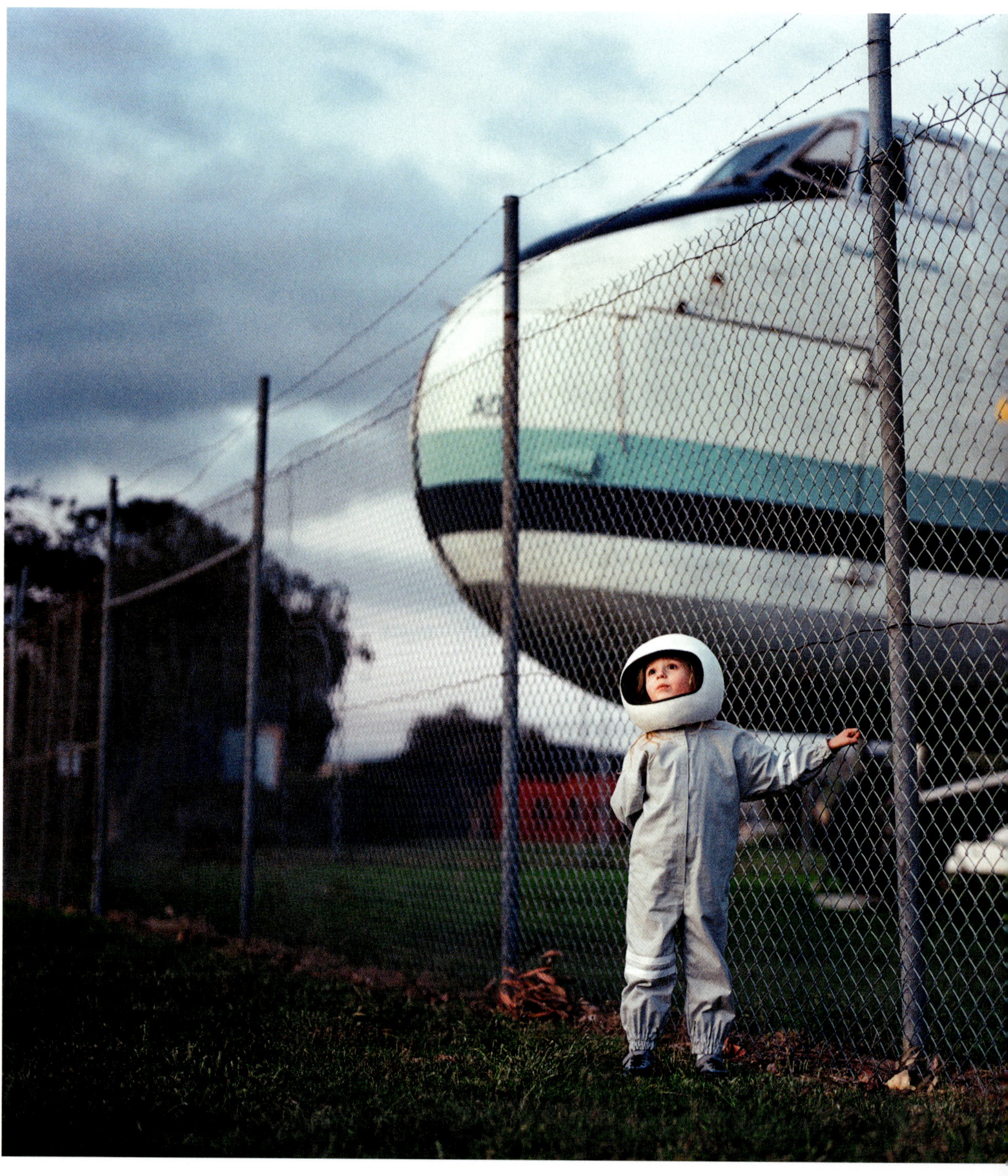

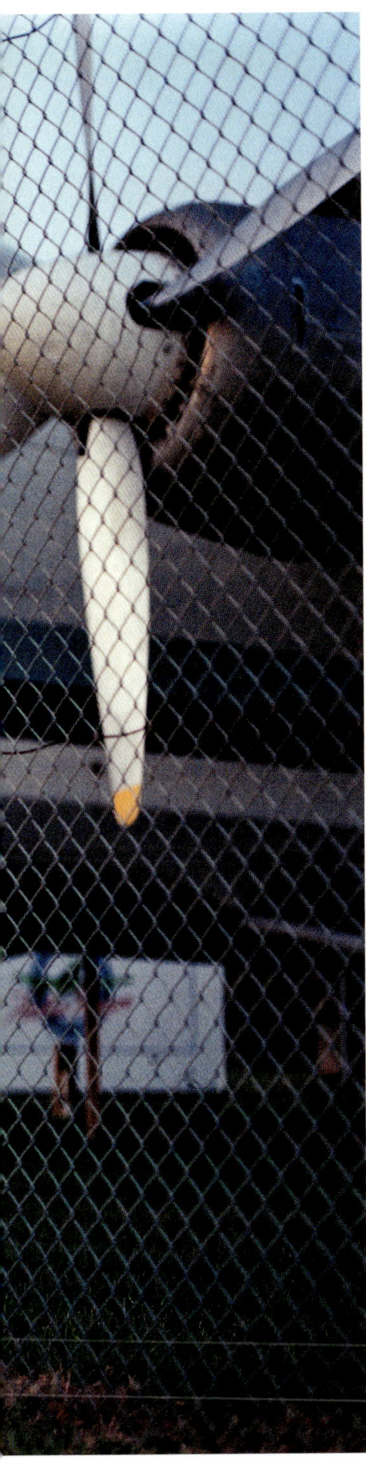

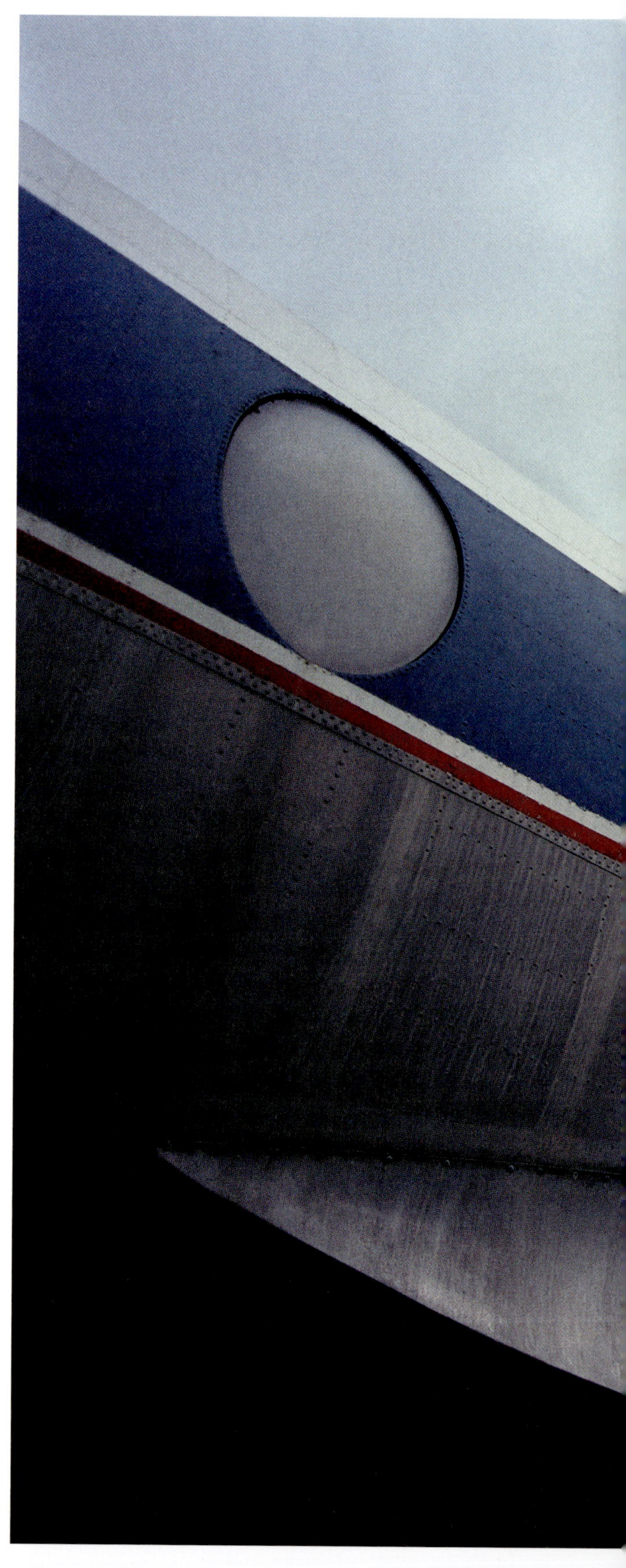

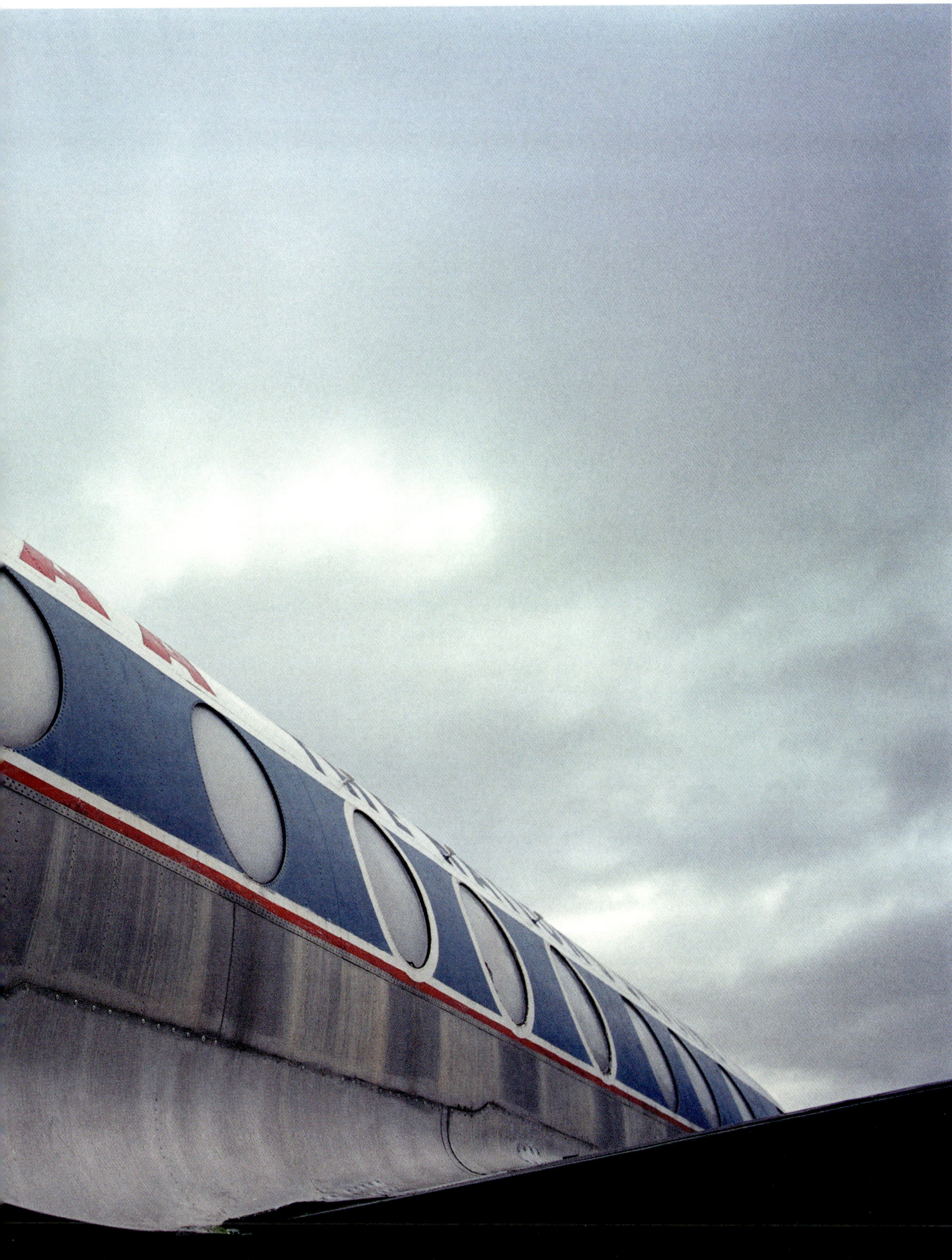

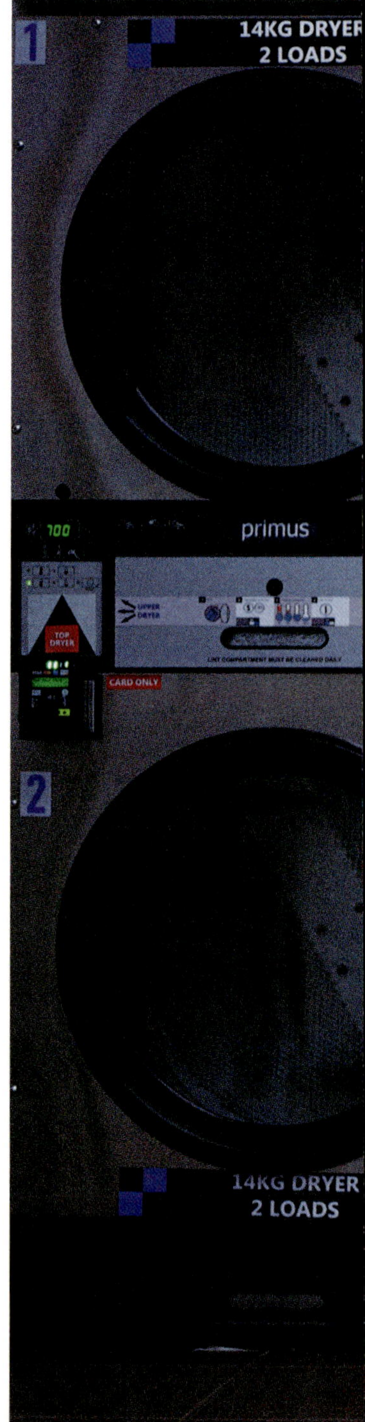
1
14KG DRYER
2 LOADS
primus
TOP DRYER
CARD ONLY
2
14KG DRYER
2 LOADS

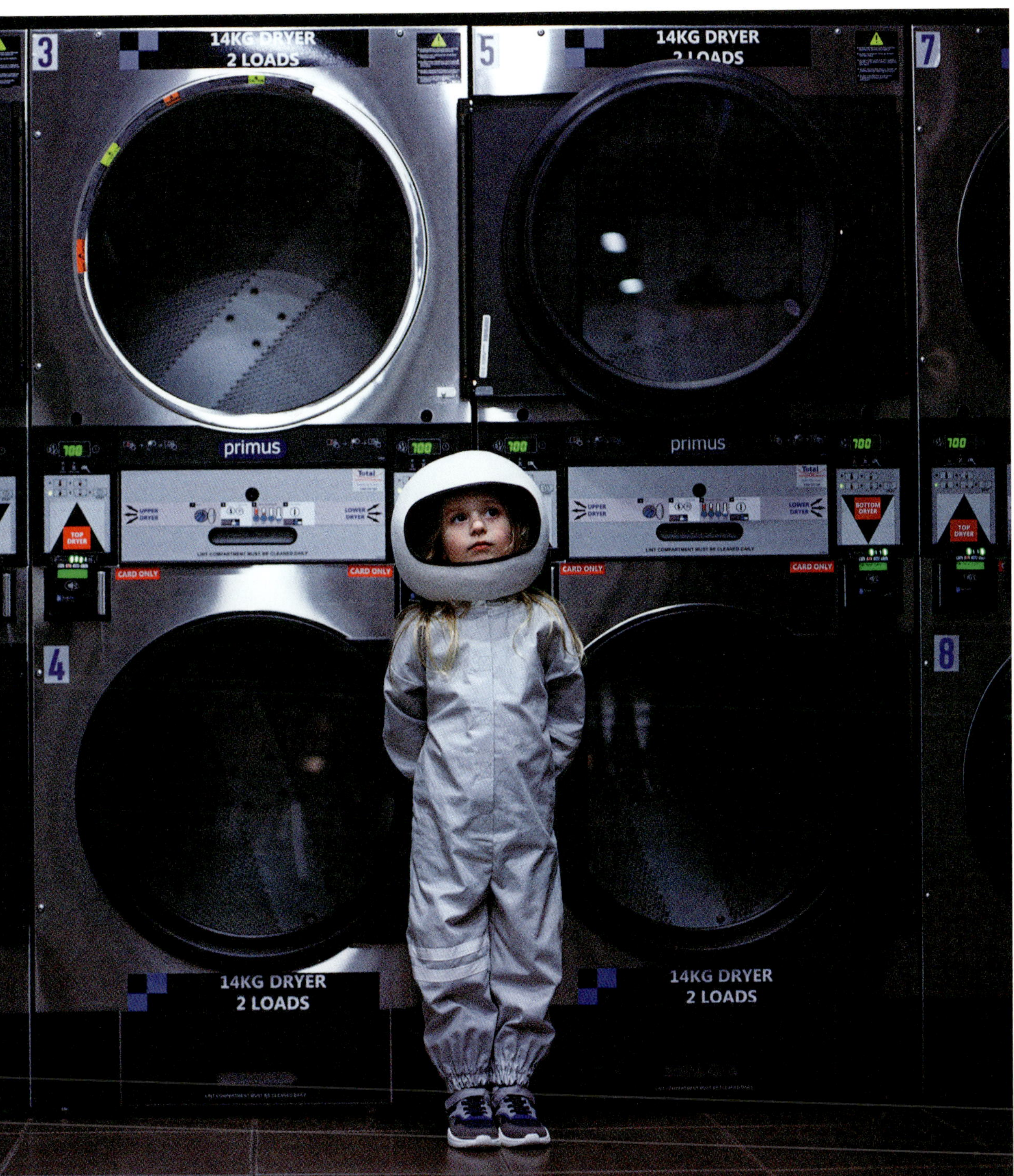
3
14KG DRYER
2 LOADS
5
14KG DRYER
7
primus
primus
CARD ONLY
CARD ONLY
CARD ONLY
CARD ONLY
4
8
14KG DRYER
2 LOADS
14KG DRYER
2 LOADS

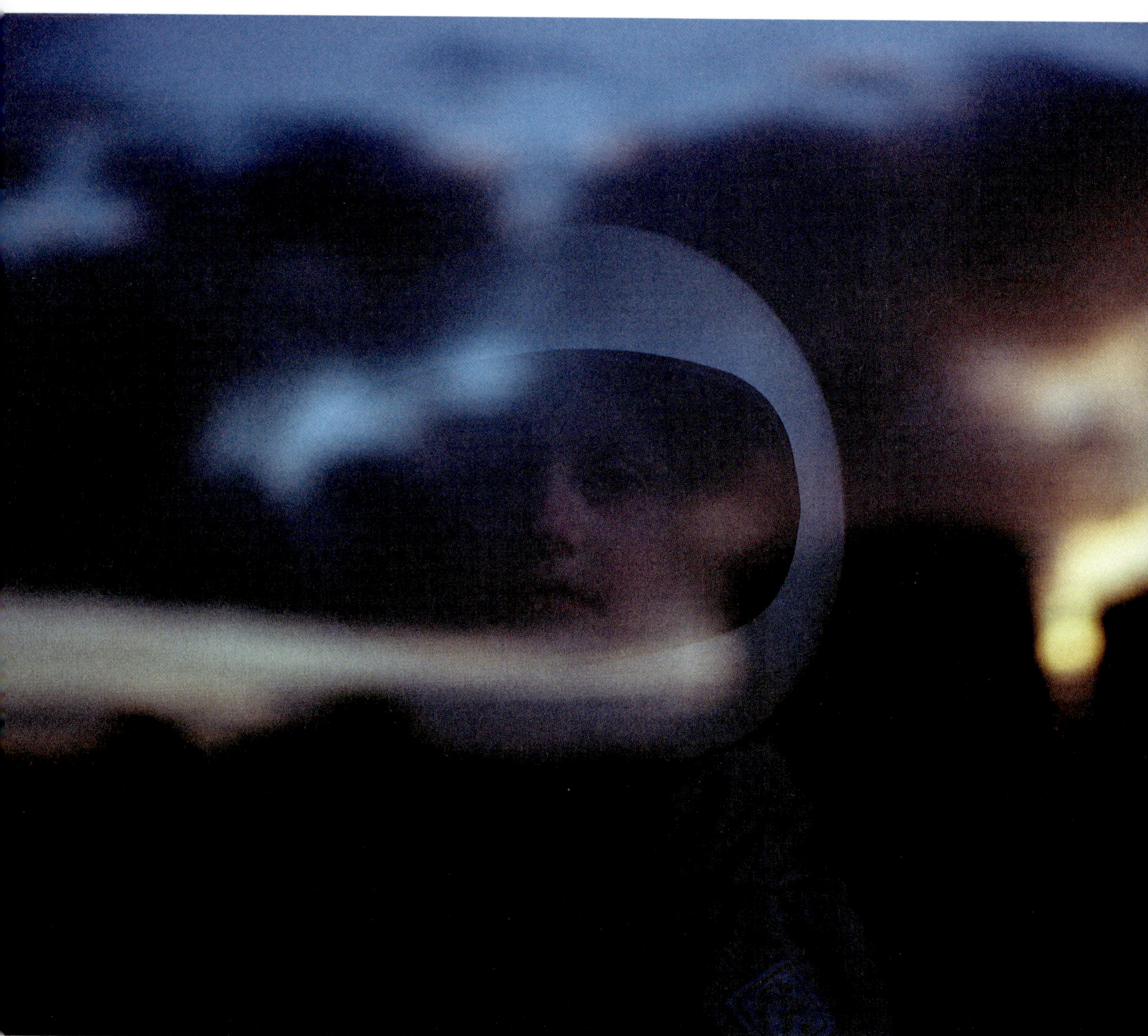

The Cabin

There is sadness here,
but sadness also signifies
the existence of hope.

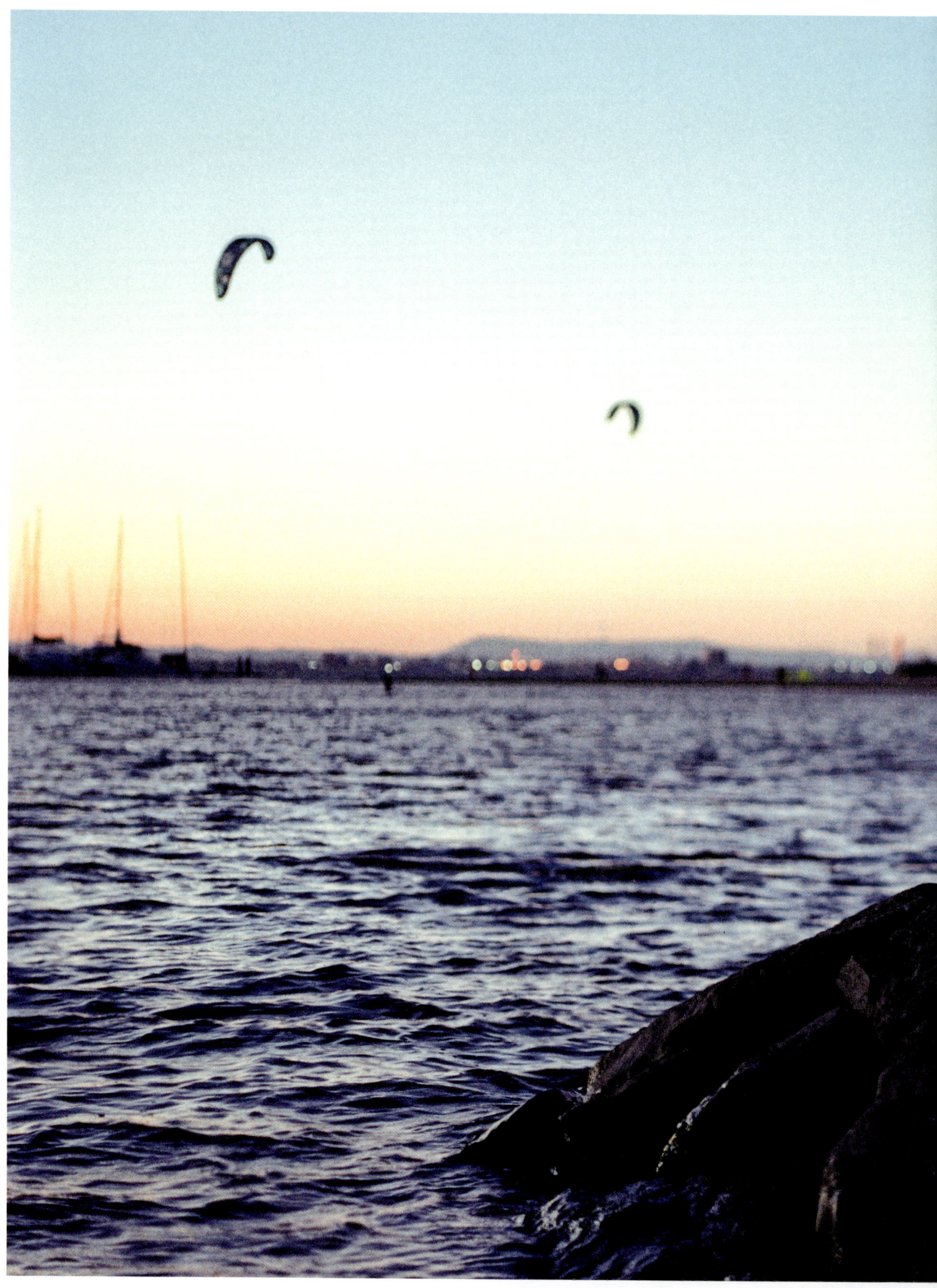

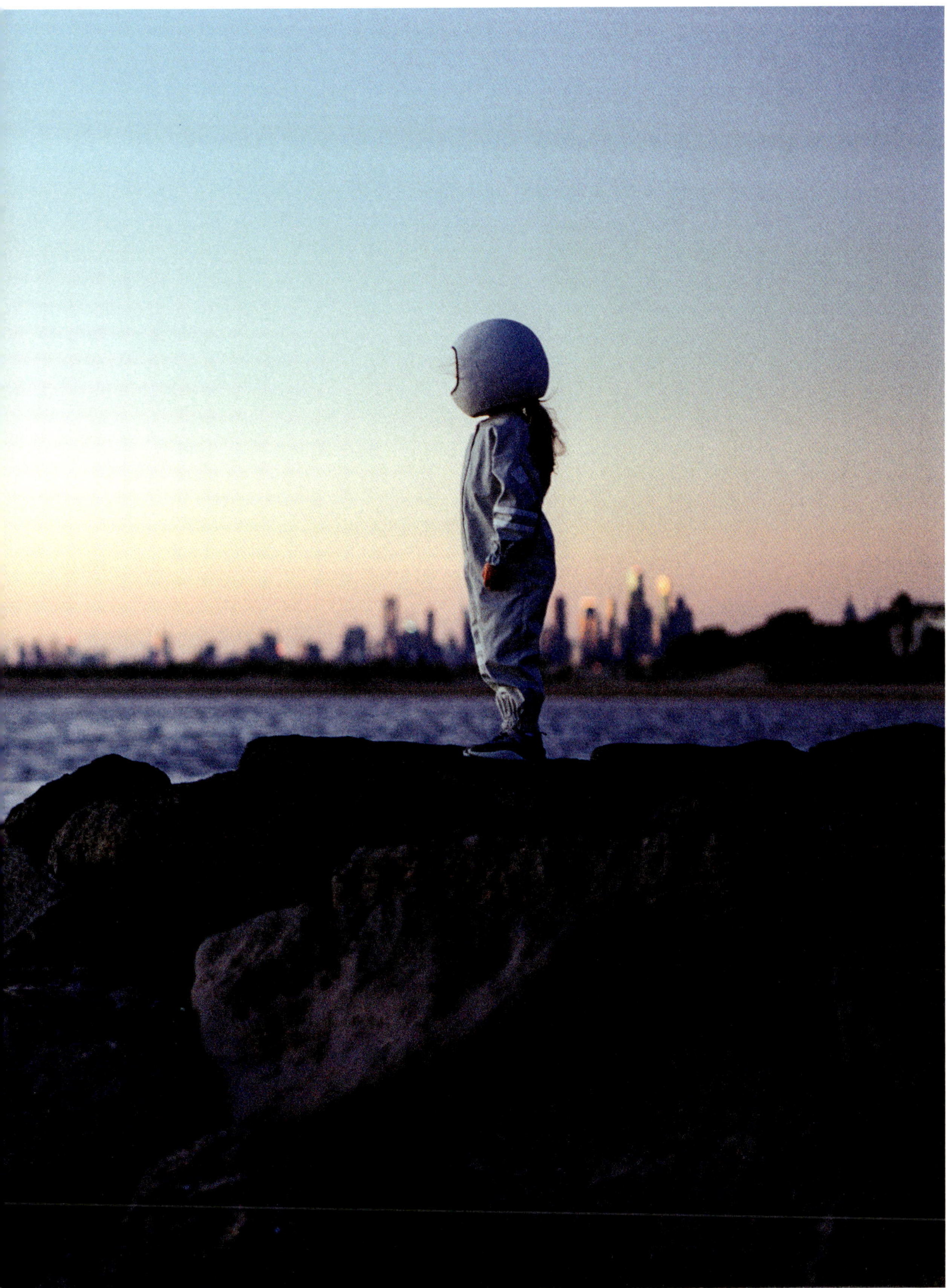

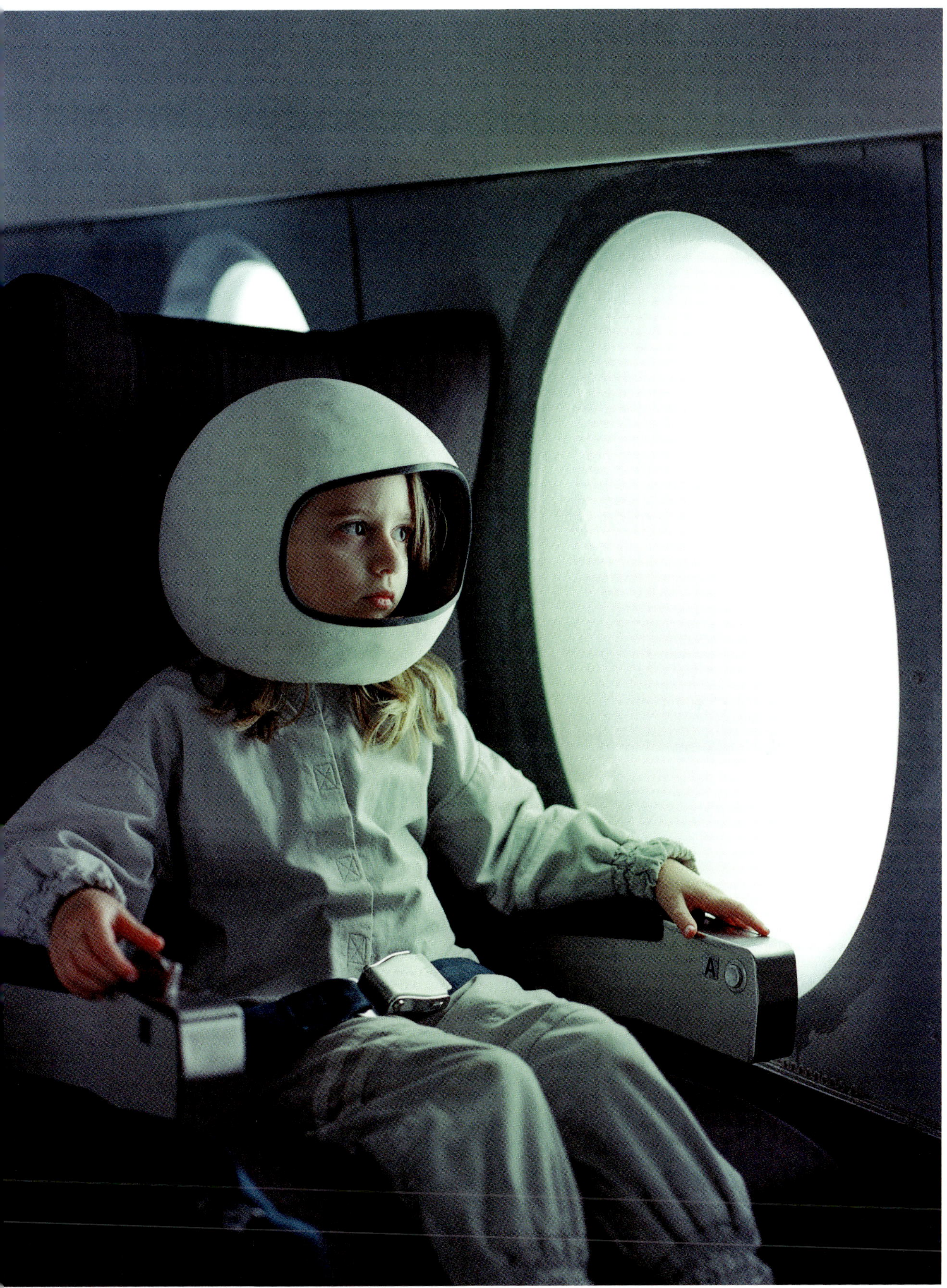
A

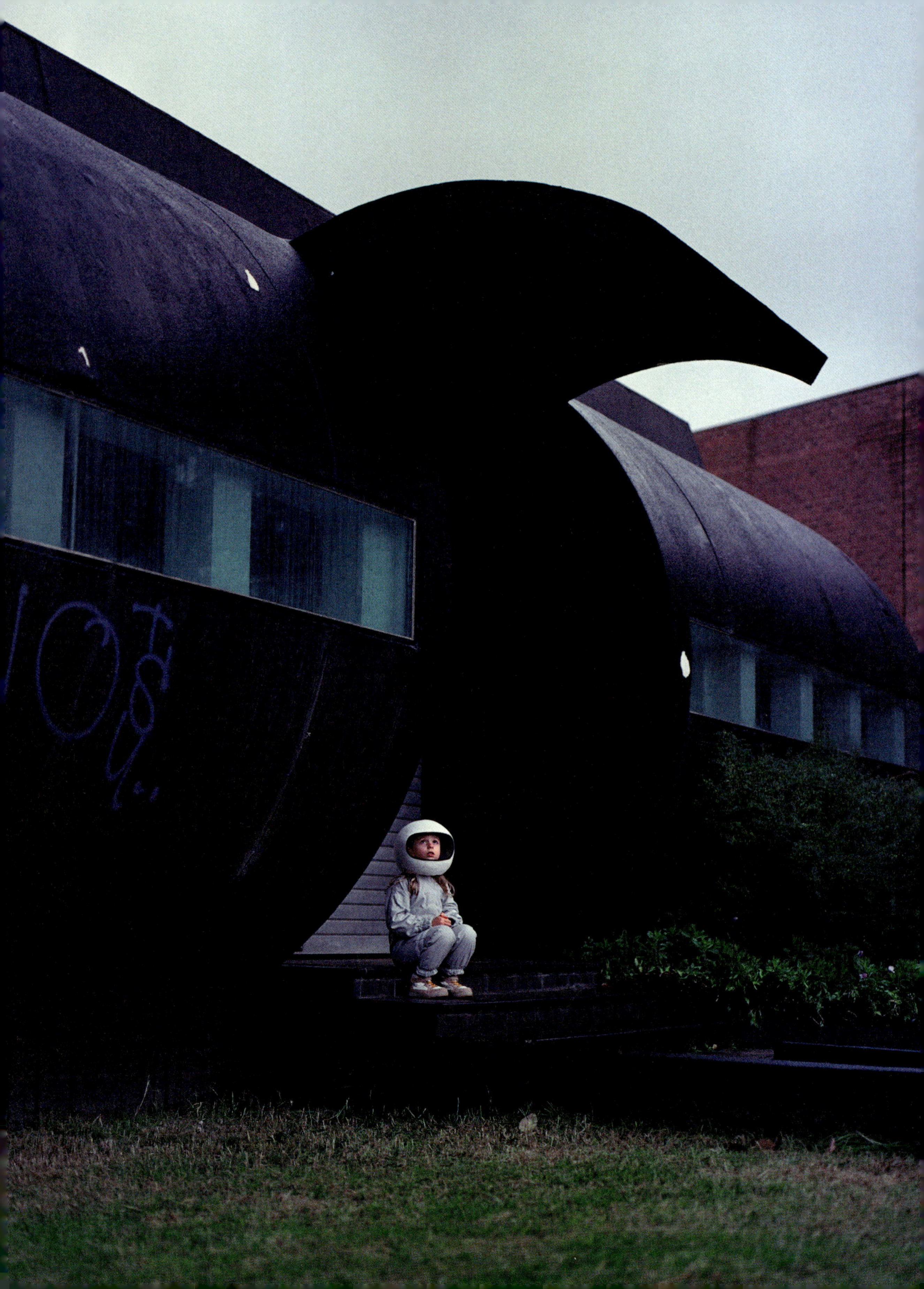

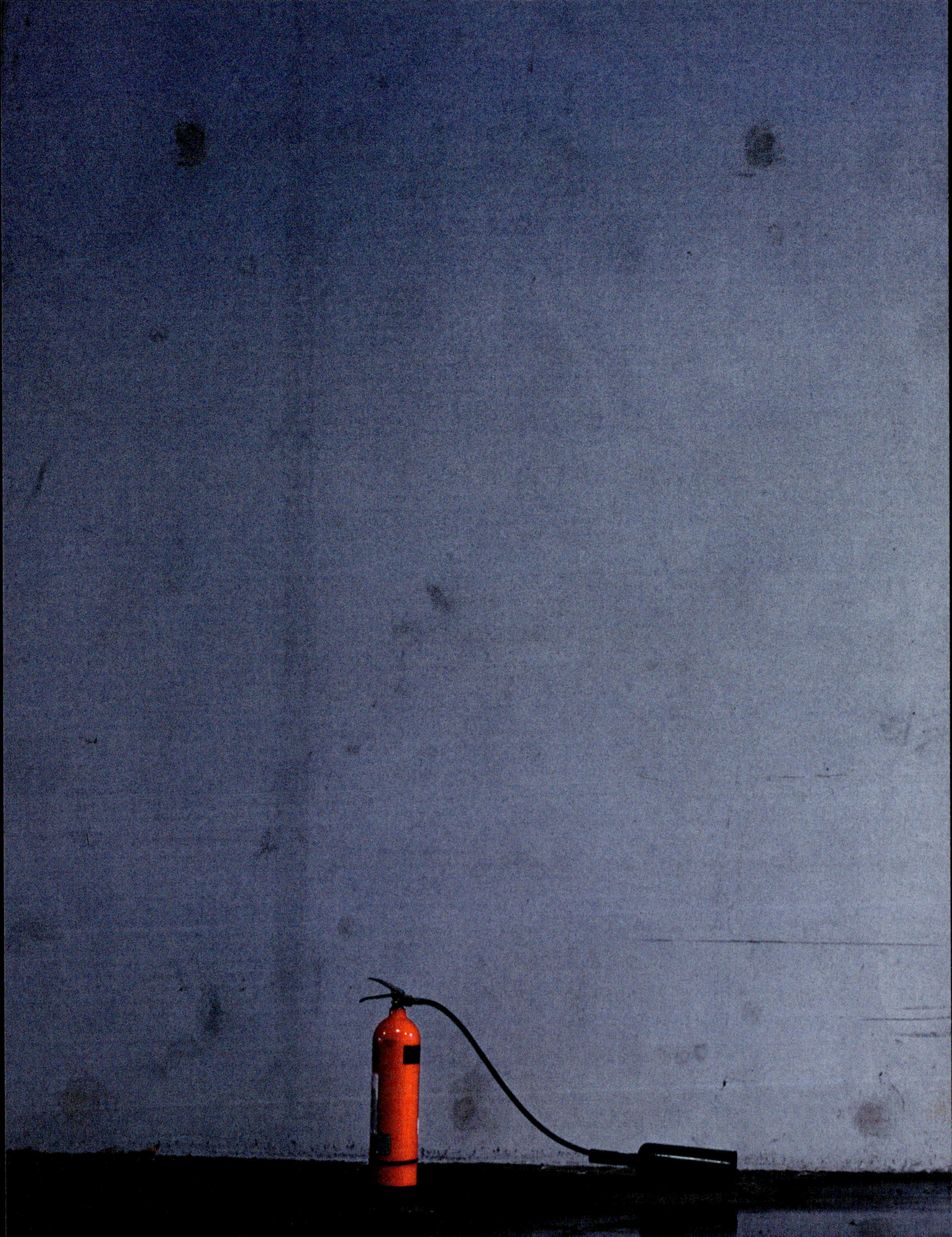

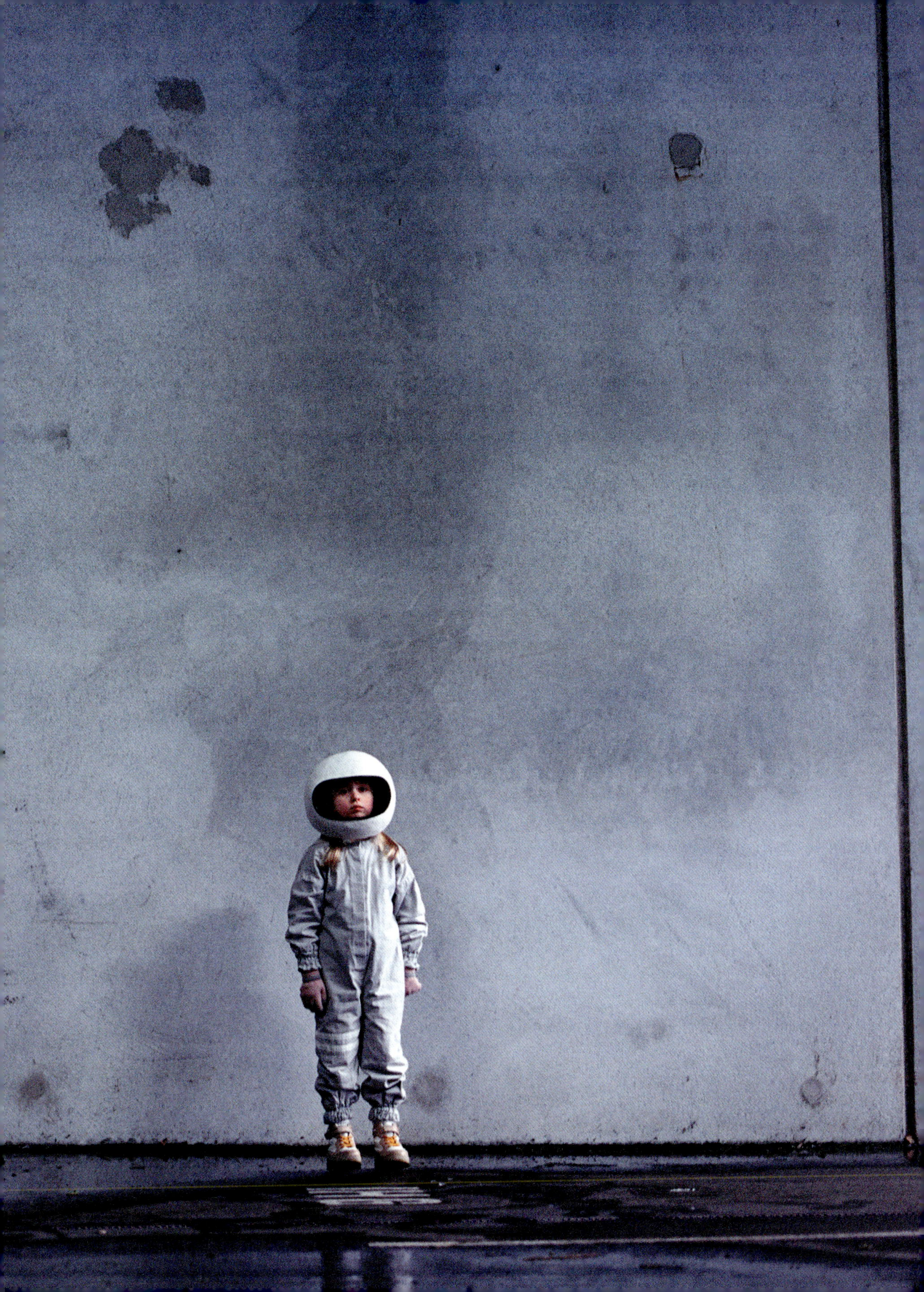

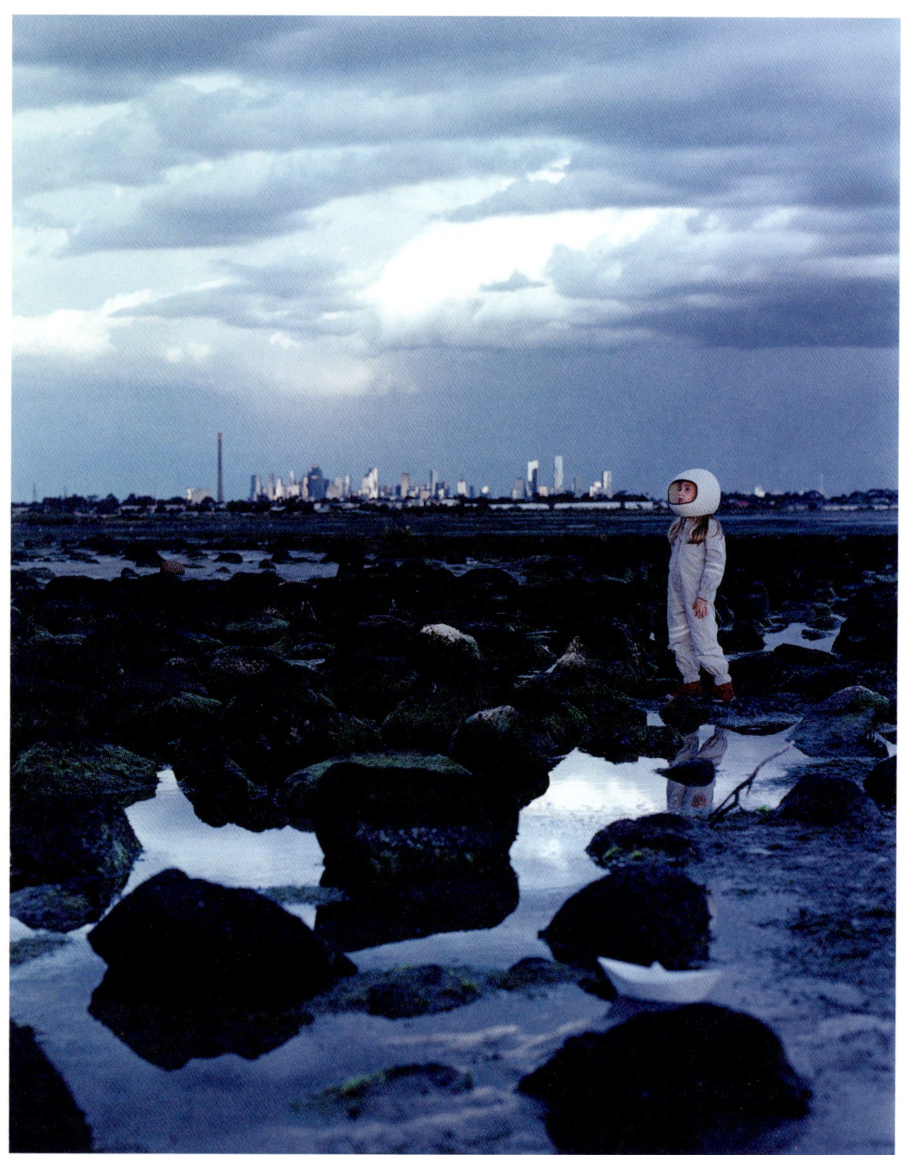

Out of Reach

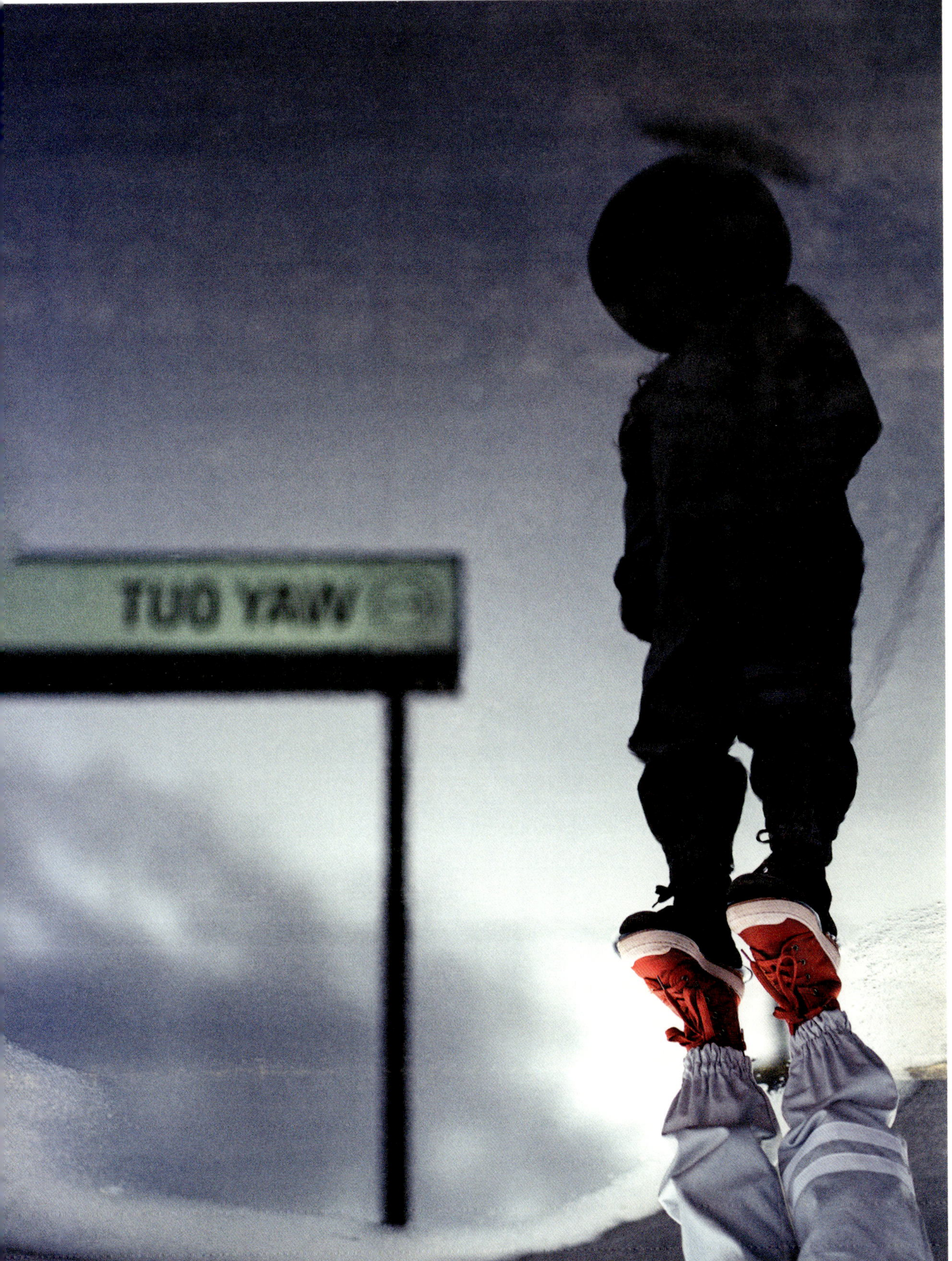
TUO YAW

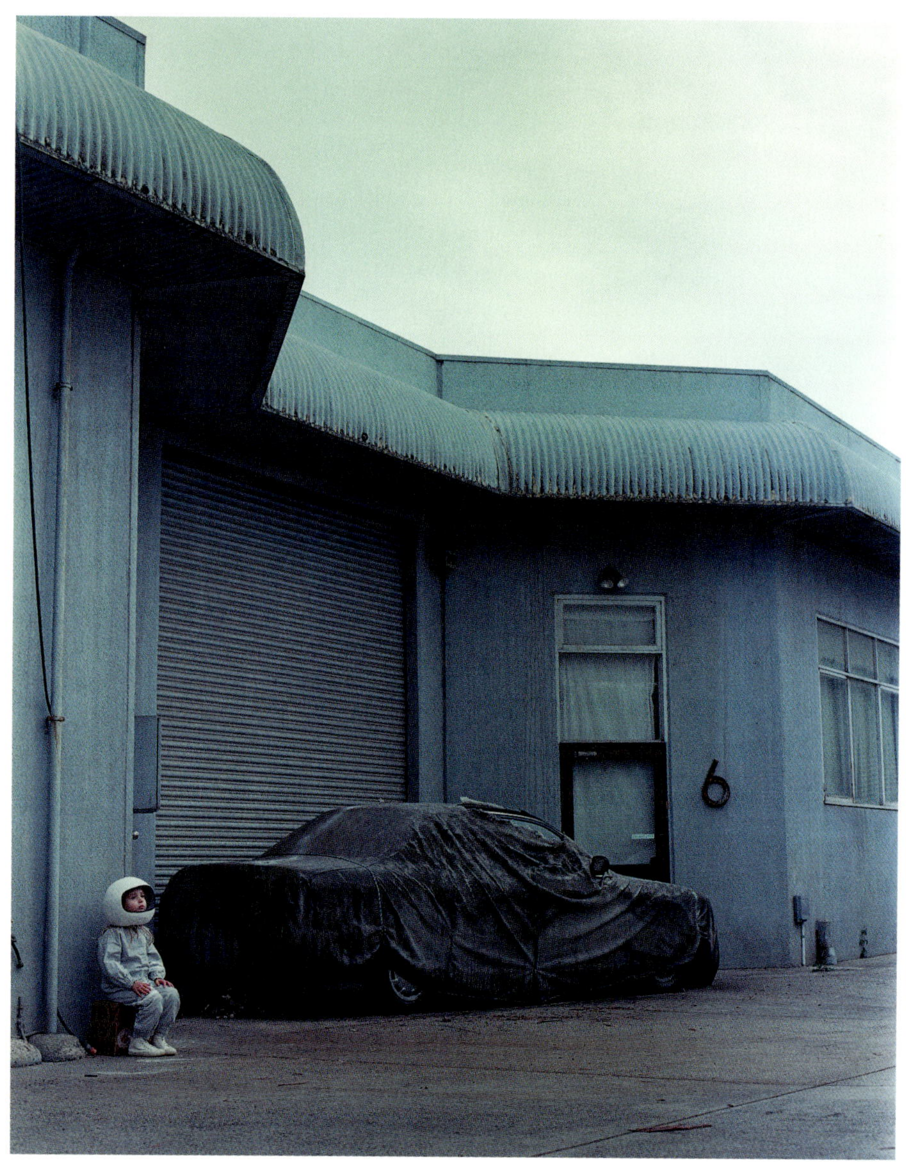

Undercover

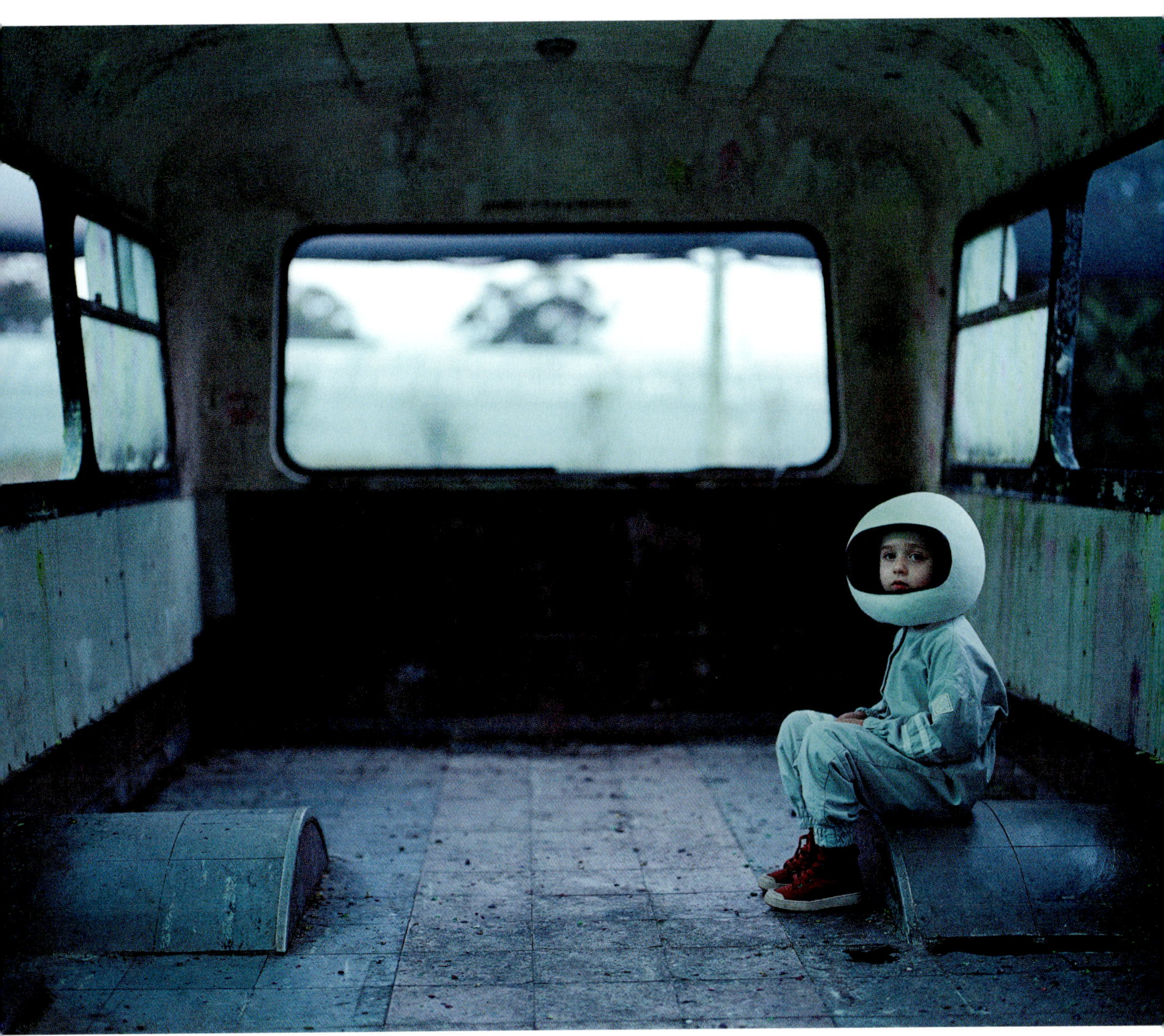

She is an explorer,
an archaeologist and a scientist.
She is a Victorian opening
the Pharaoh's tomb.

The Carriage

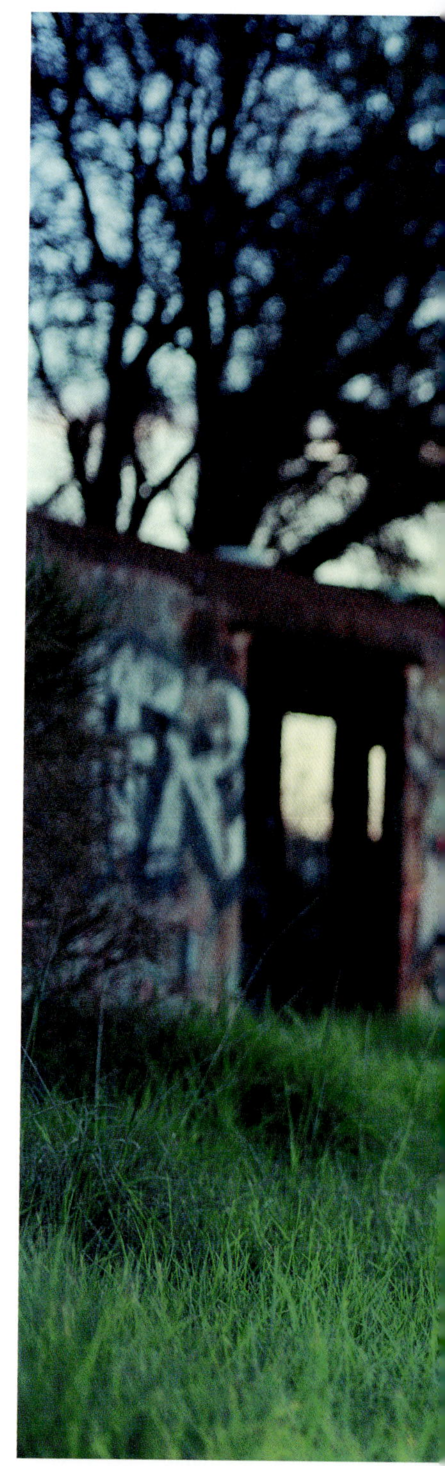

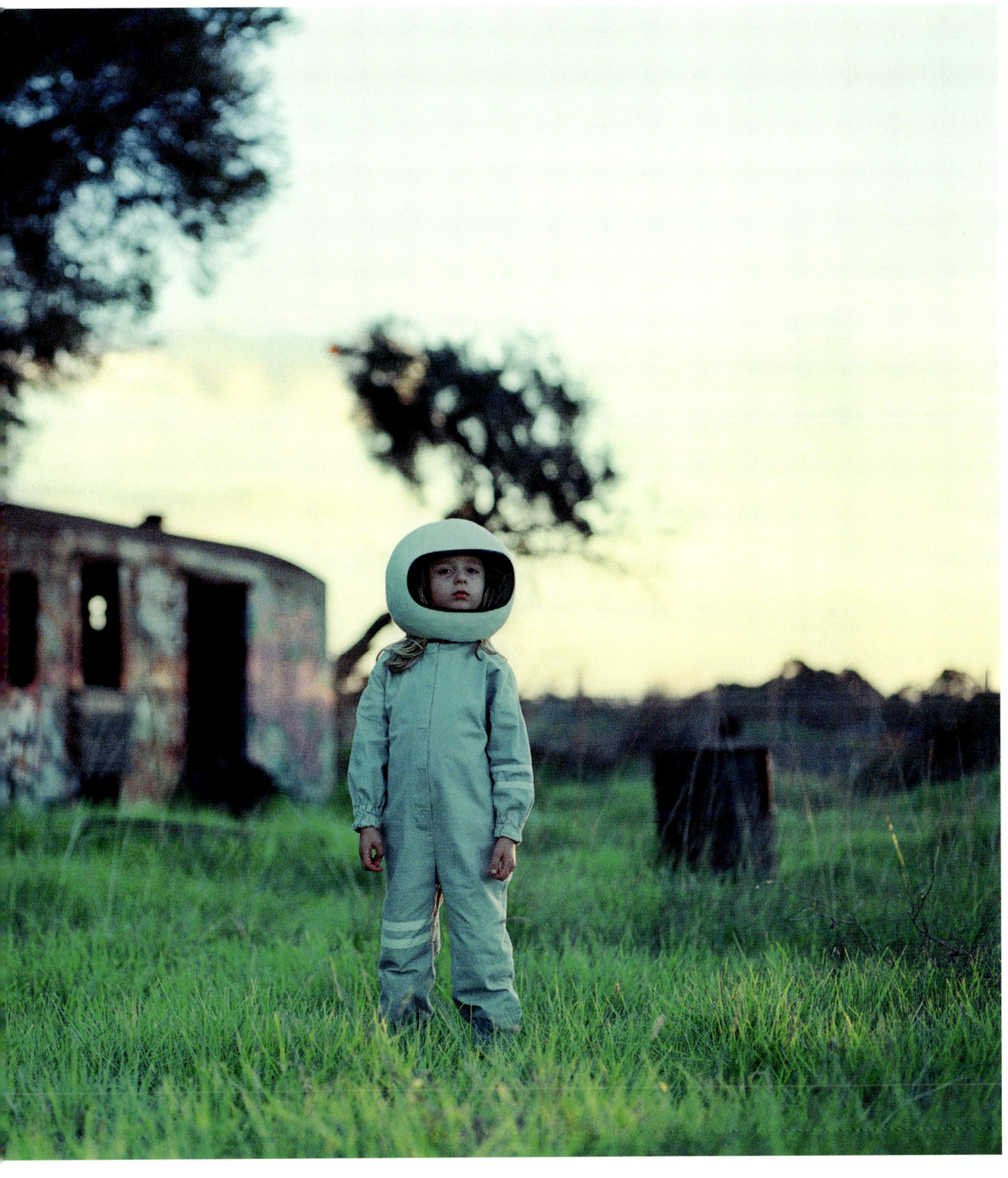

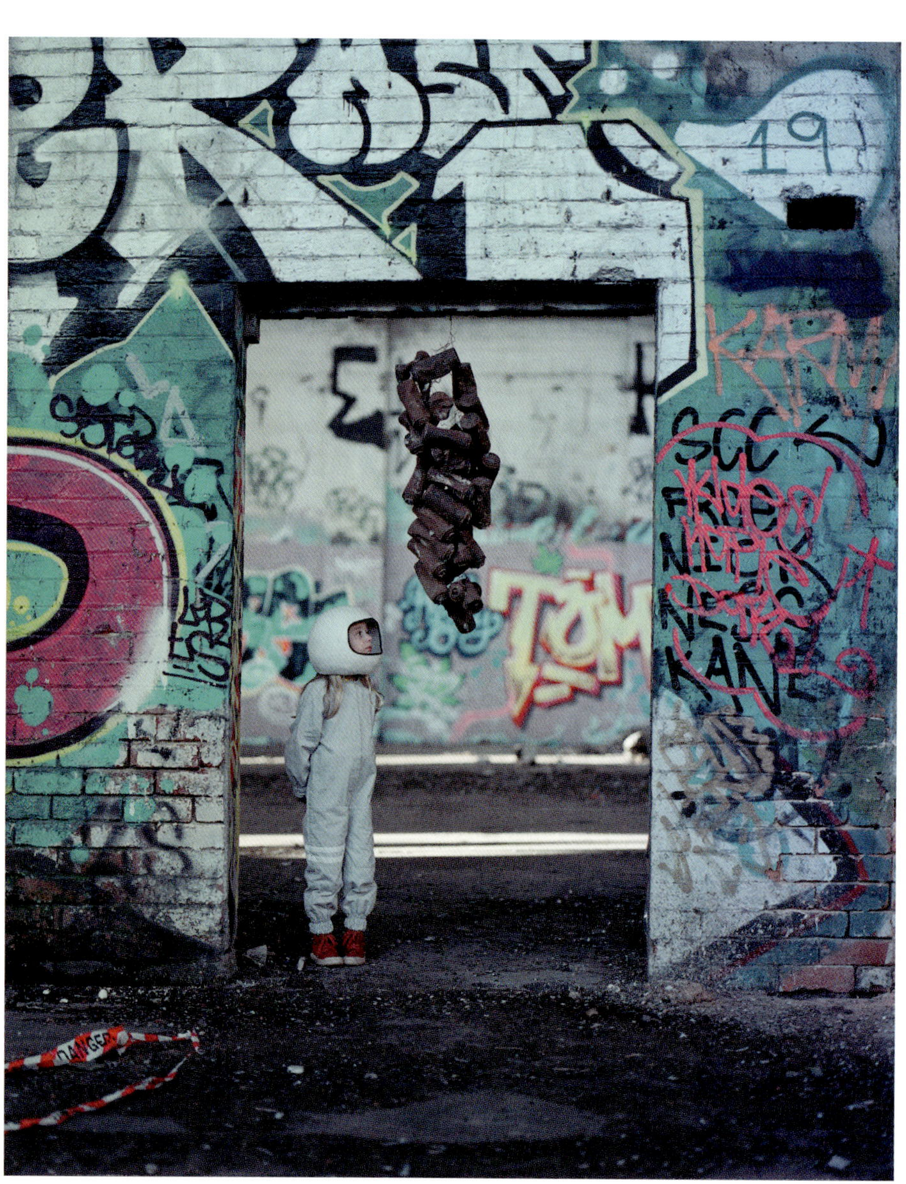
19
KANE

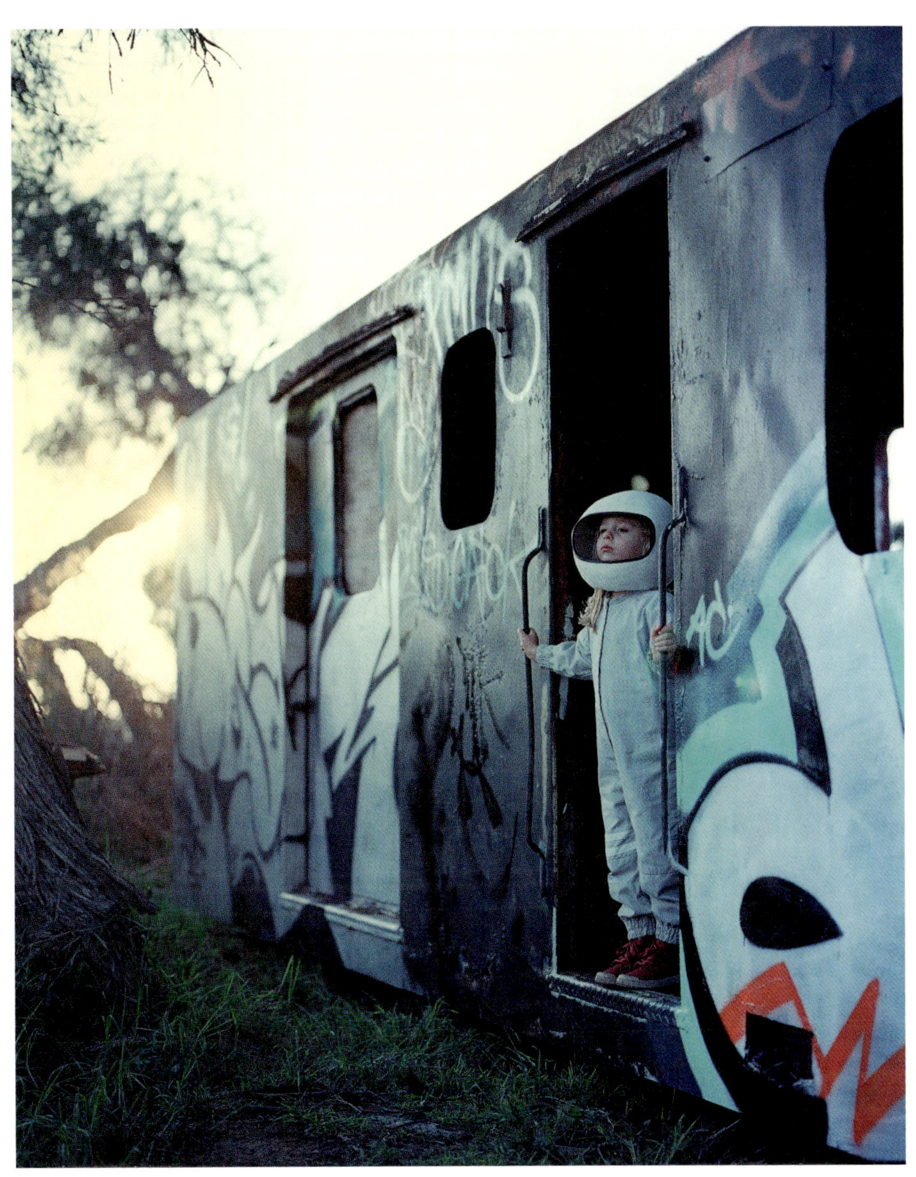

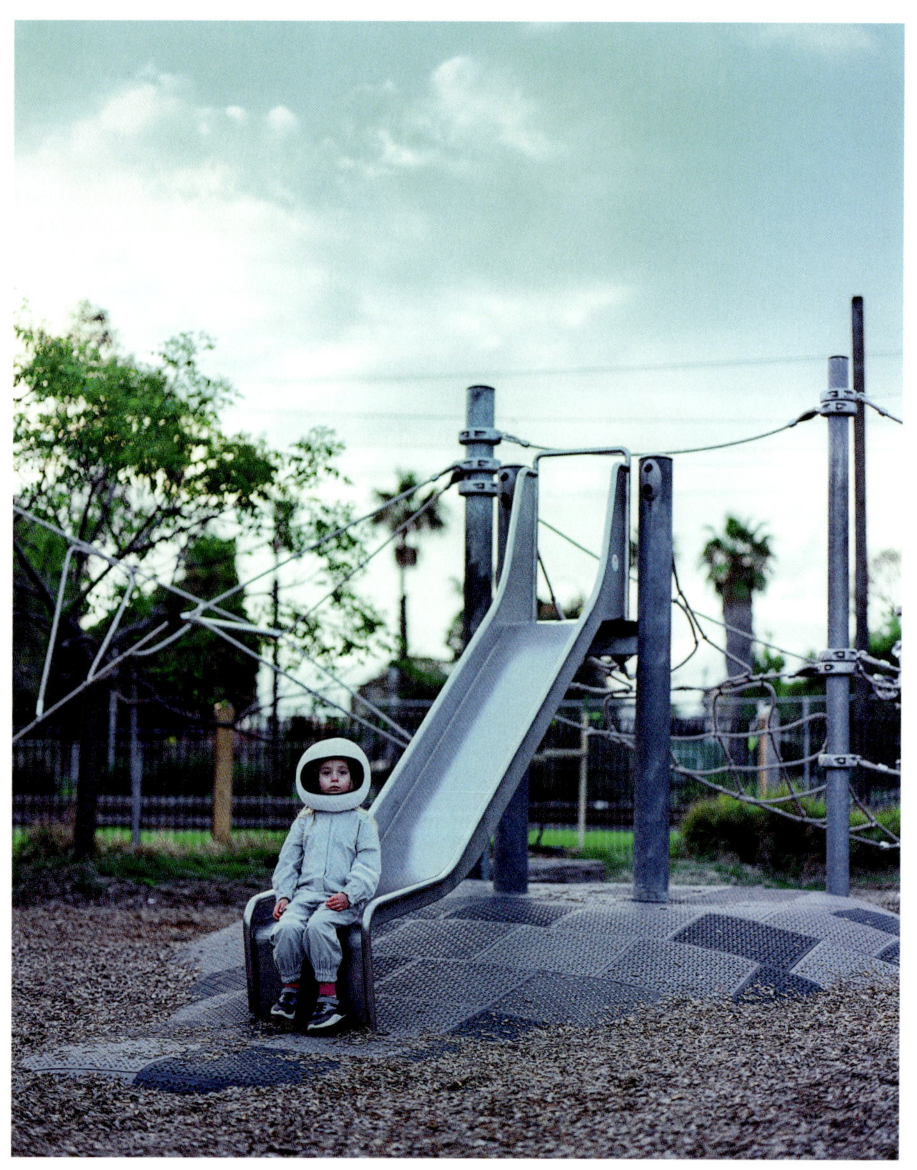

> City Line

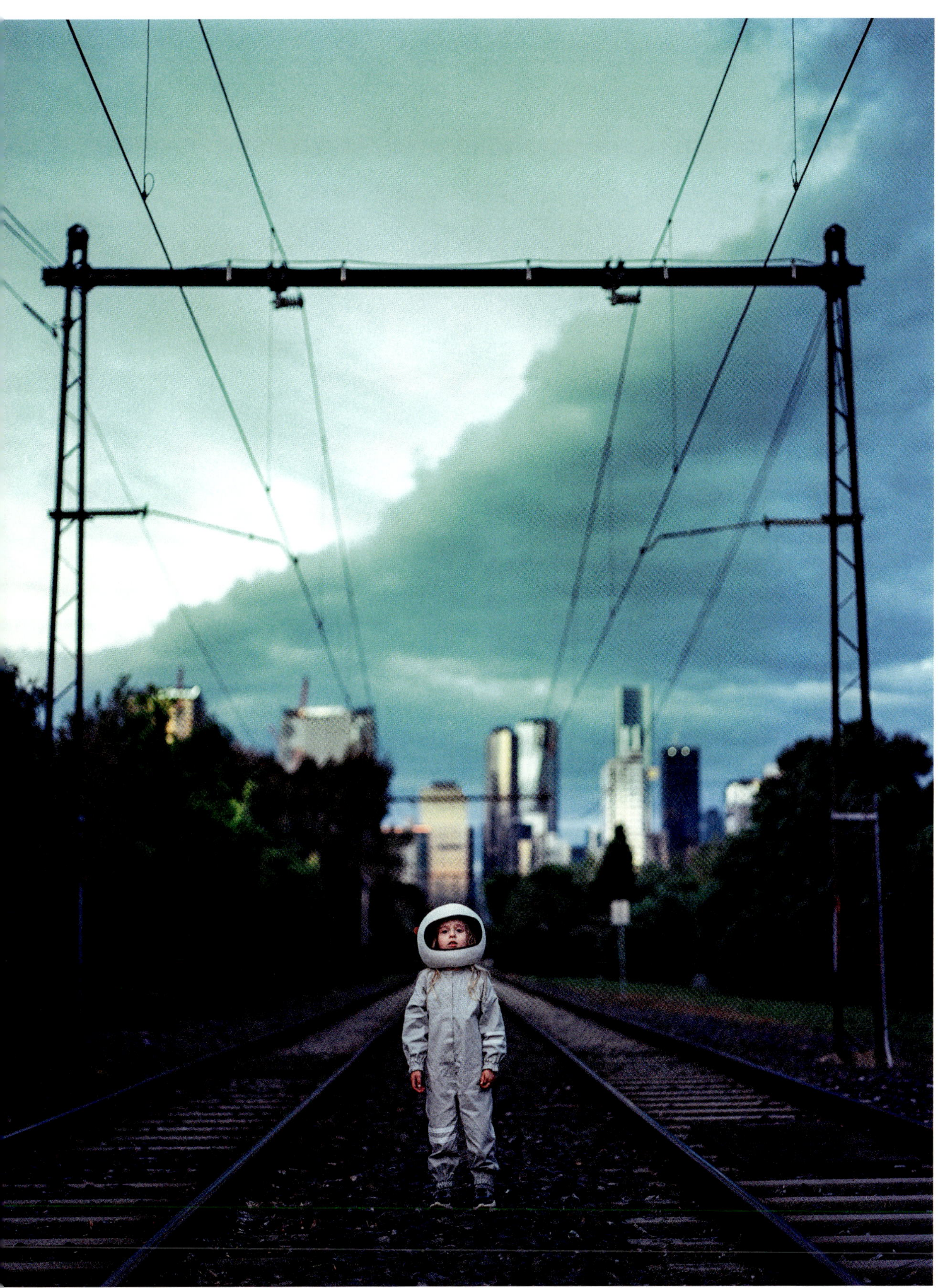

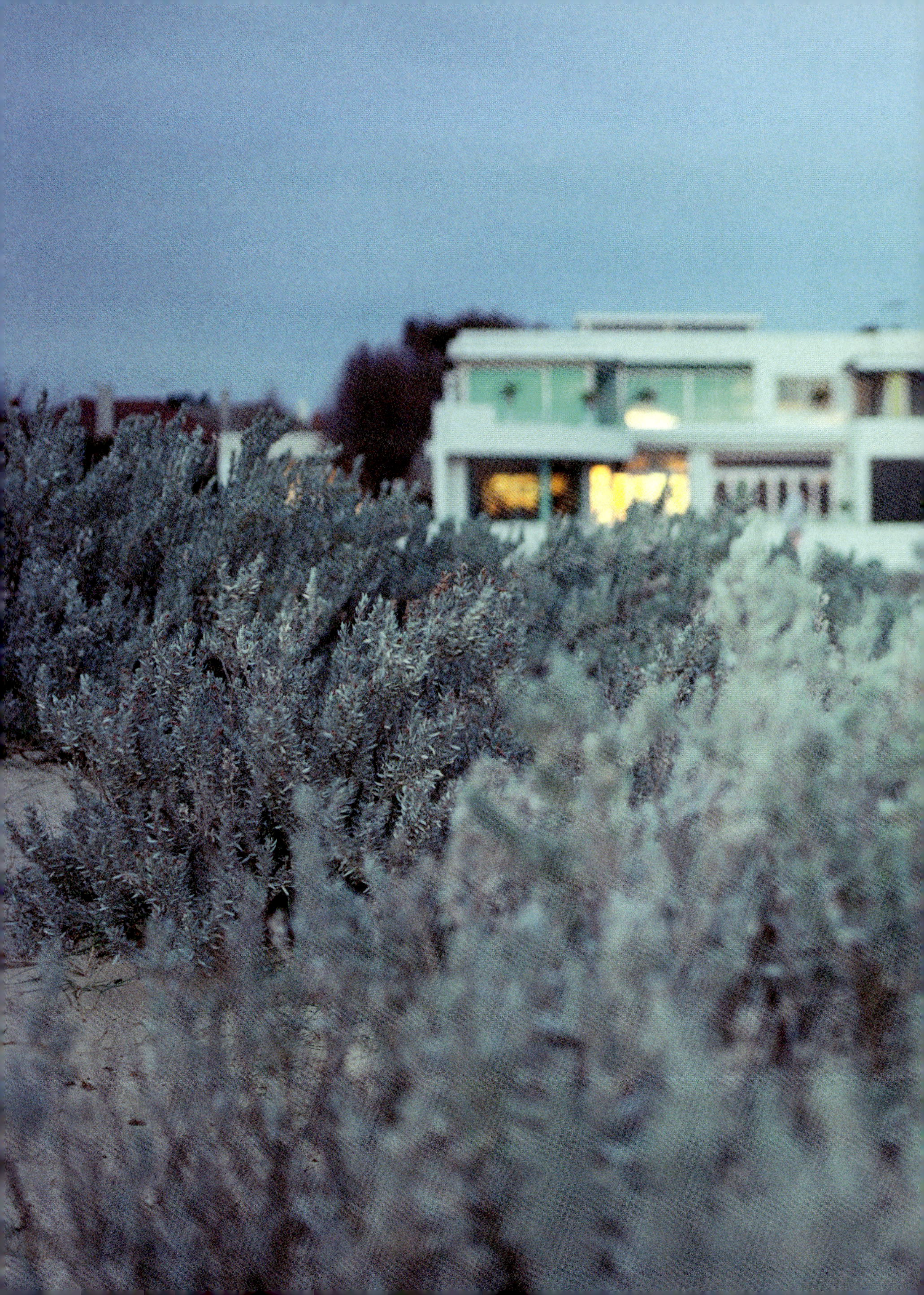

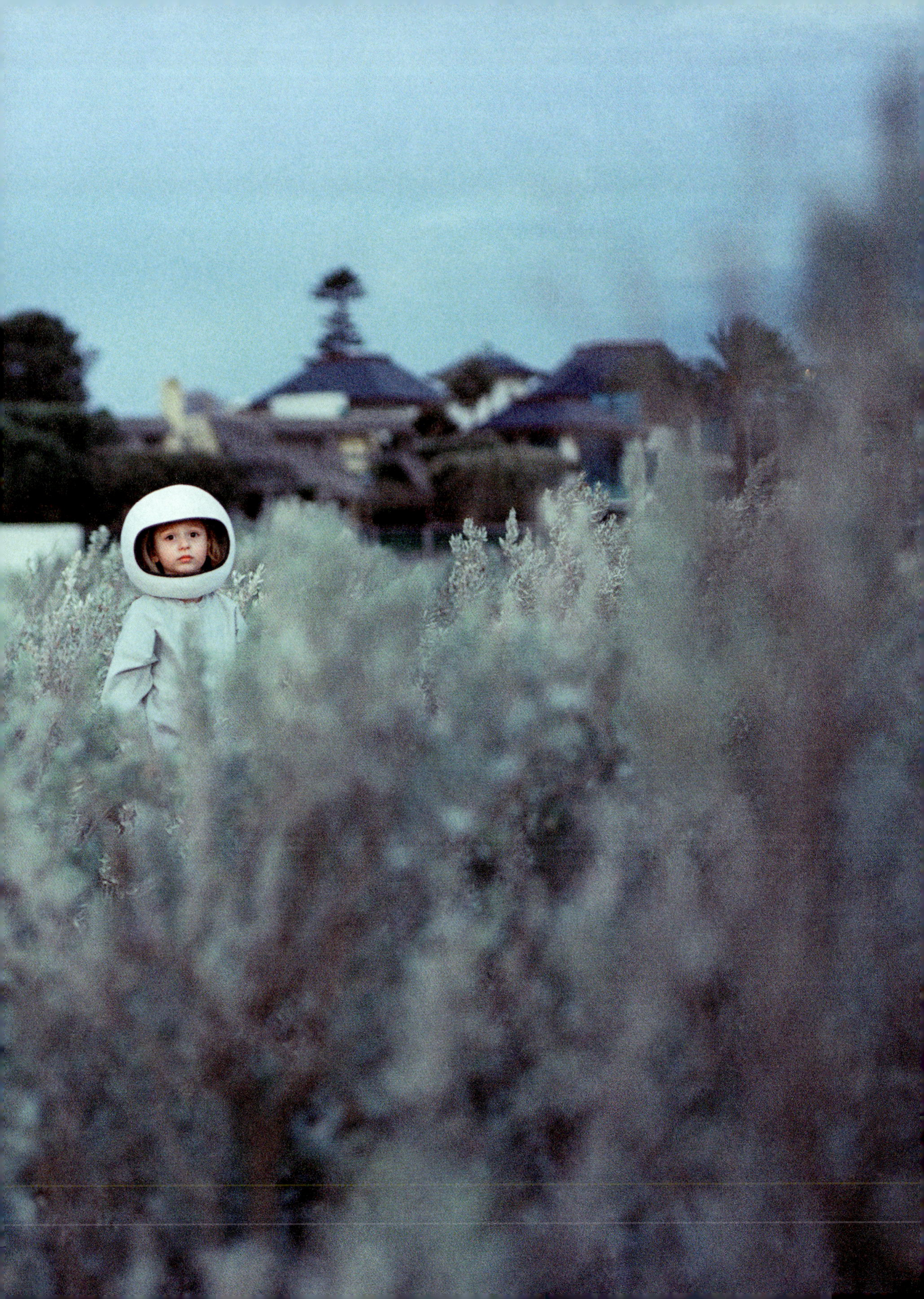

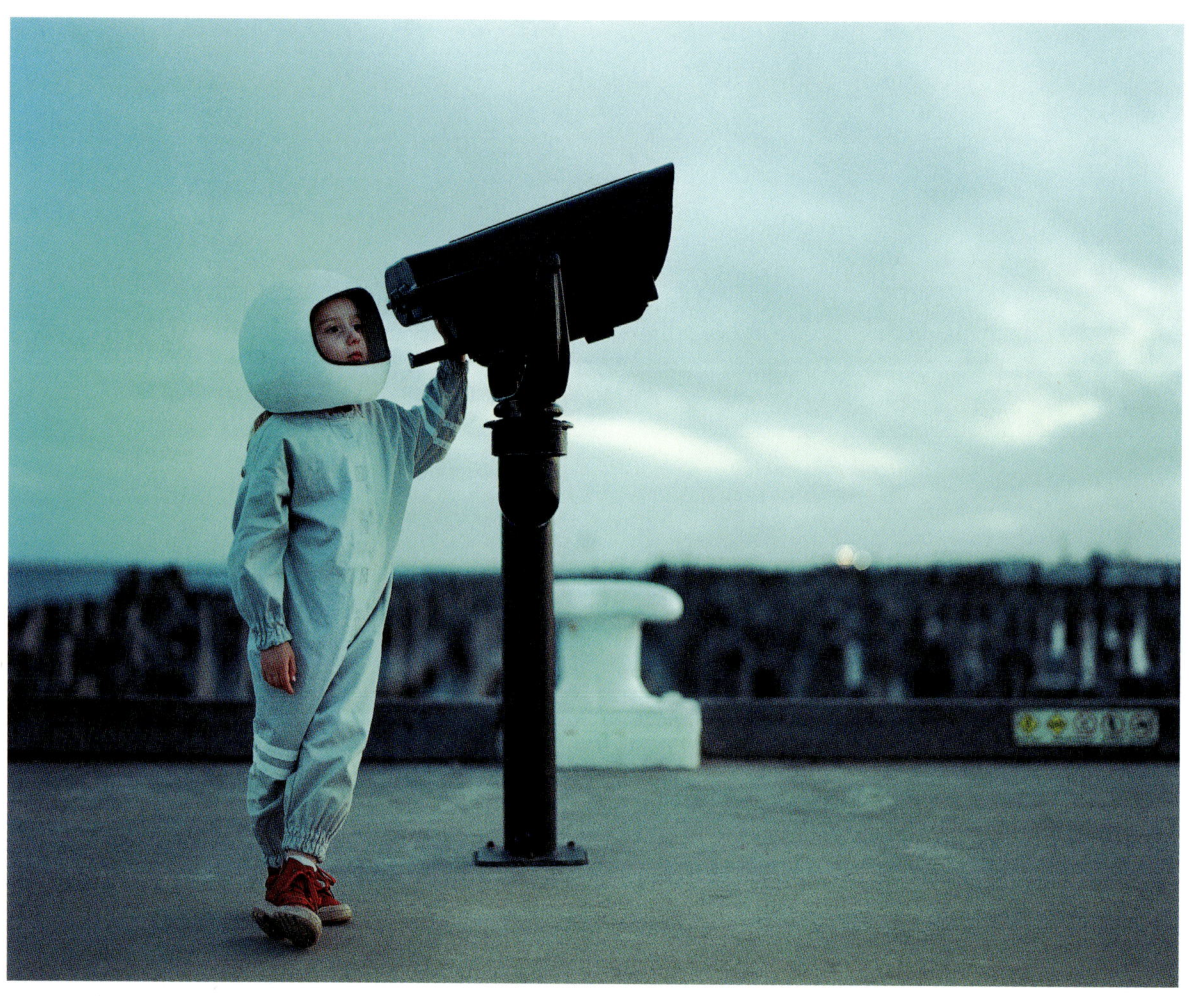

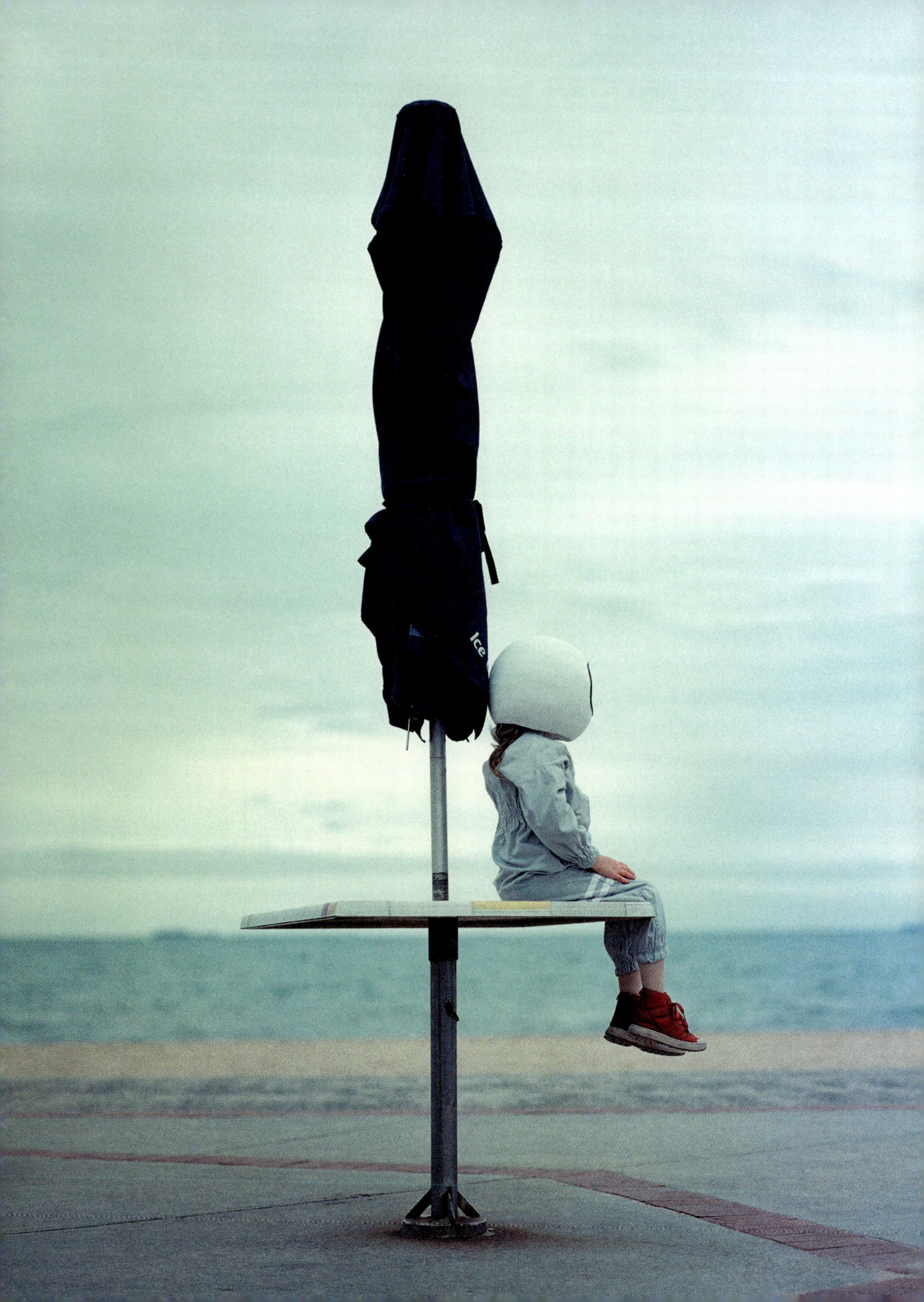
Ice

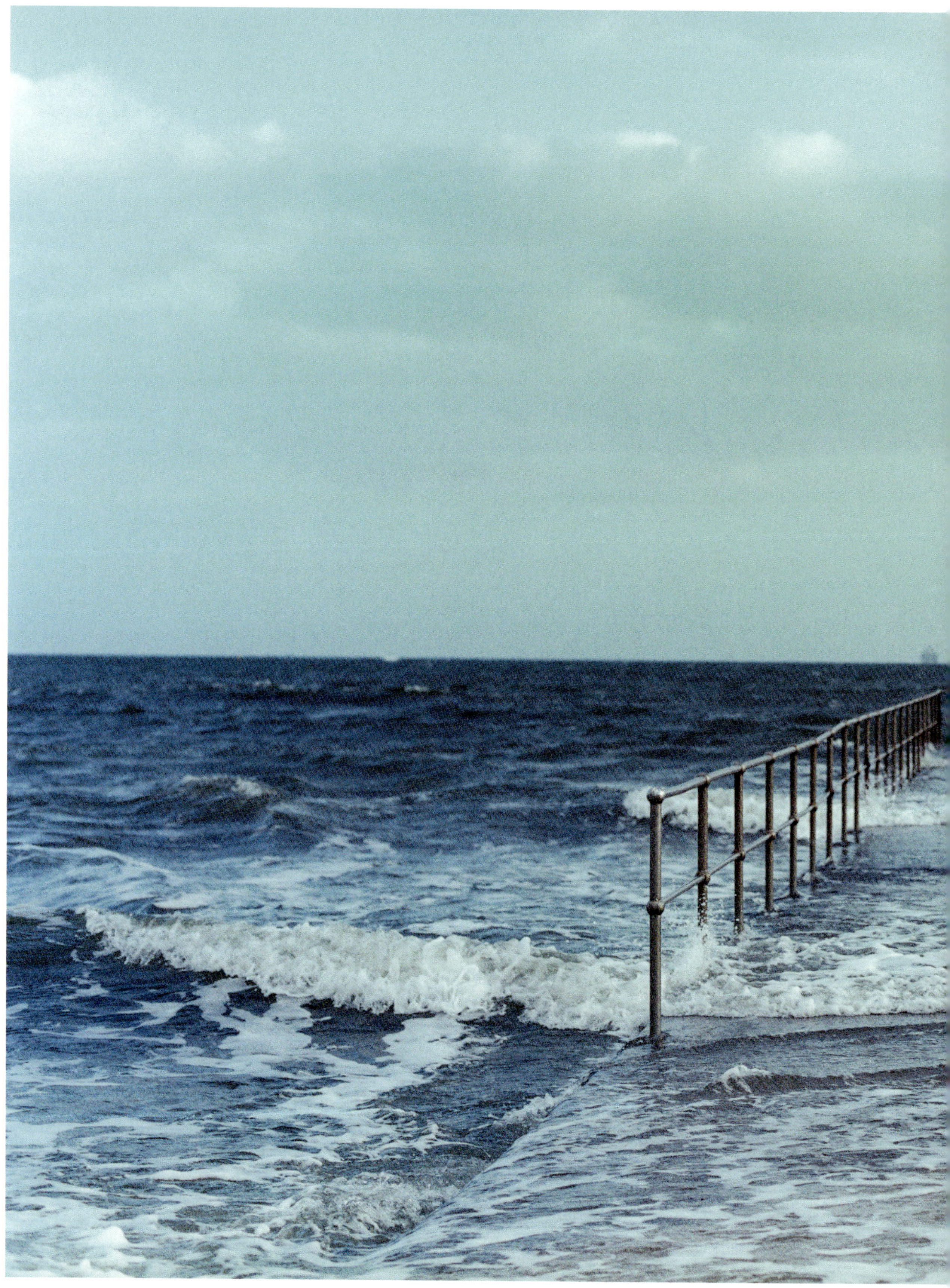

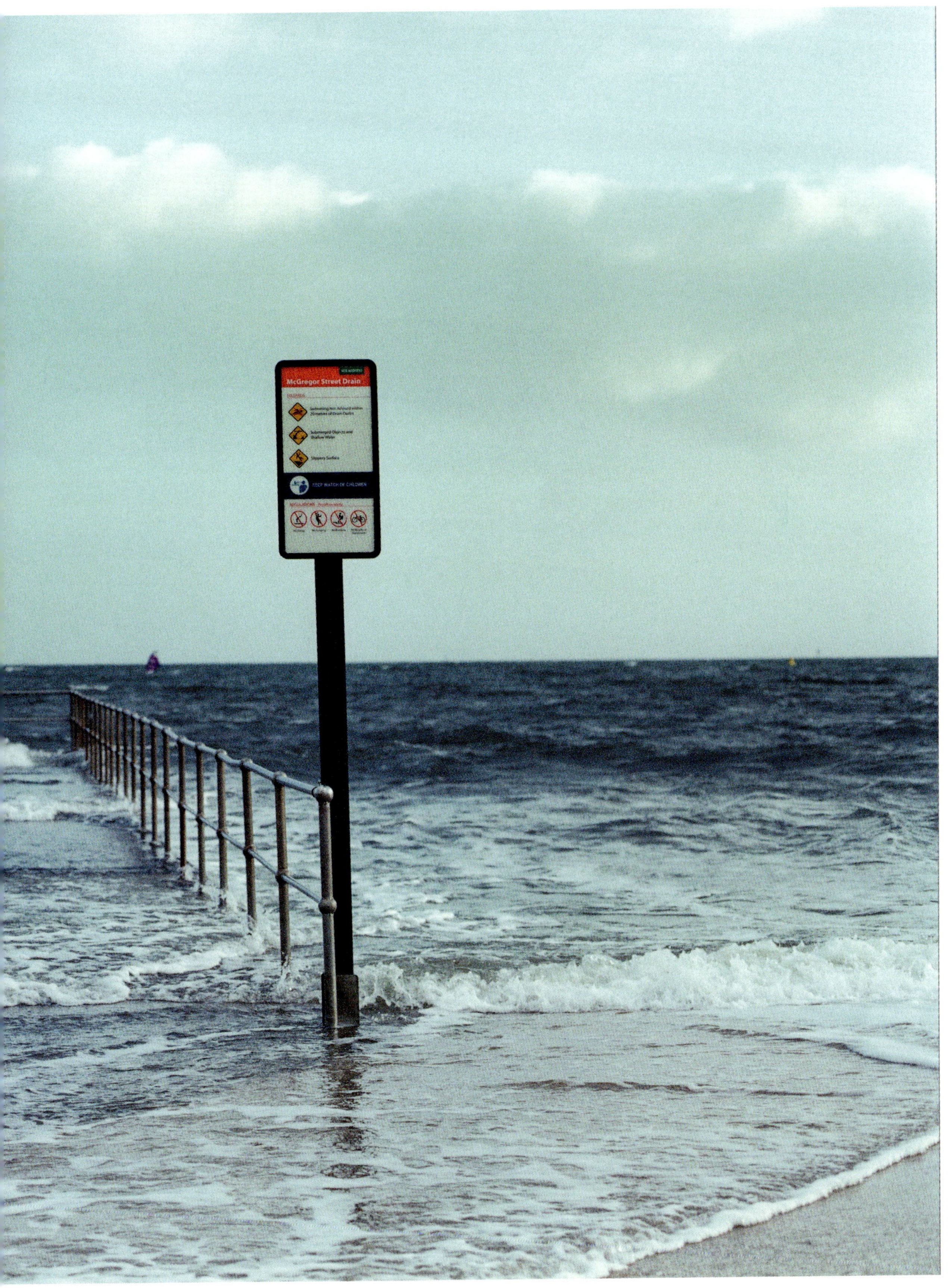
McGregor Street Drain
KEEP WATCH OF CHILDREN

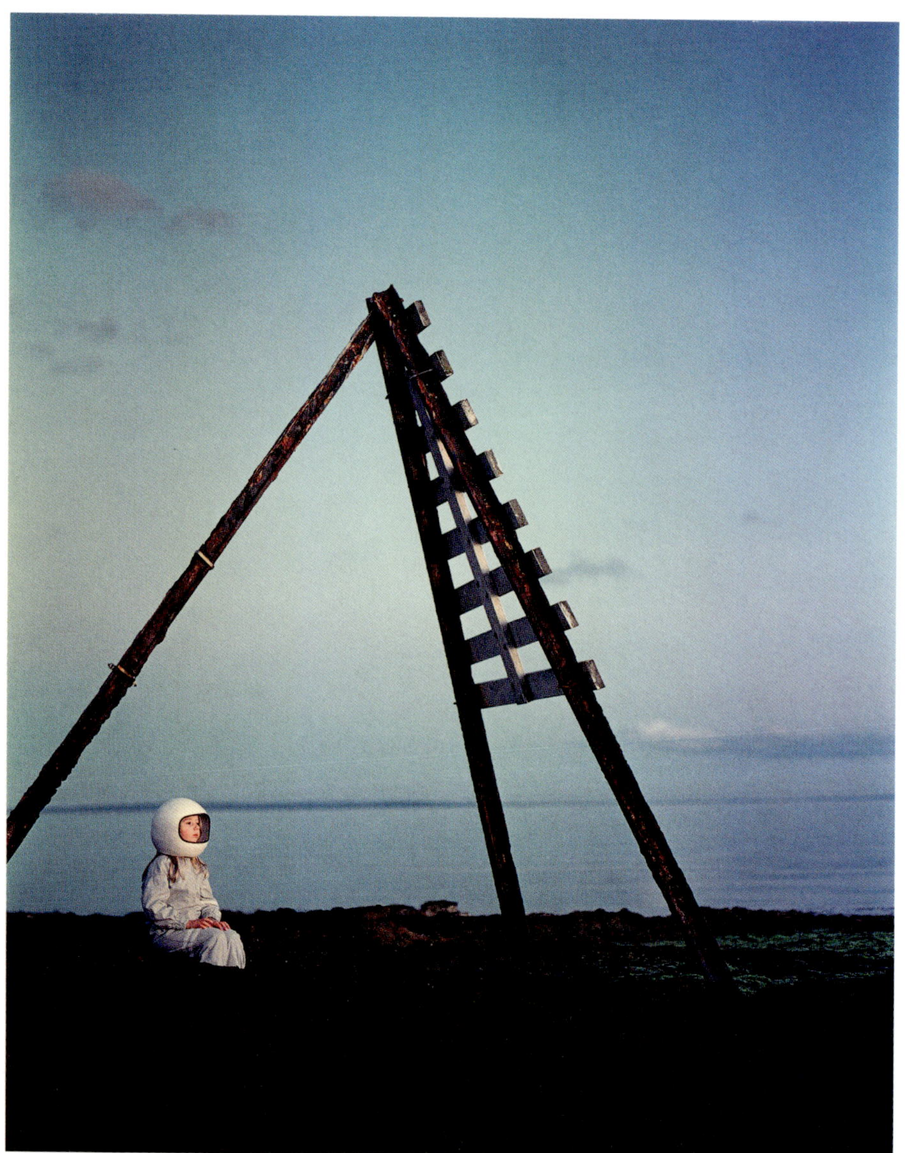

The Pyramid

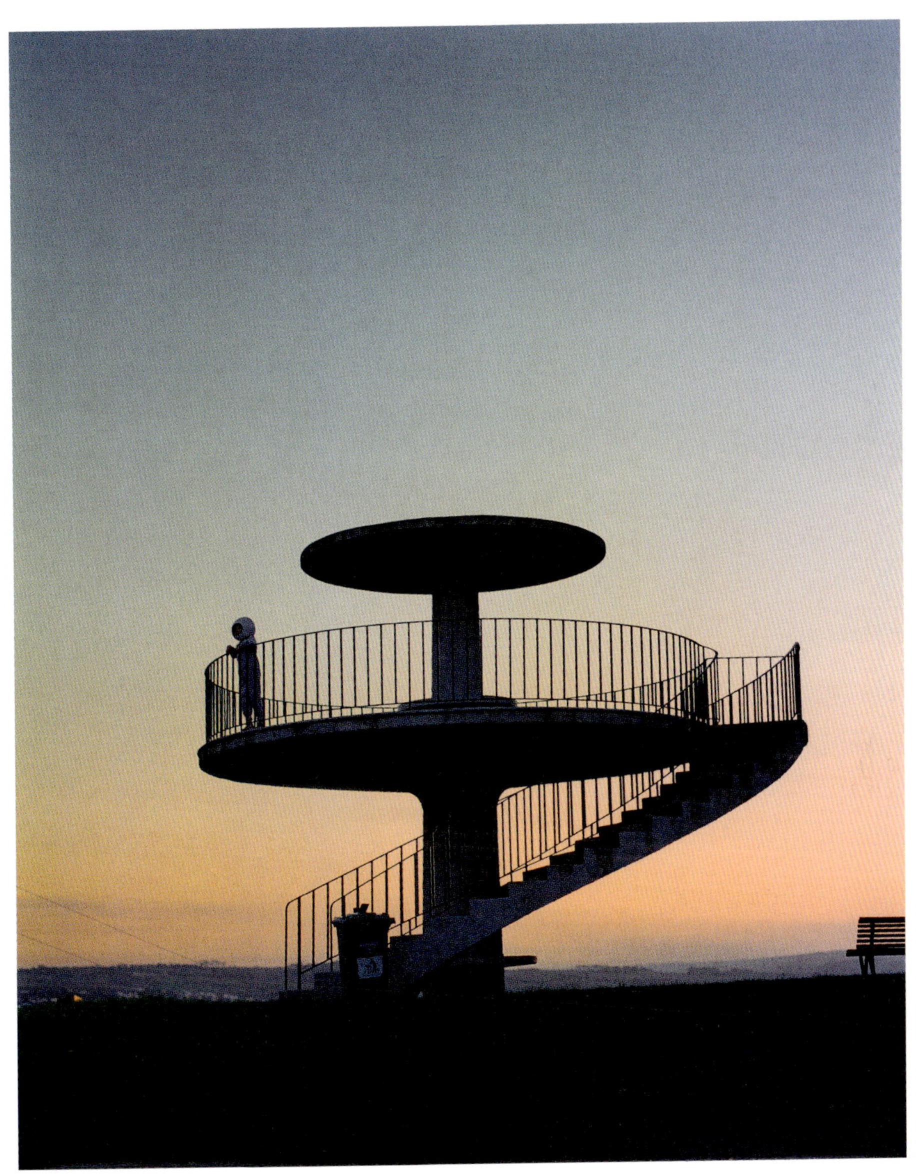

The Tower

> Firekeeper

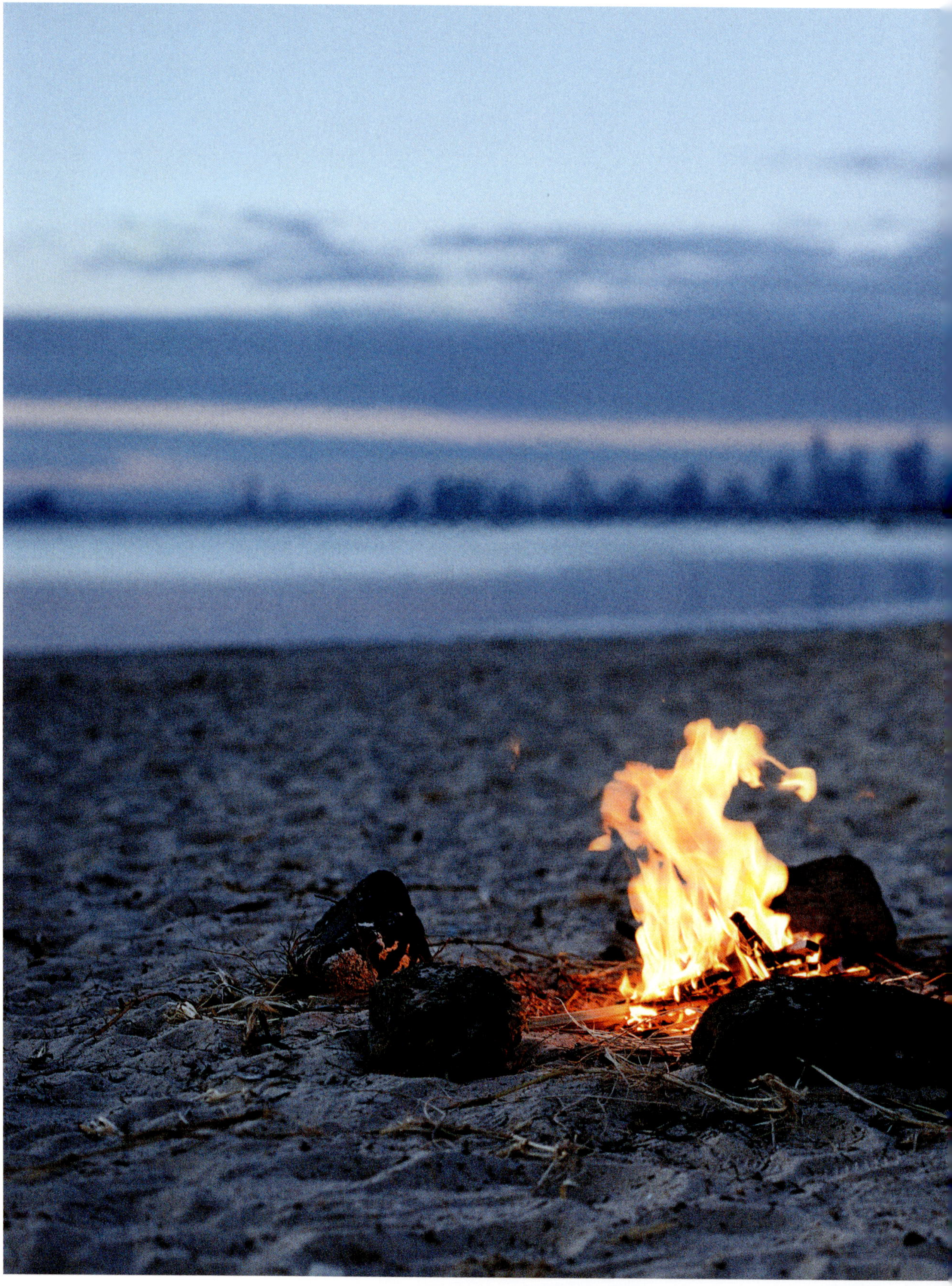

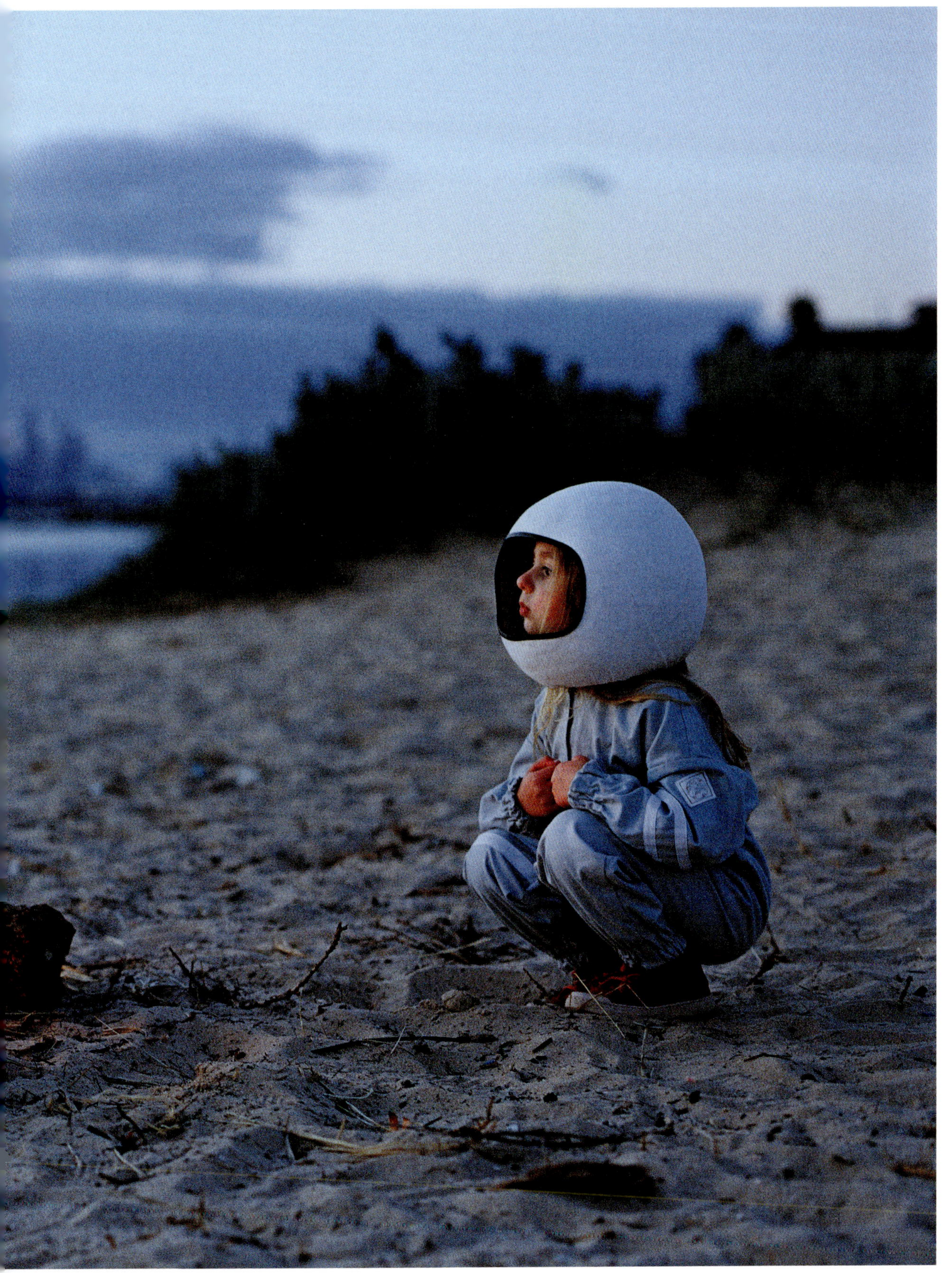

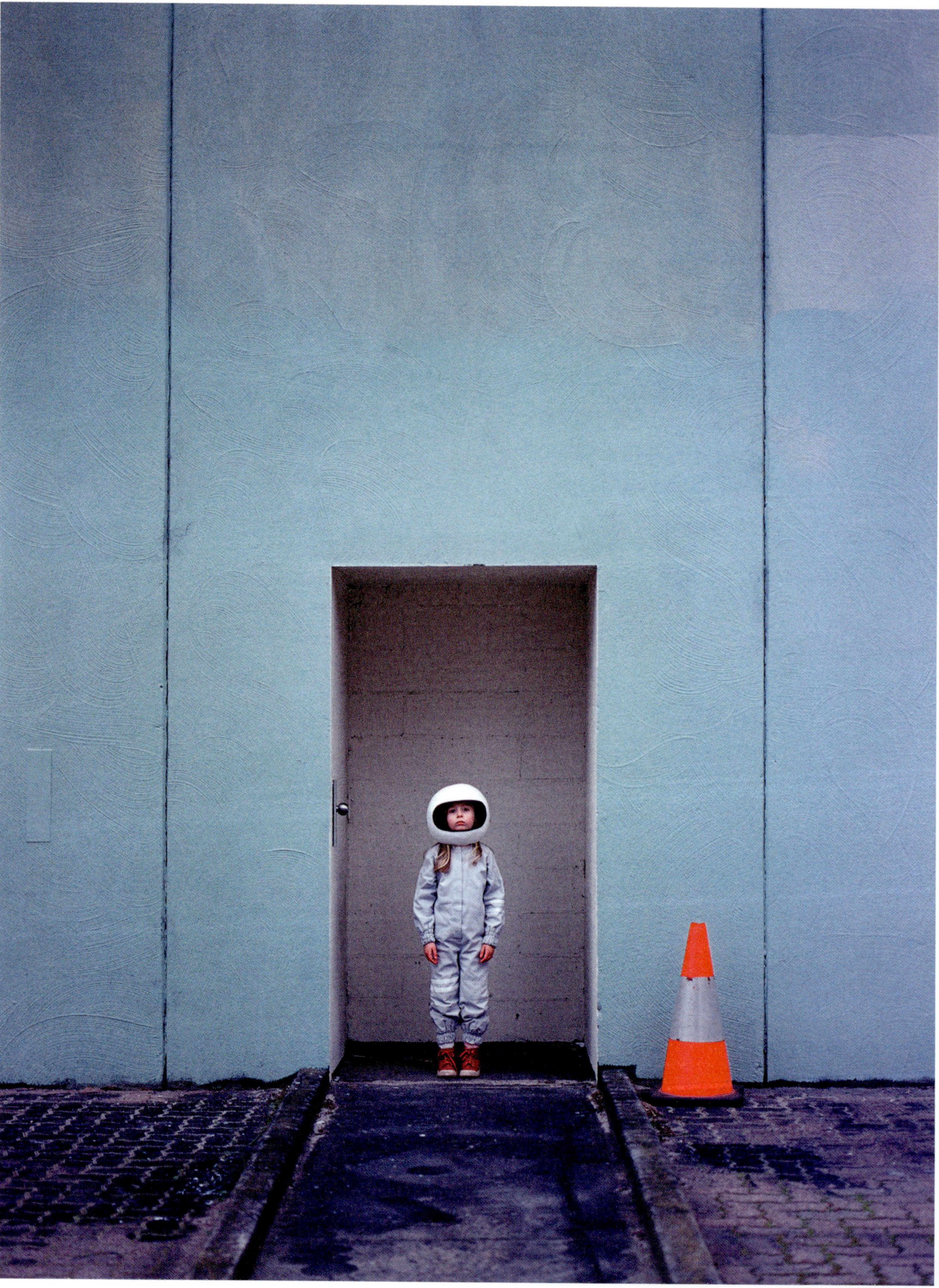

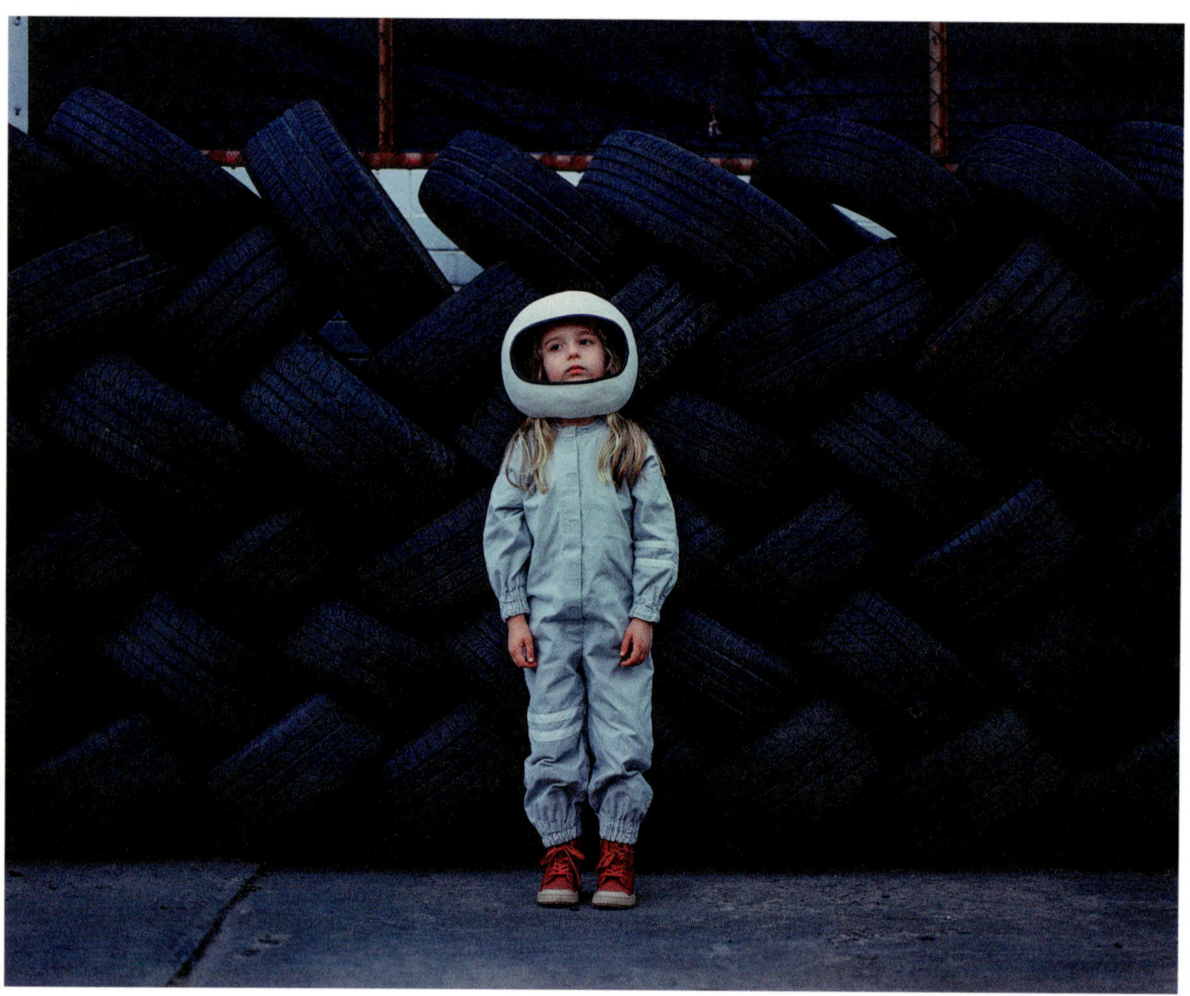

Tired

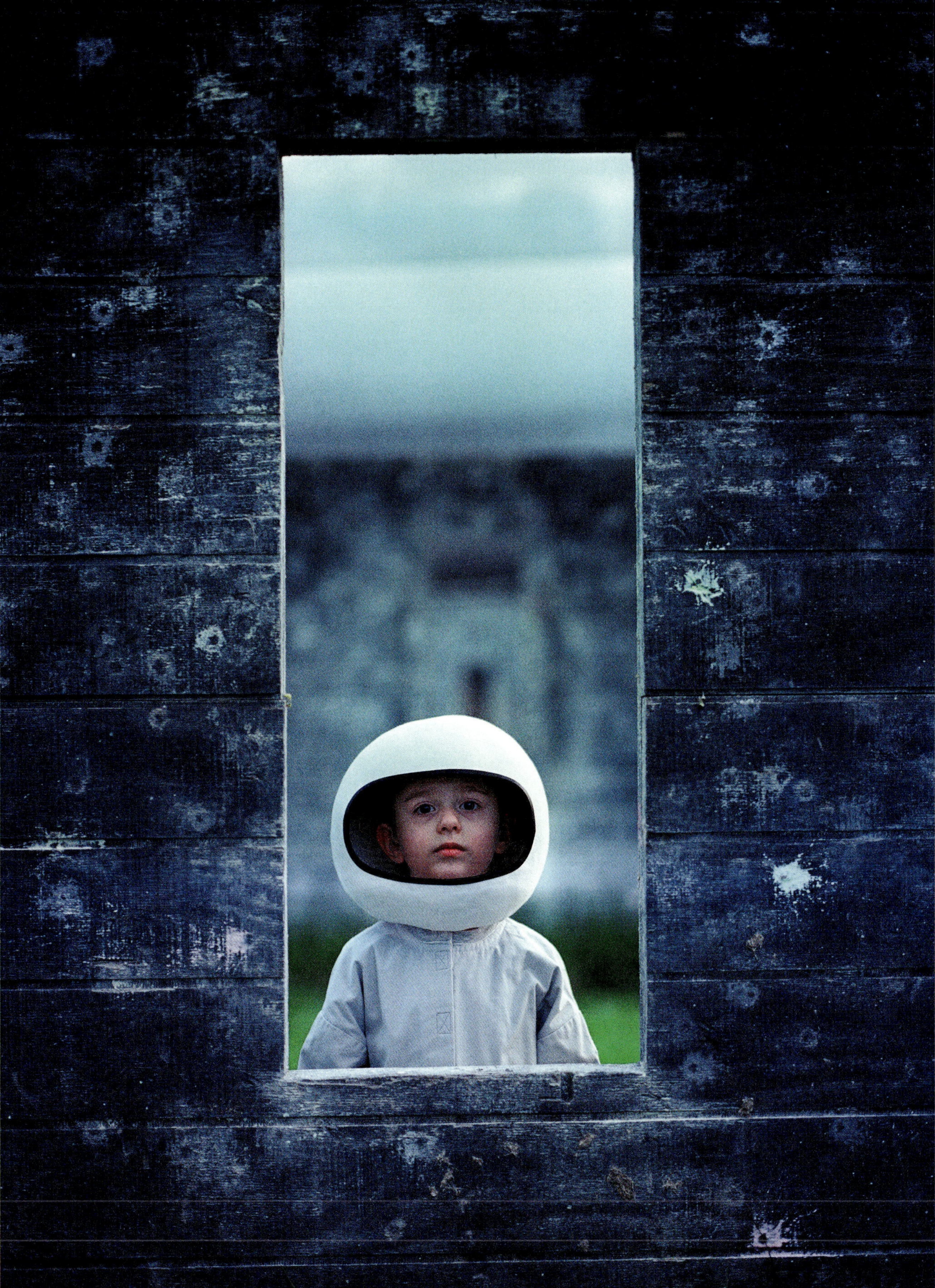

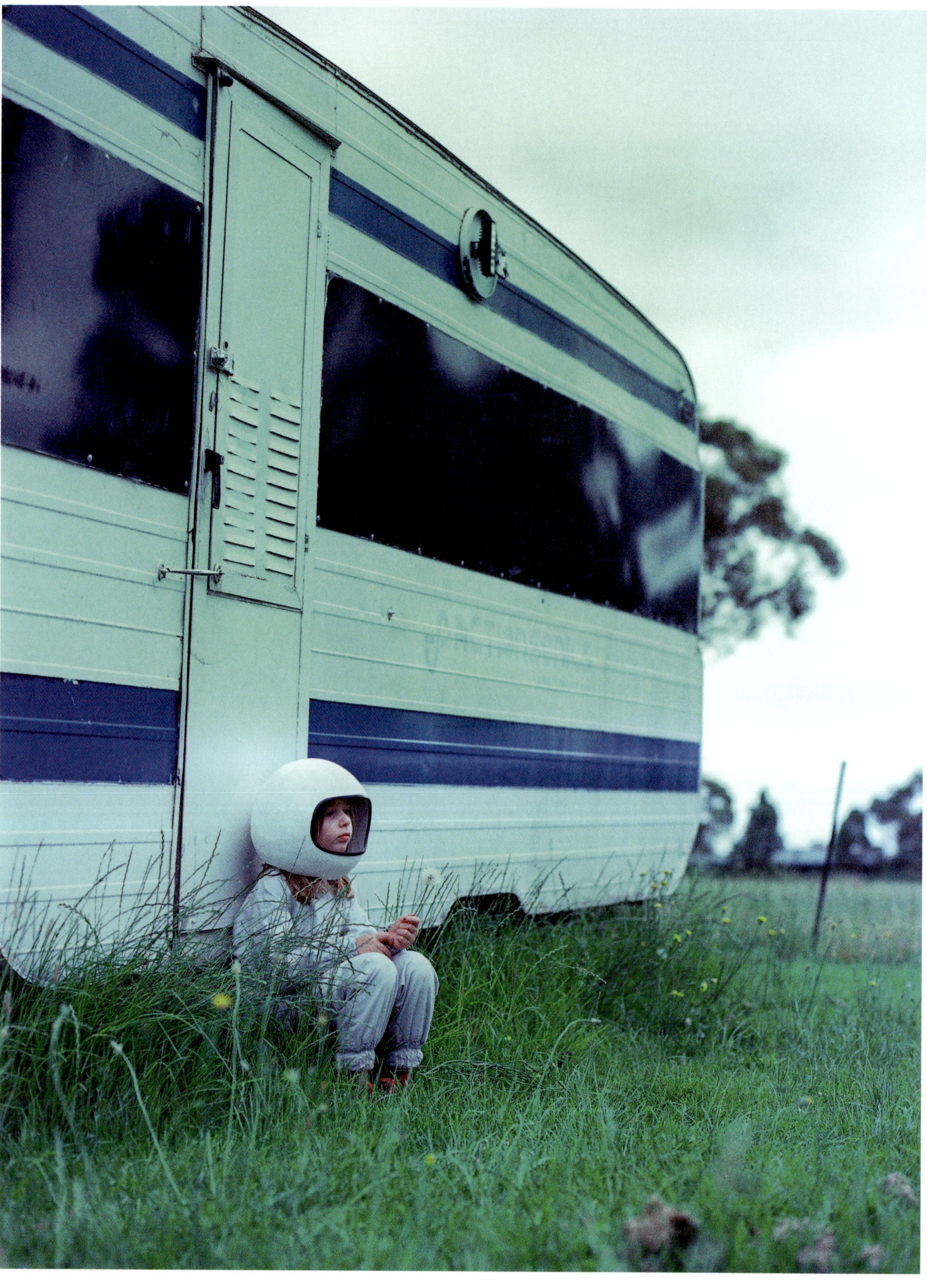

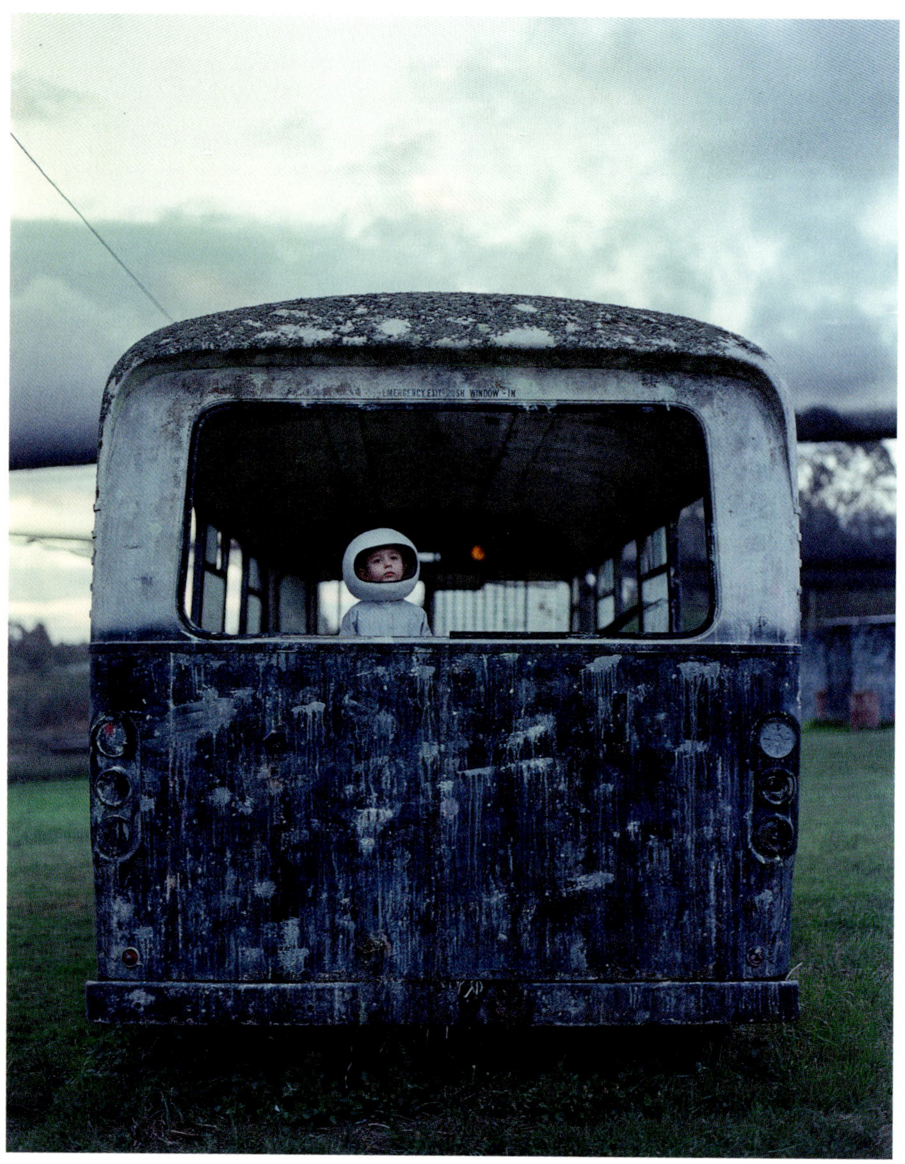
EMERGENCY EXIT
WINDOW - IN

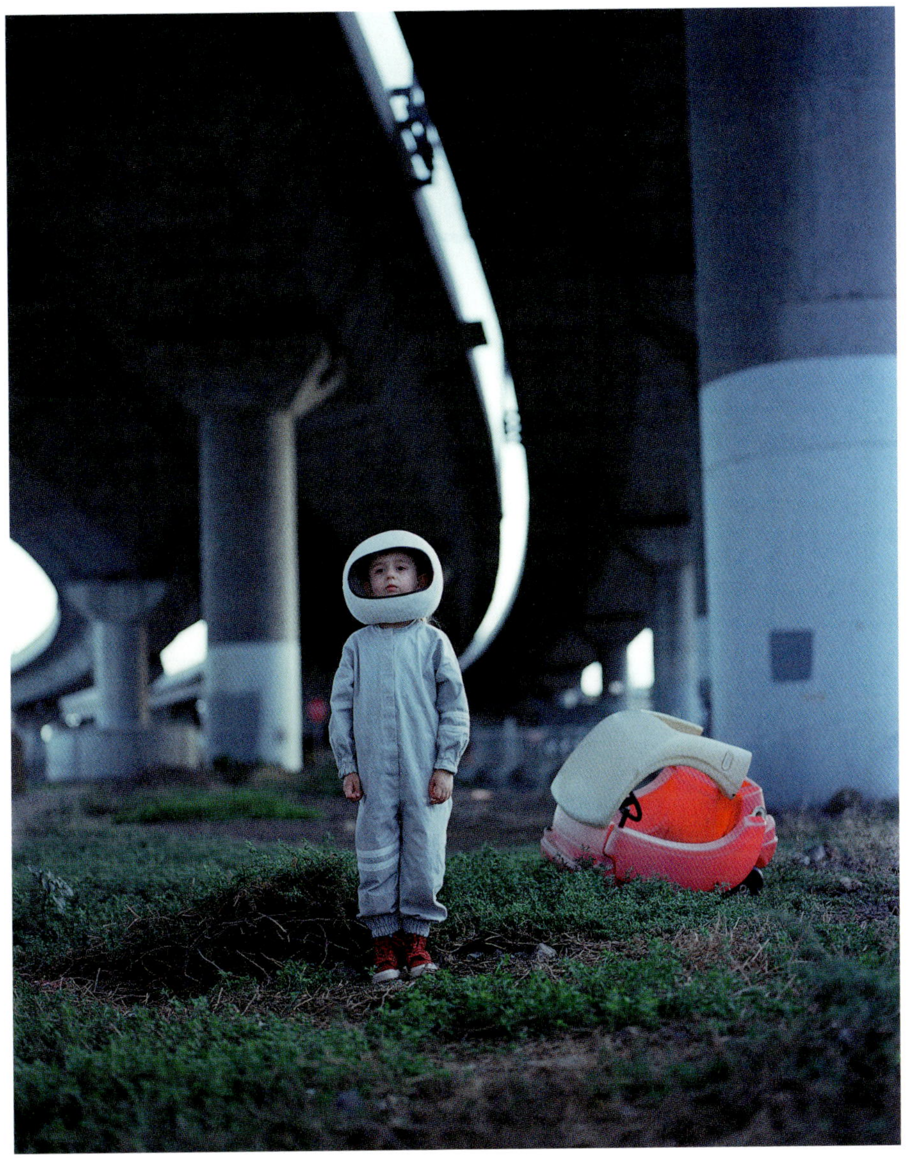

Underway

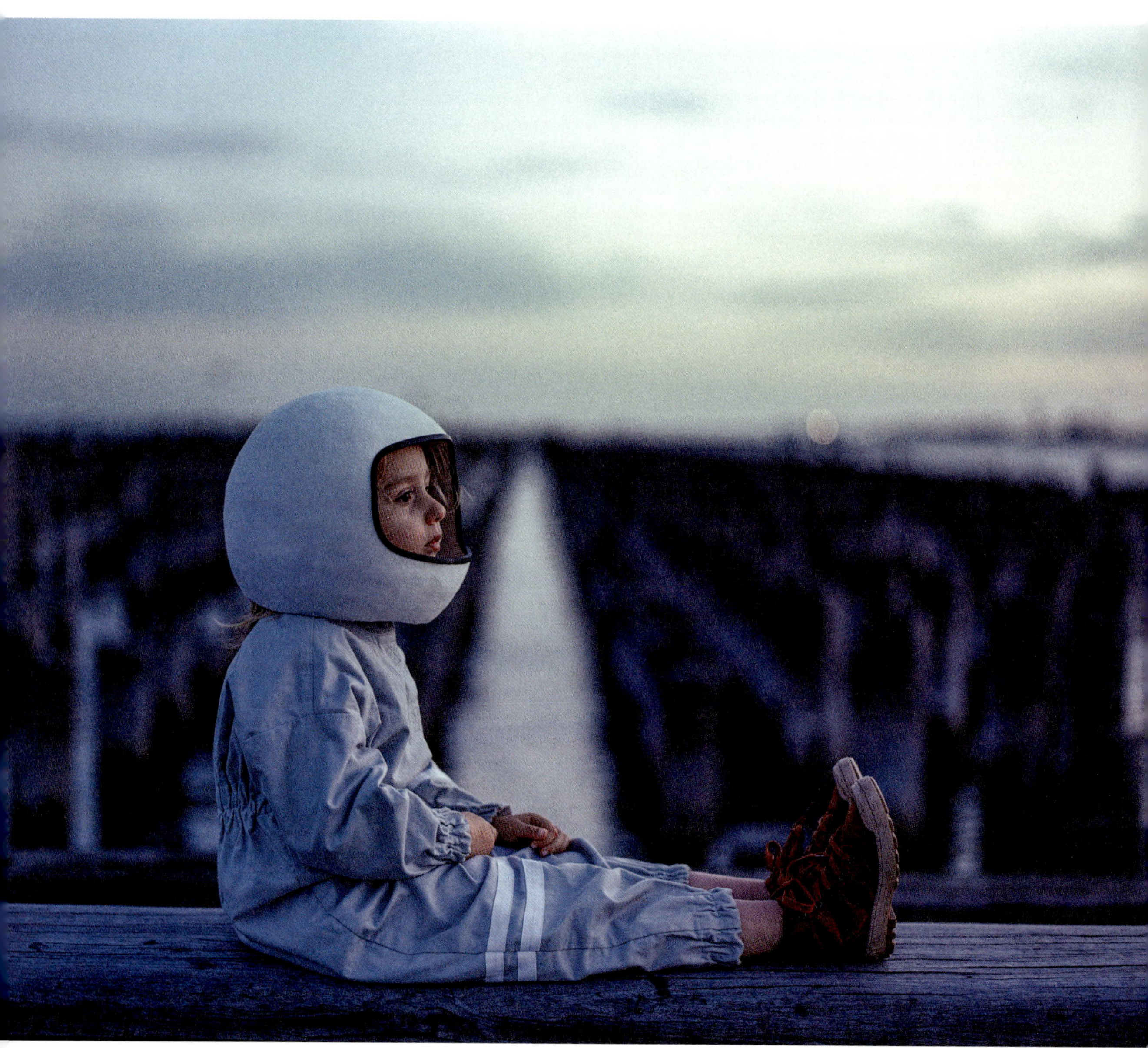

The Pier

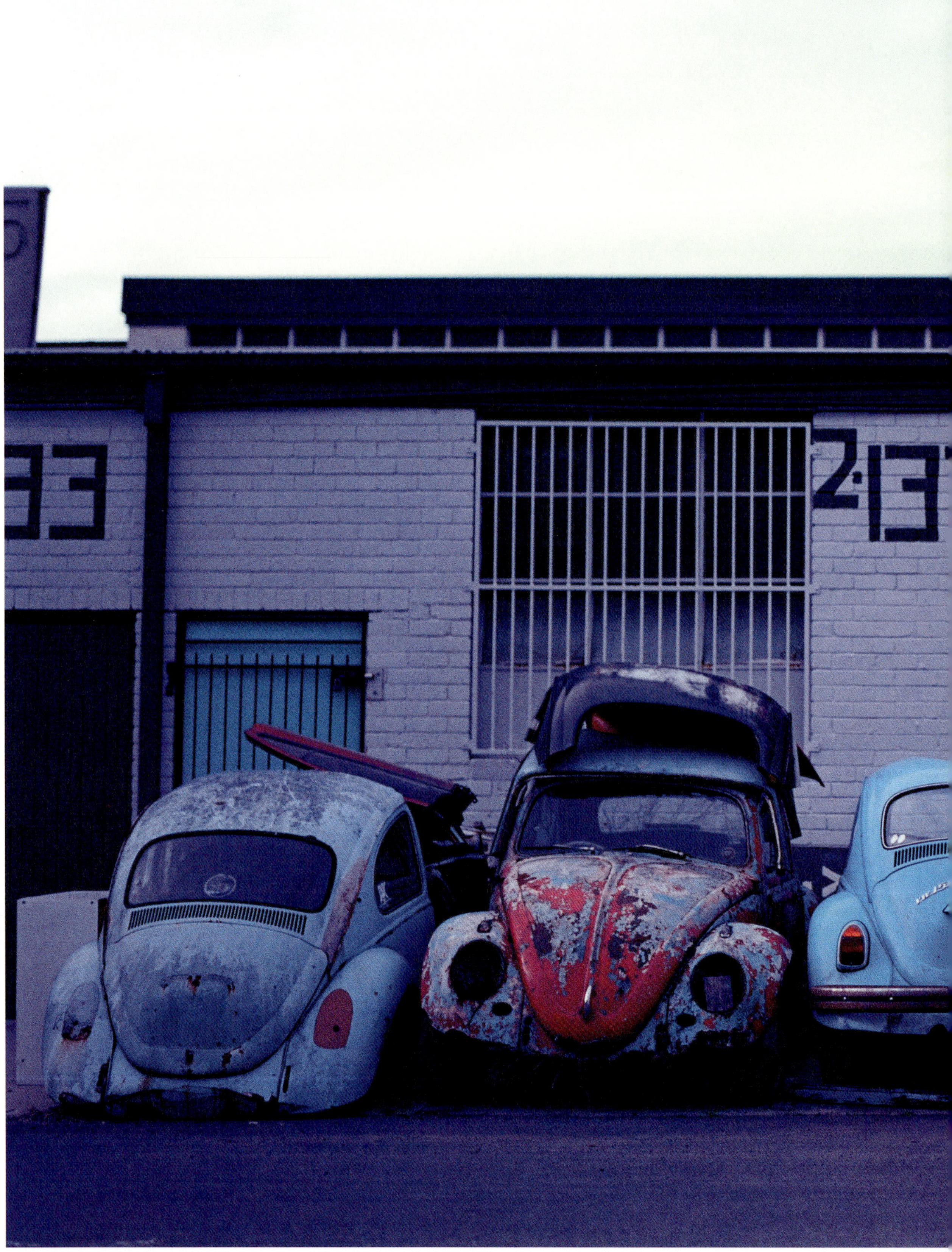
33
2·13

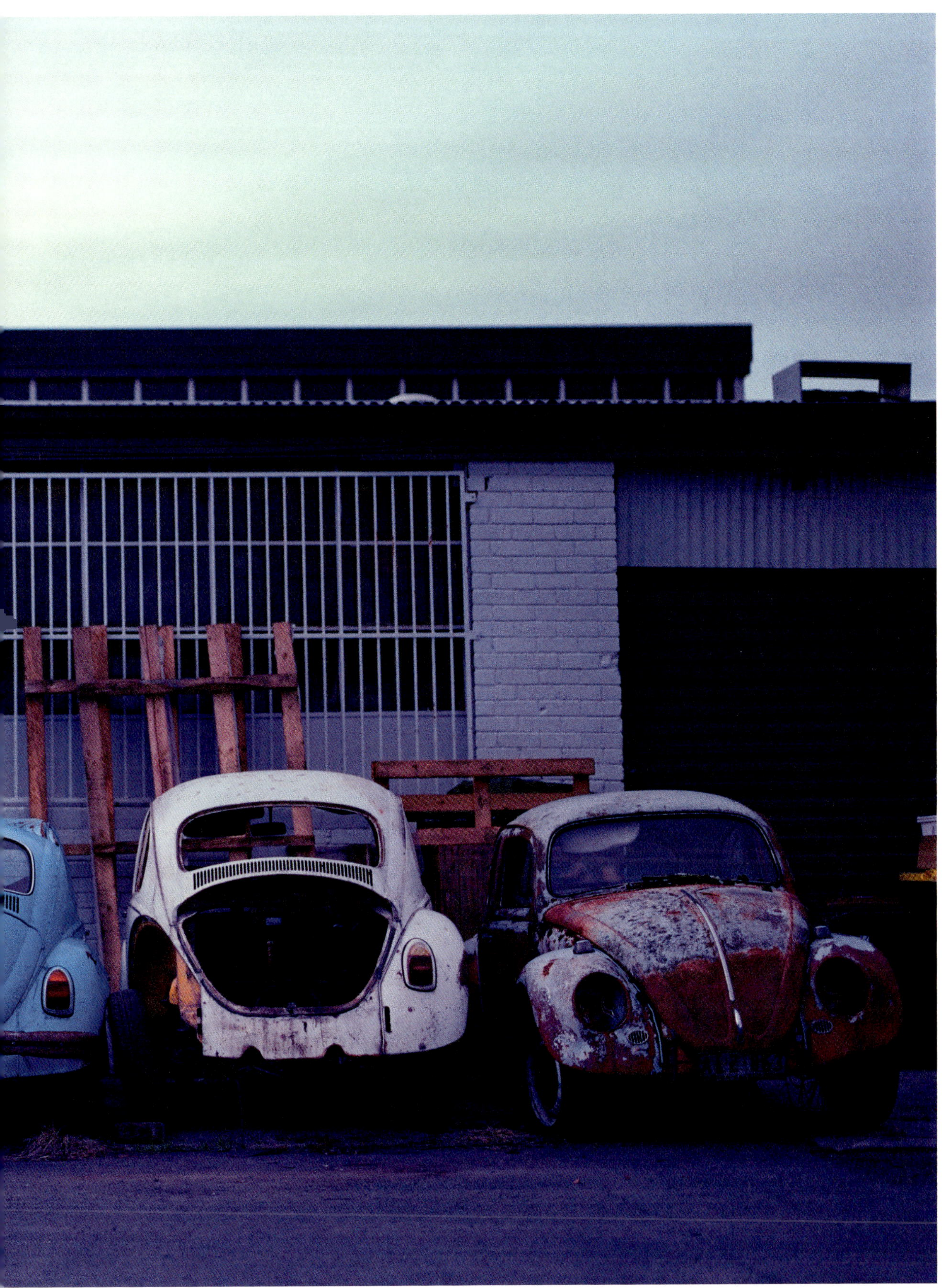

Someone once cared for those cars – washed them, polished them, kissed in them, tinkered with their engines – and now they are abandoned.

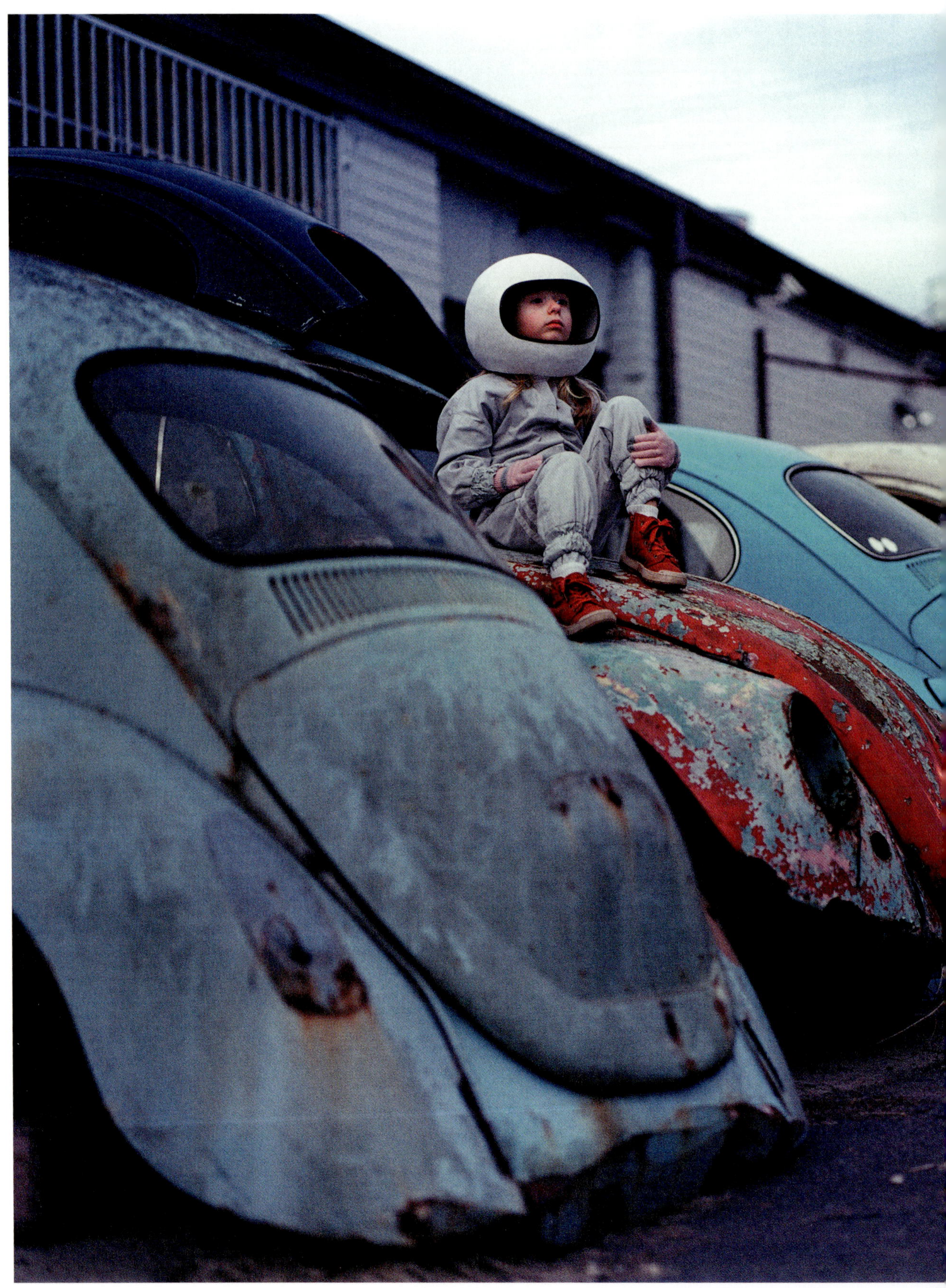

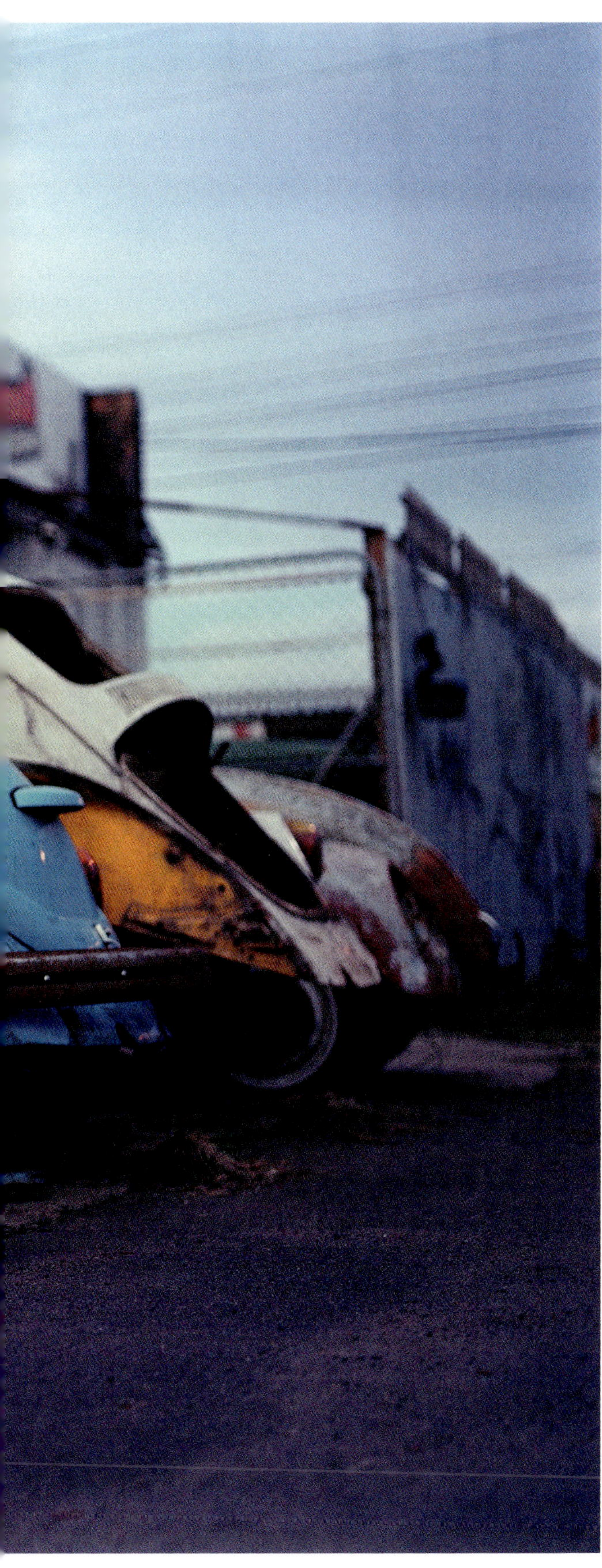

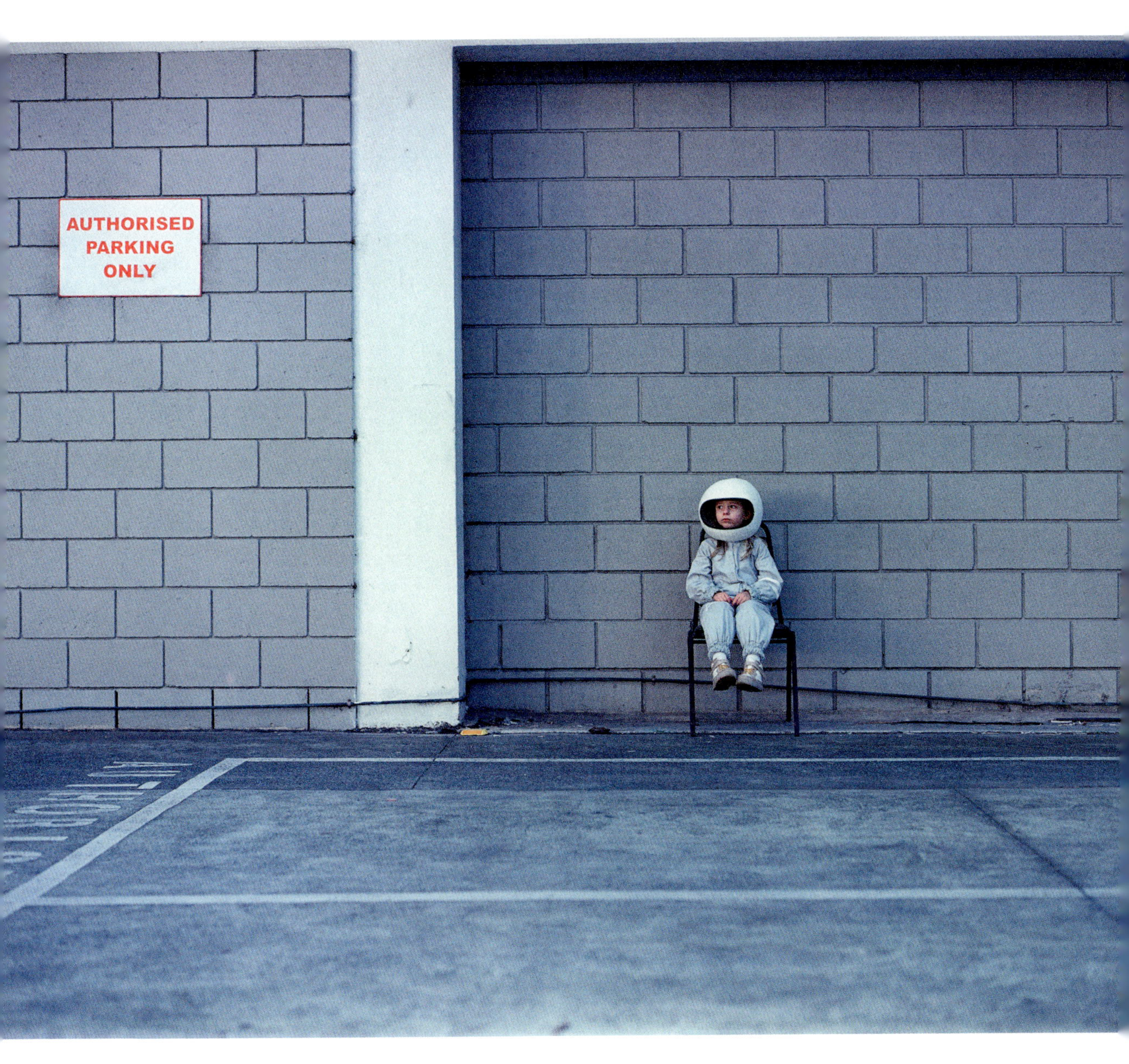
AUTHORISED
PARKING
ONLY

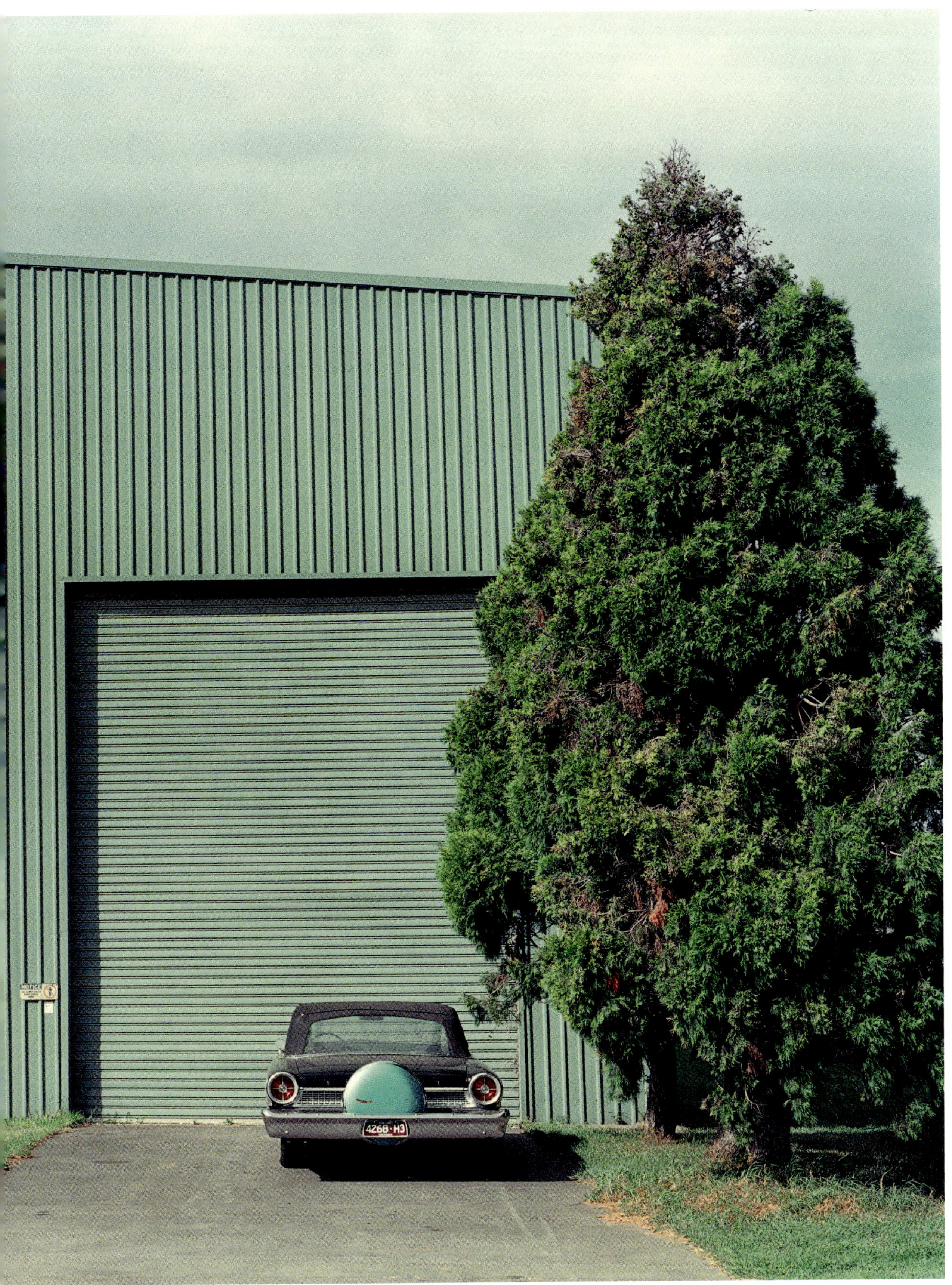
NOTICE
4268·H3

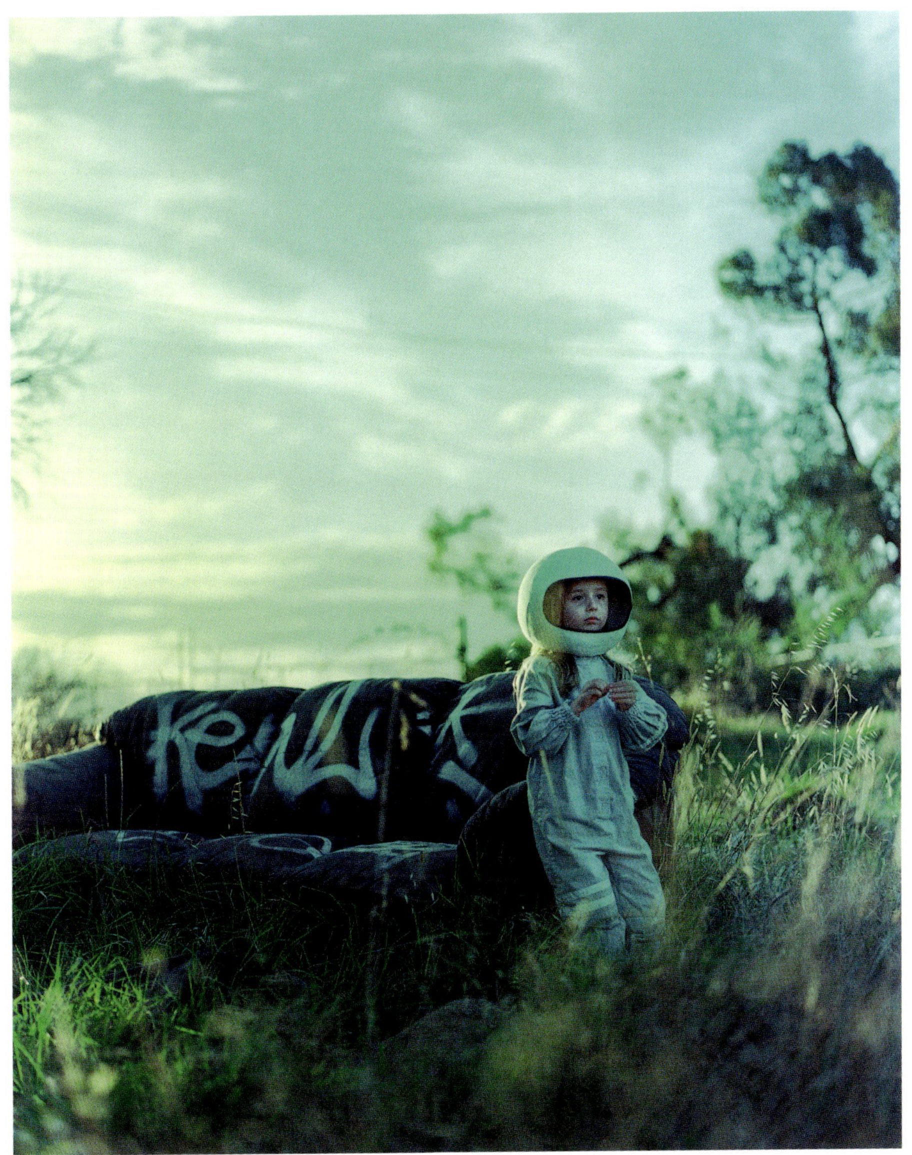

Country Comfort

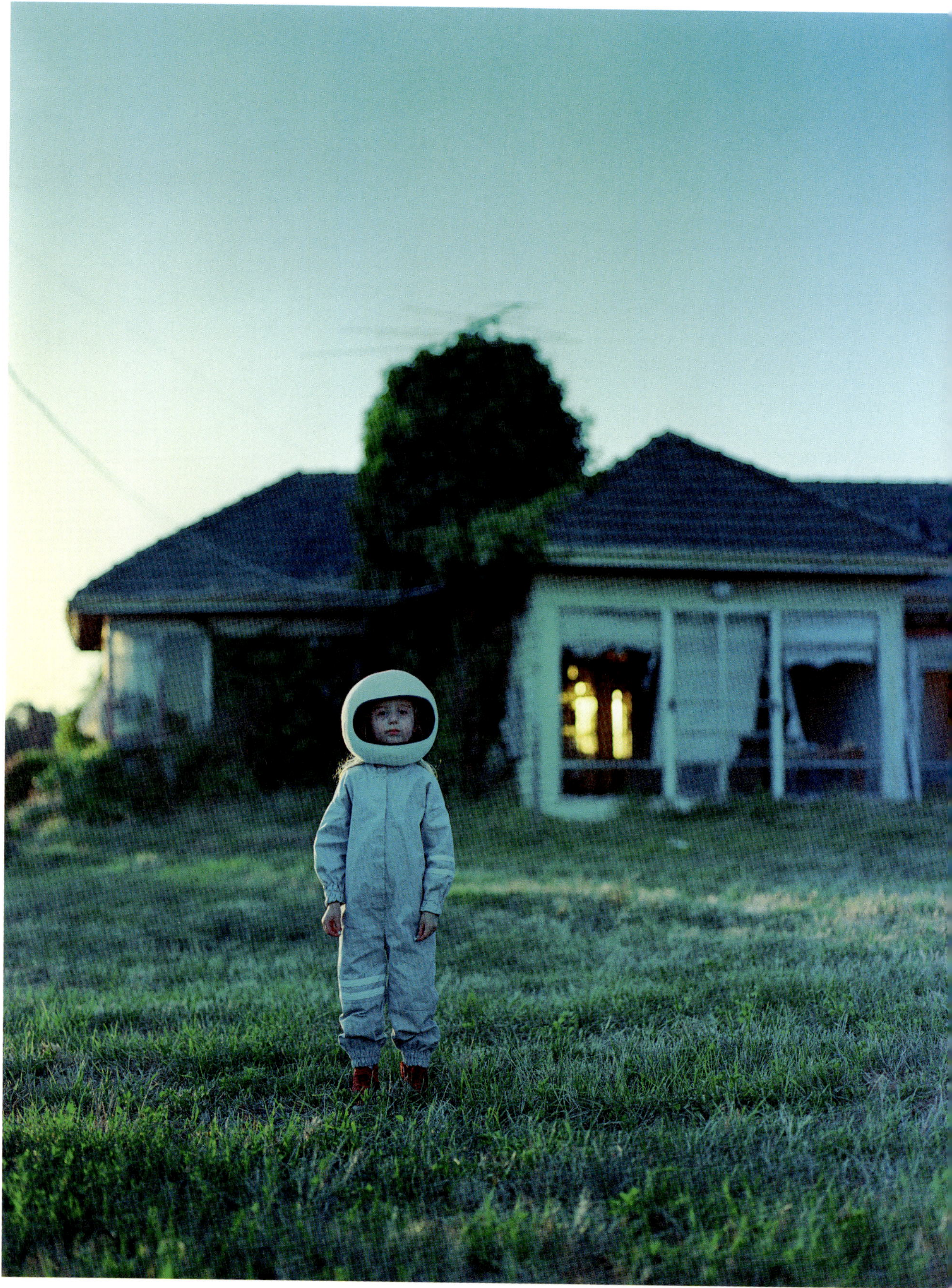

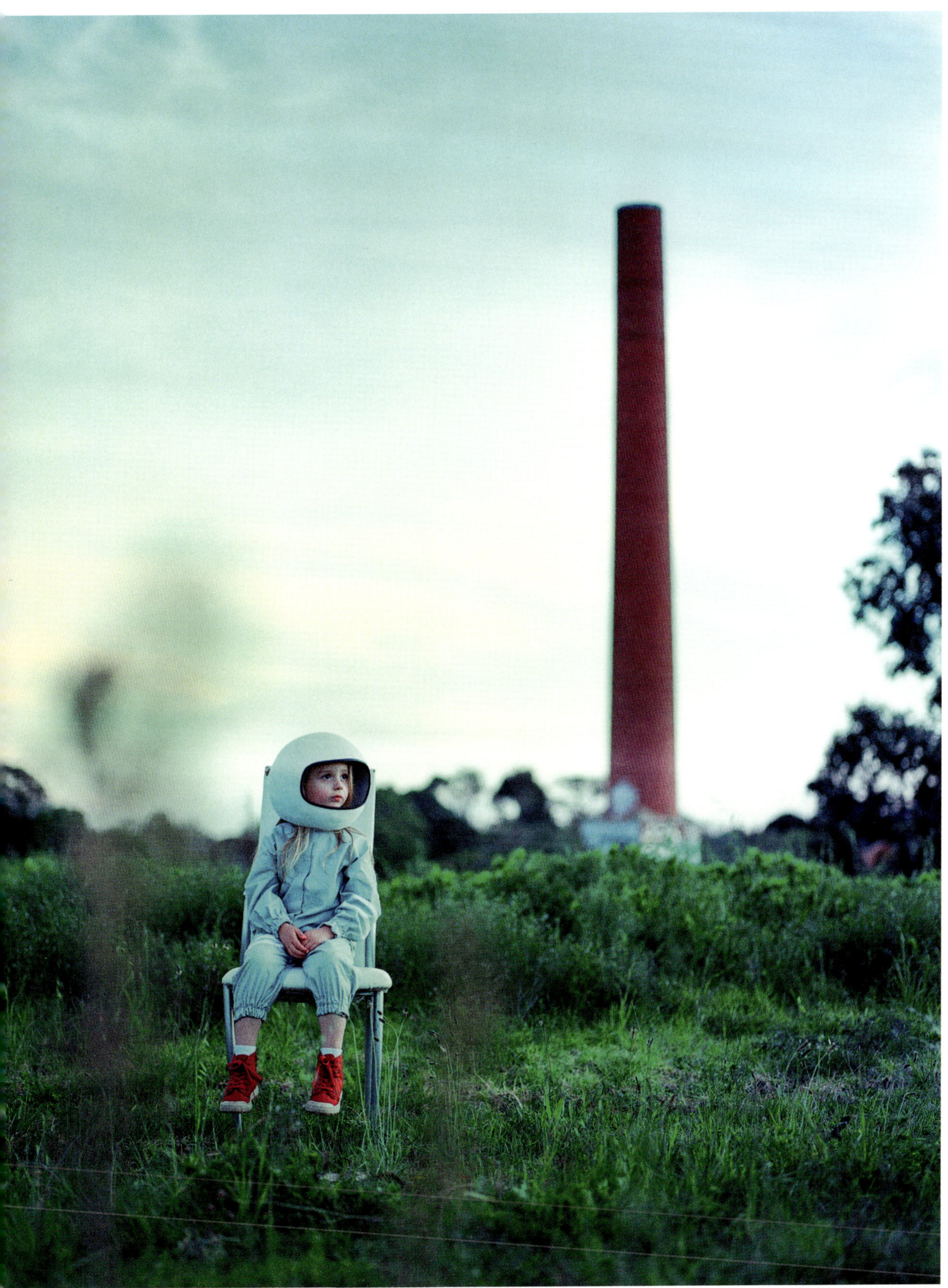

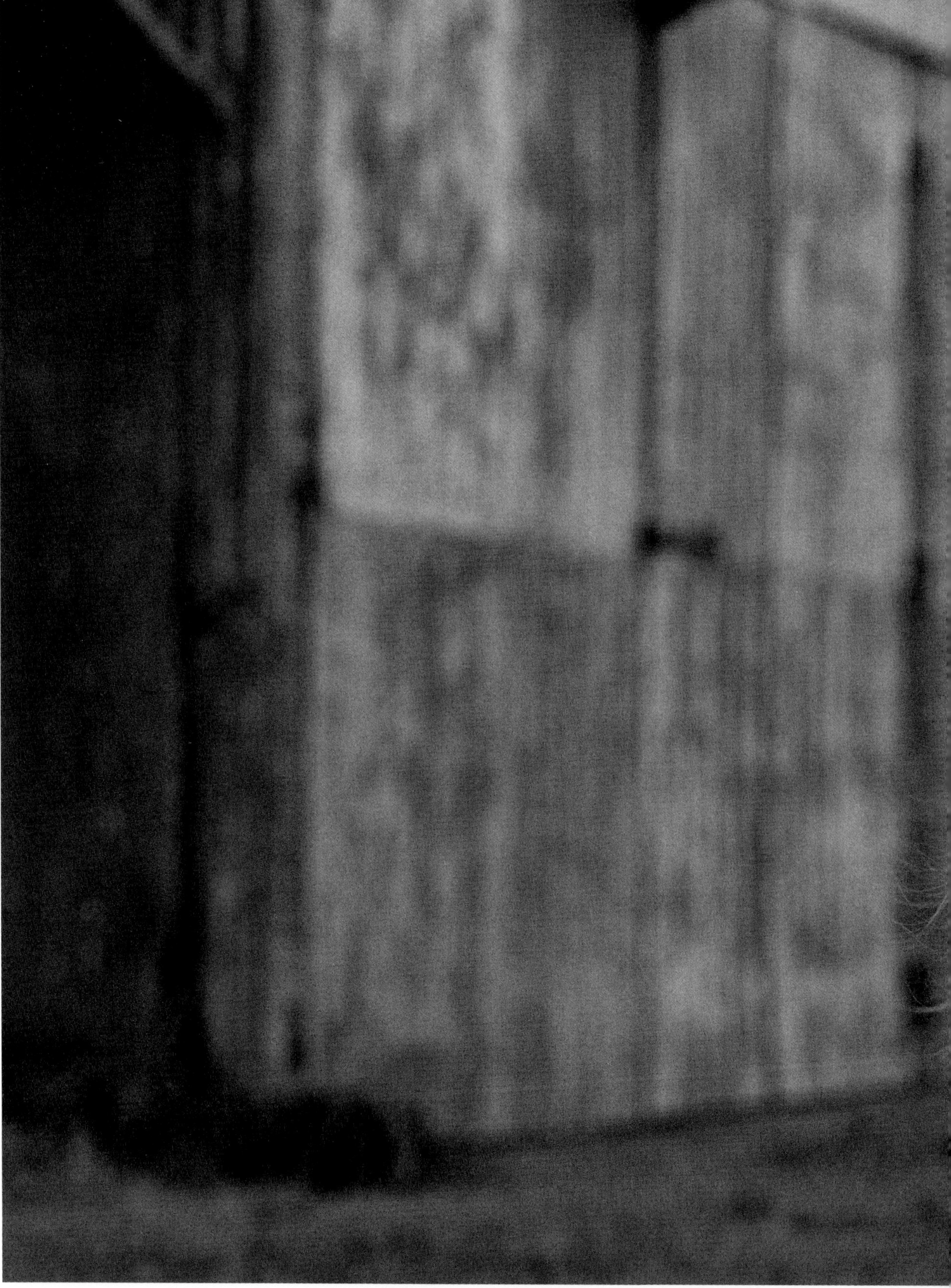

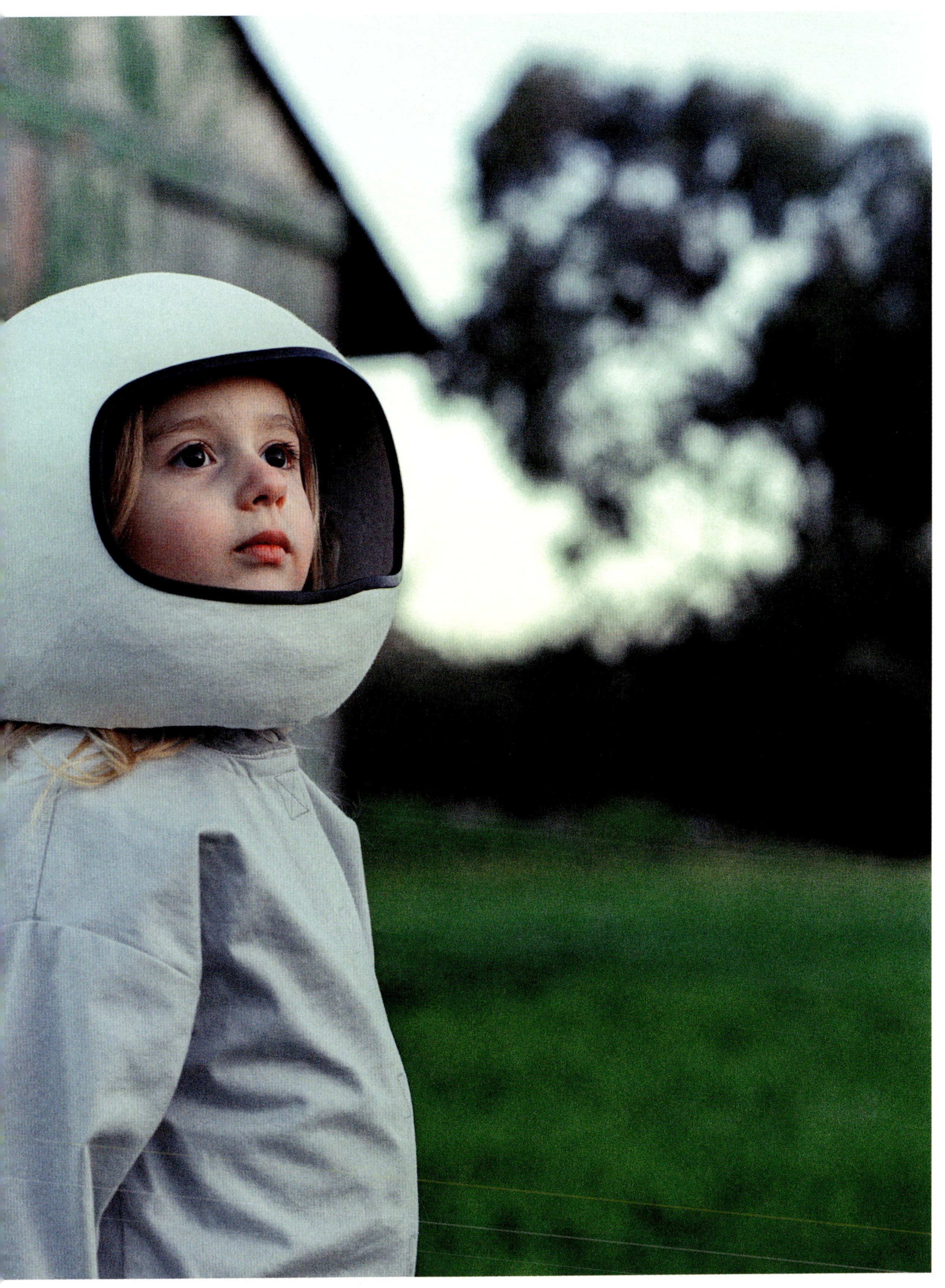

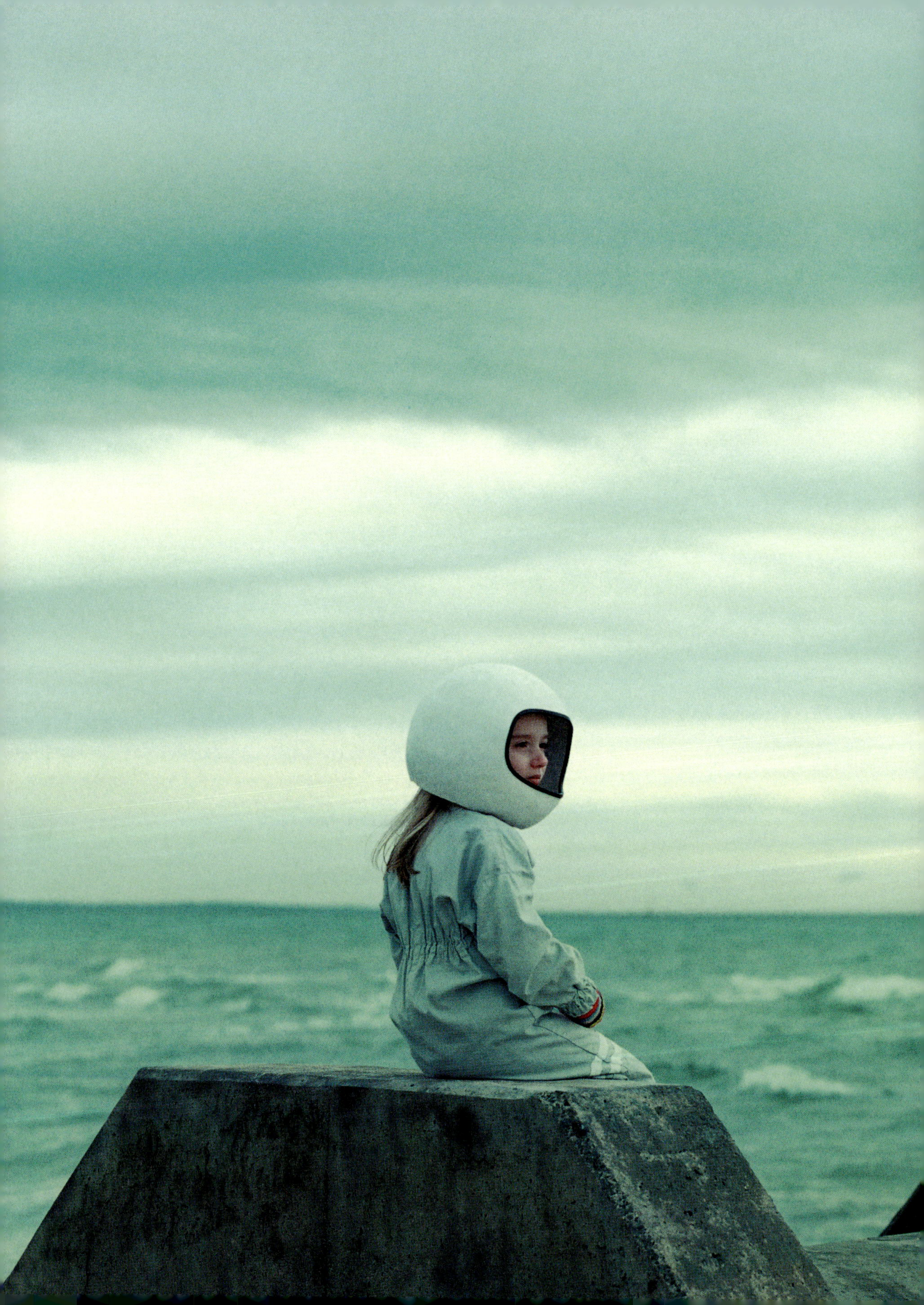

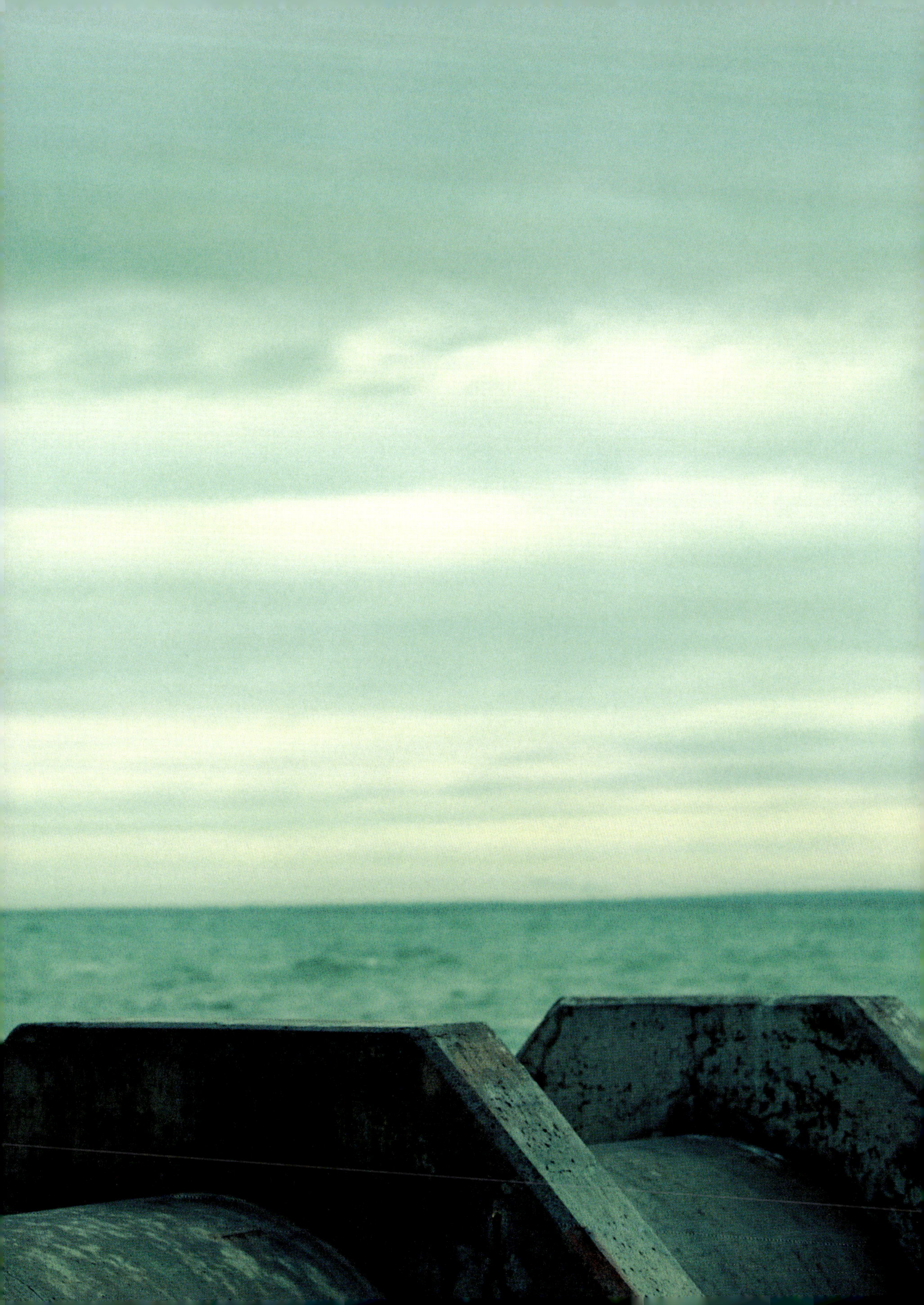

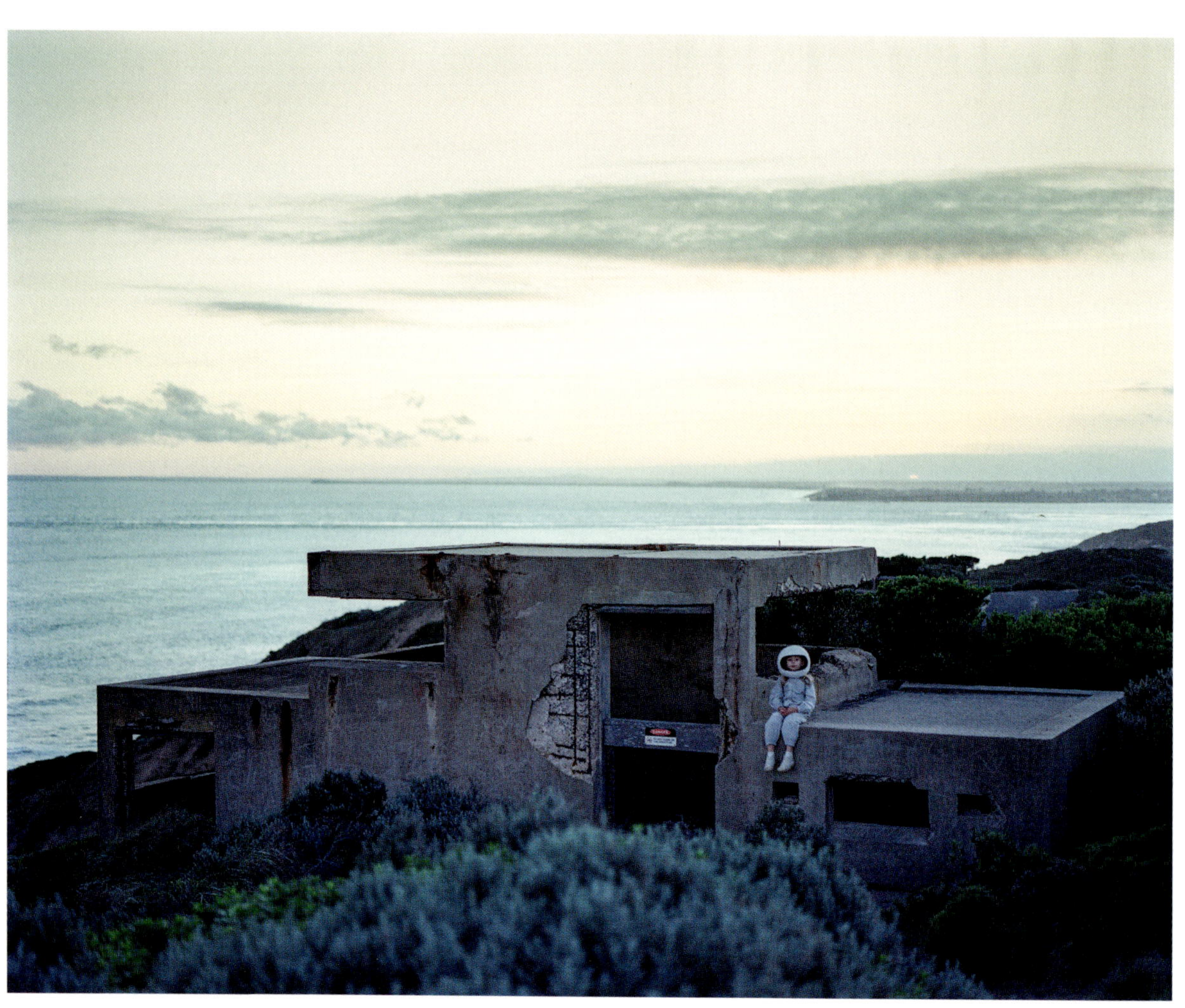

< Solaris

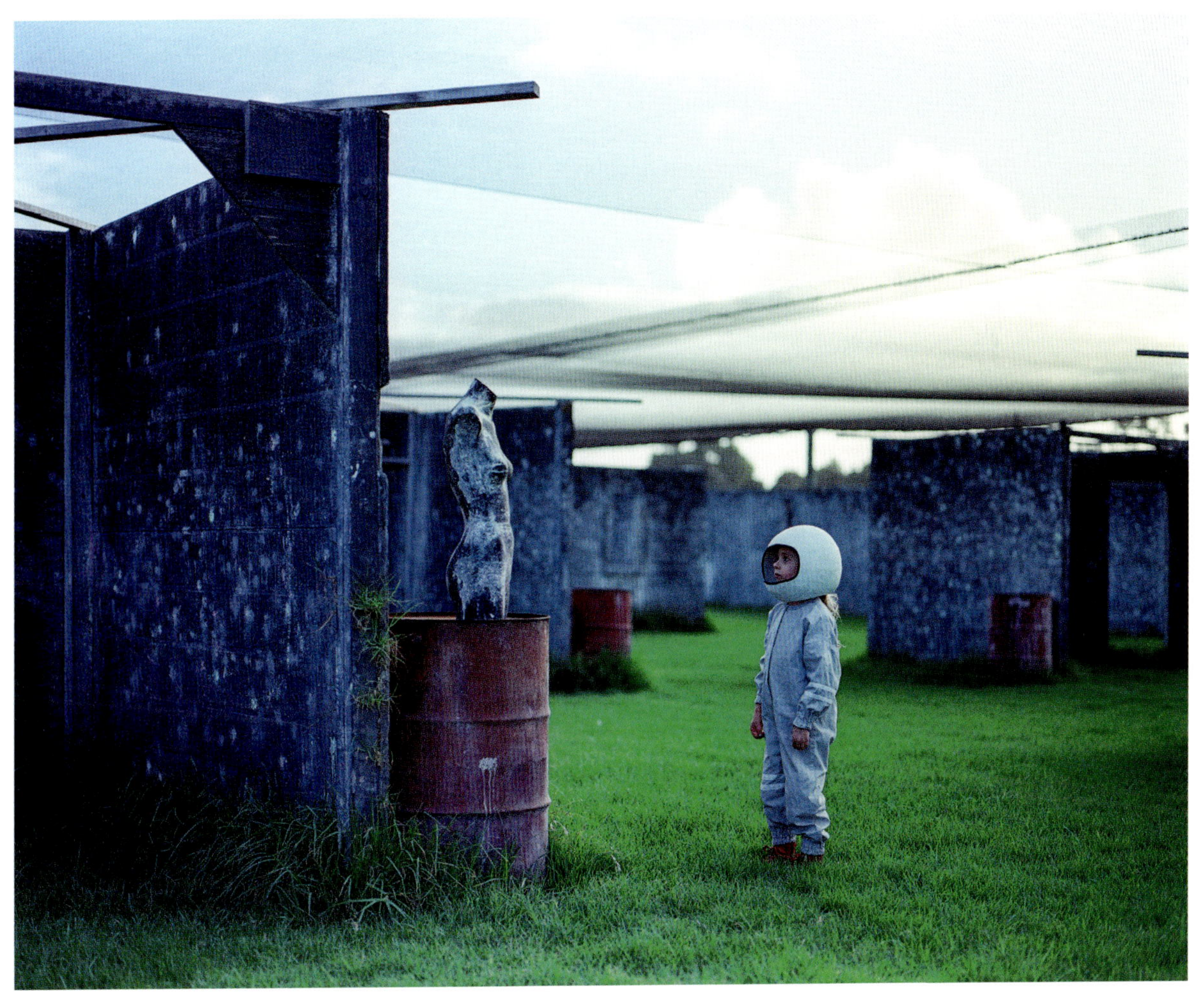

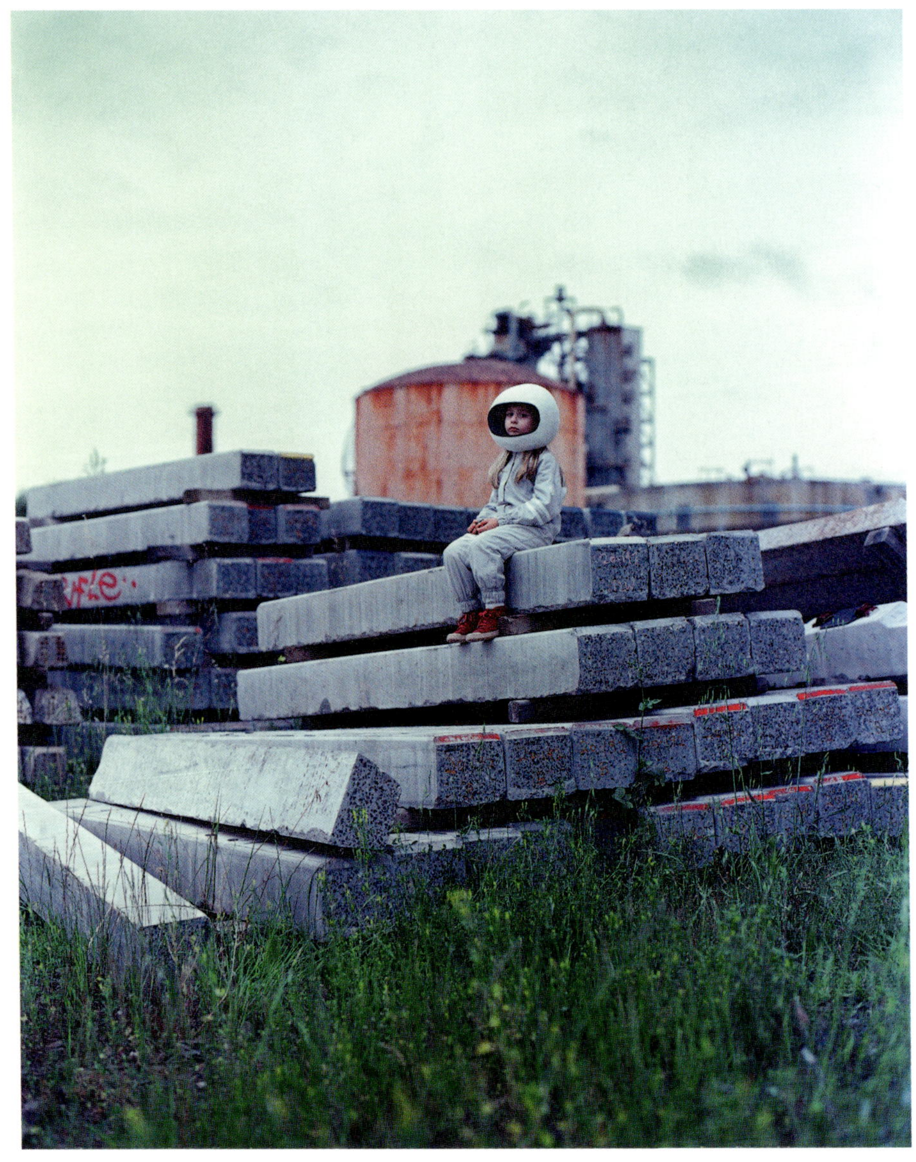

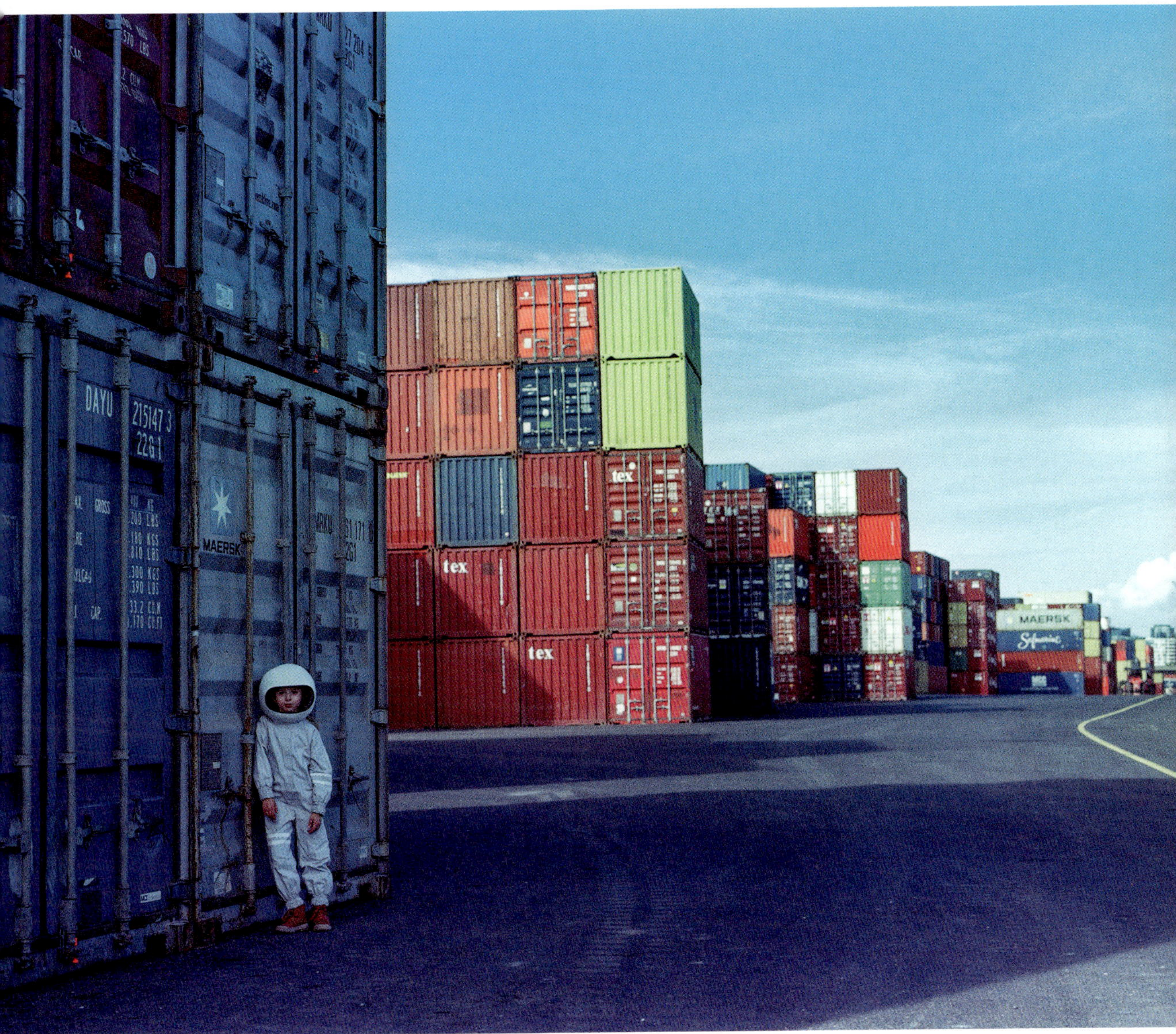

The Cargo

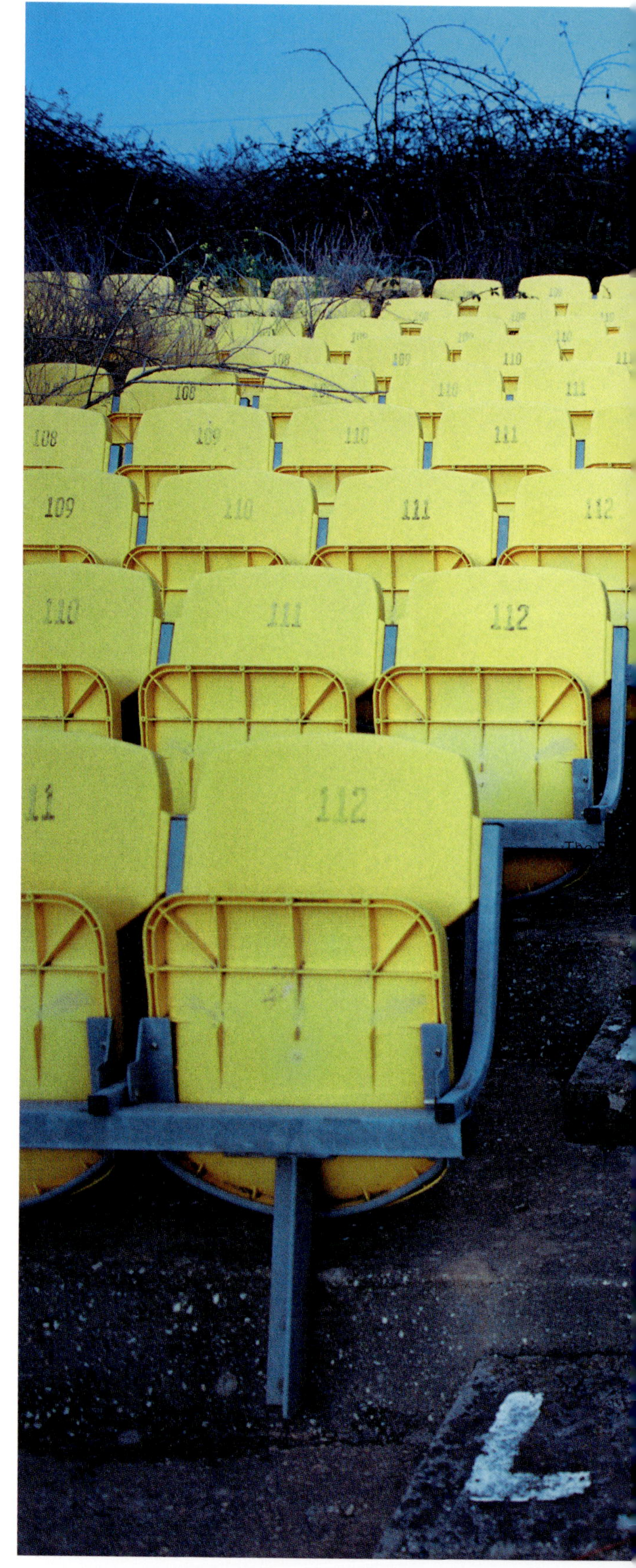

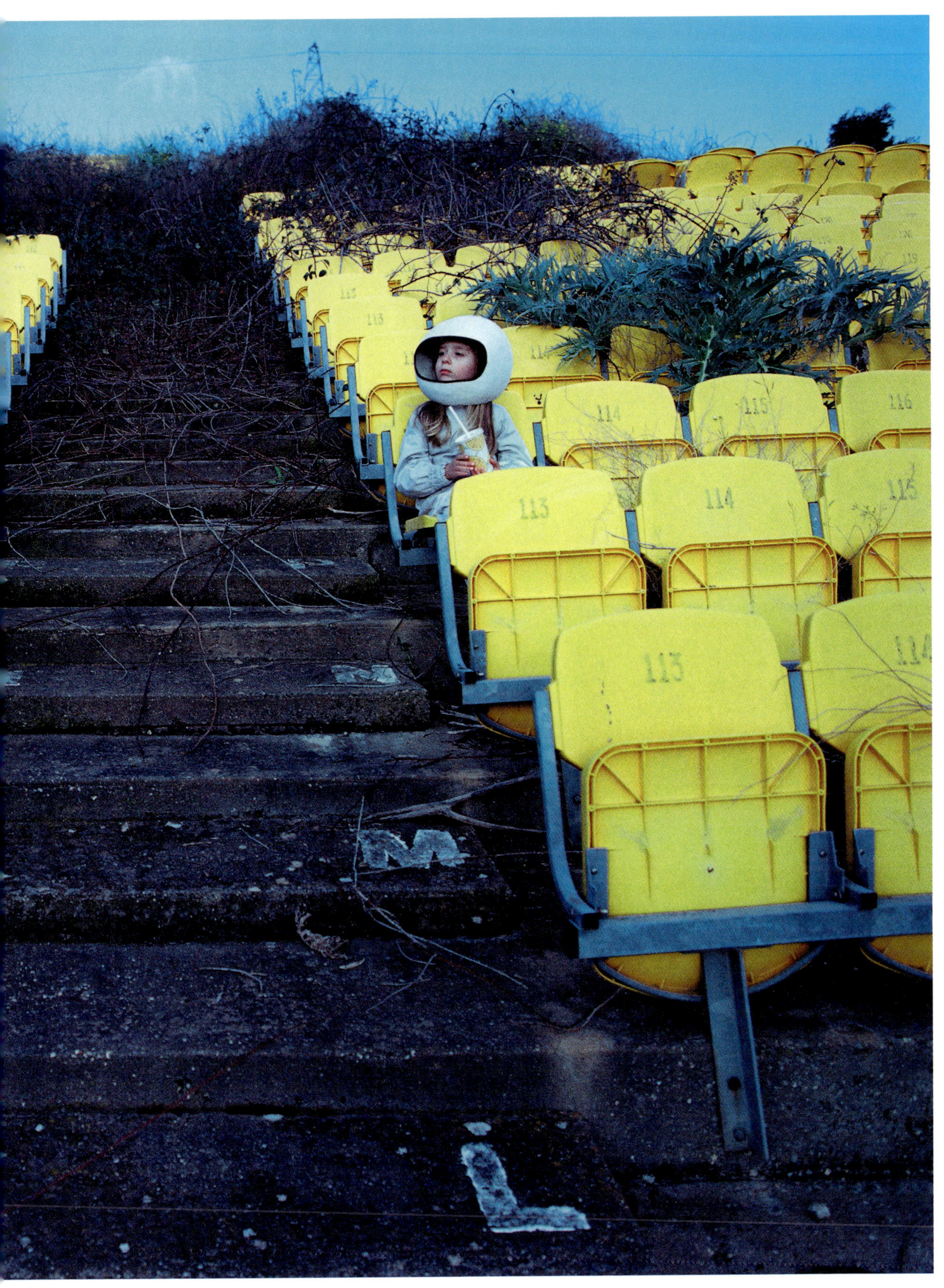
113
114
115
116
M
L

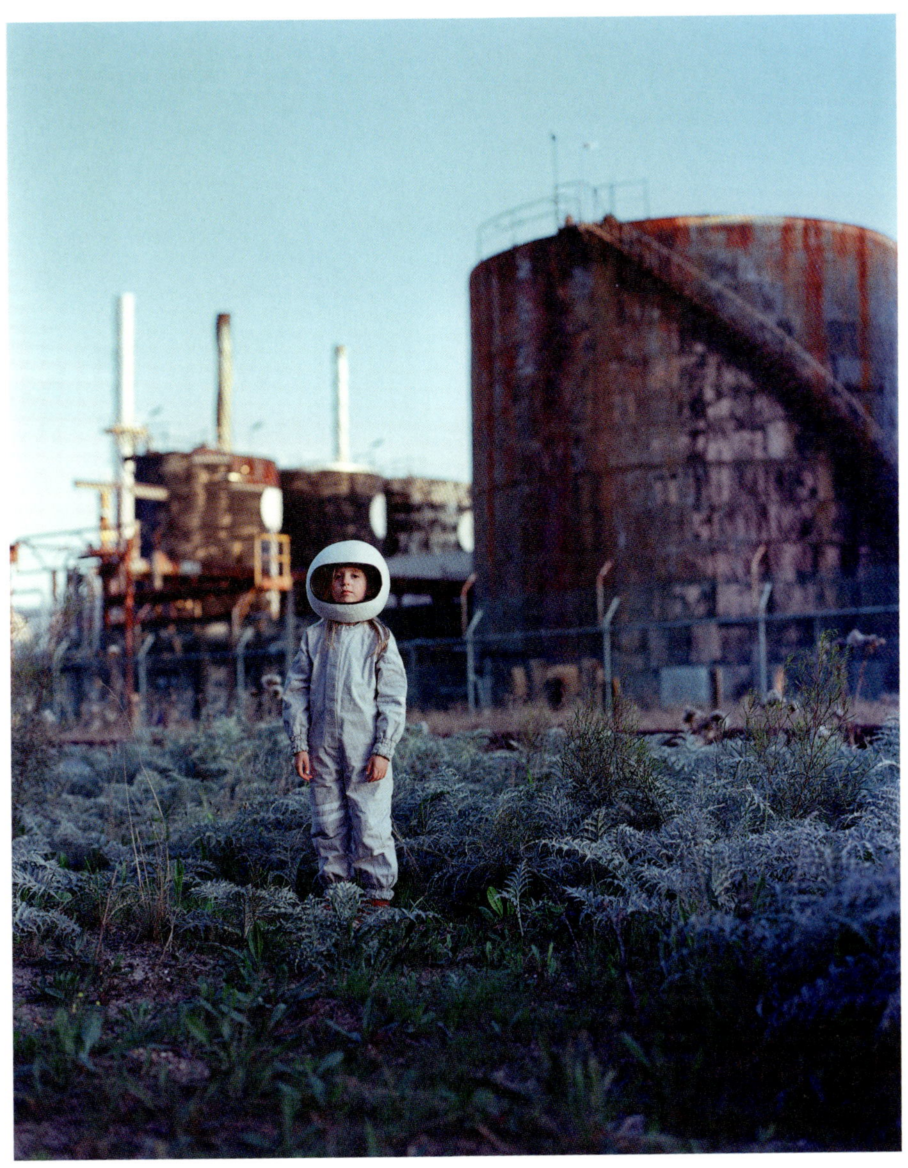

The Barrel

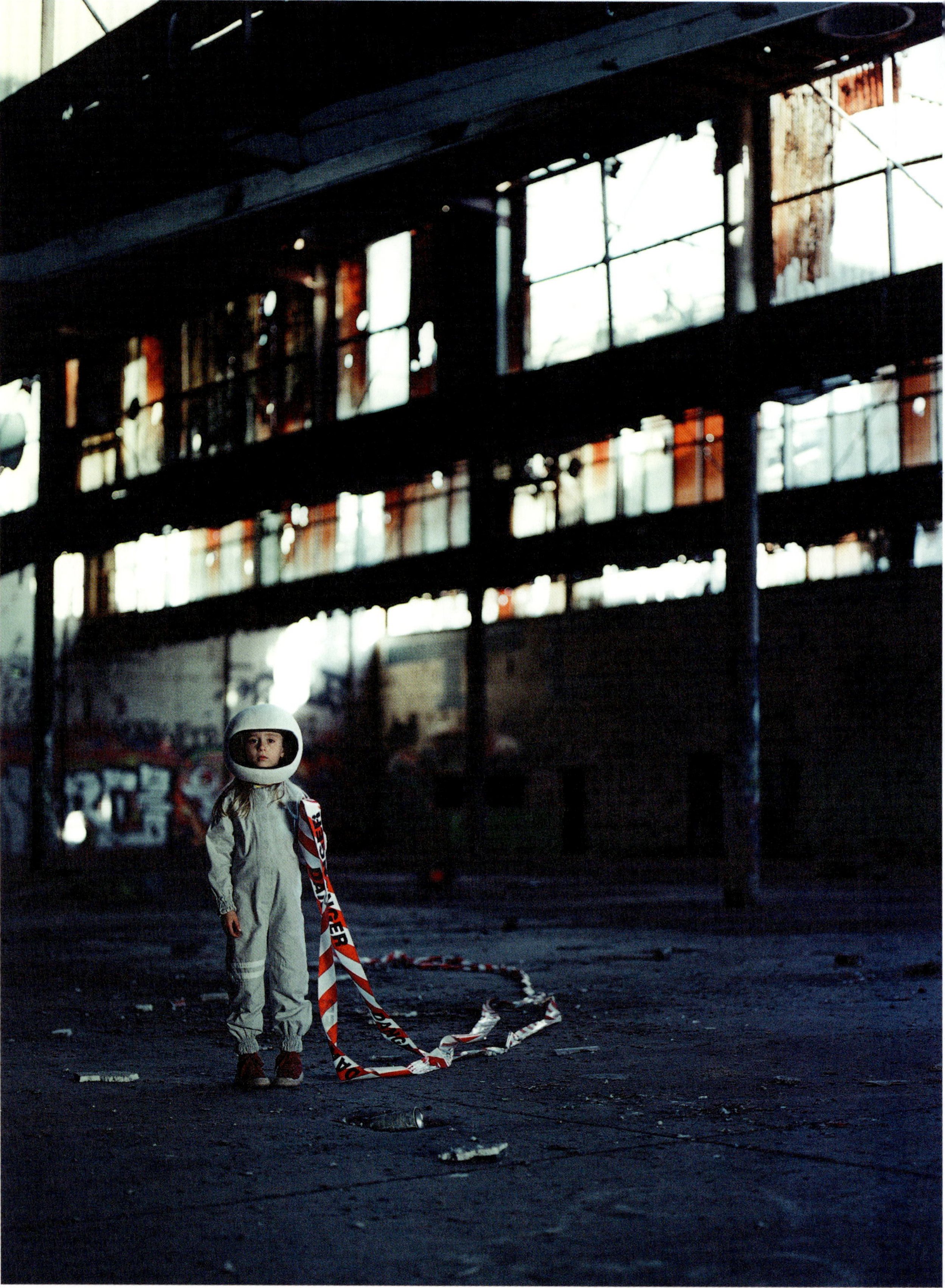
DANGER

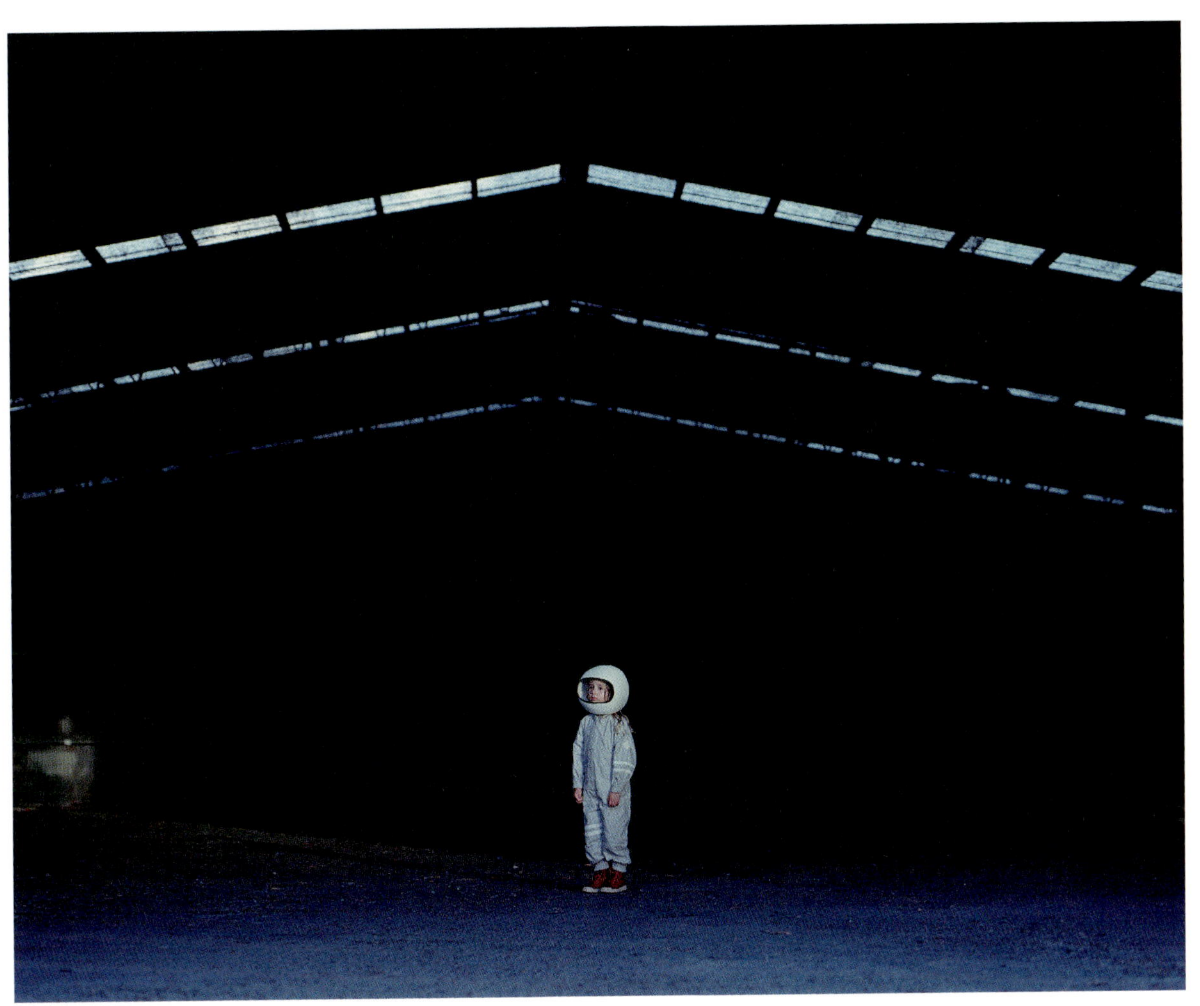

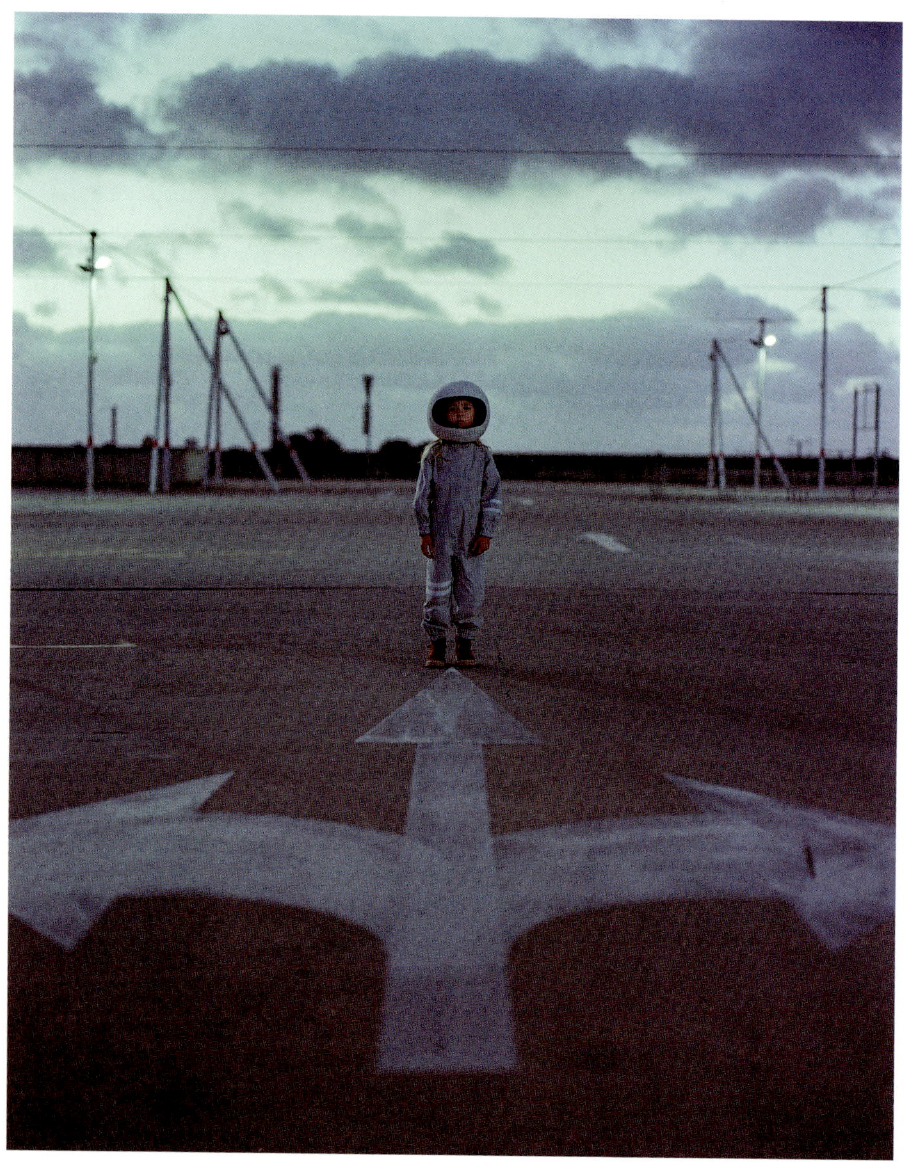

The Trident

> The Tide

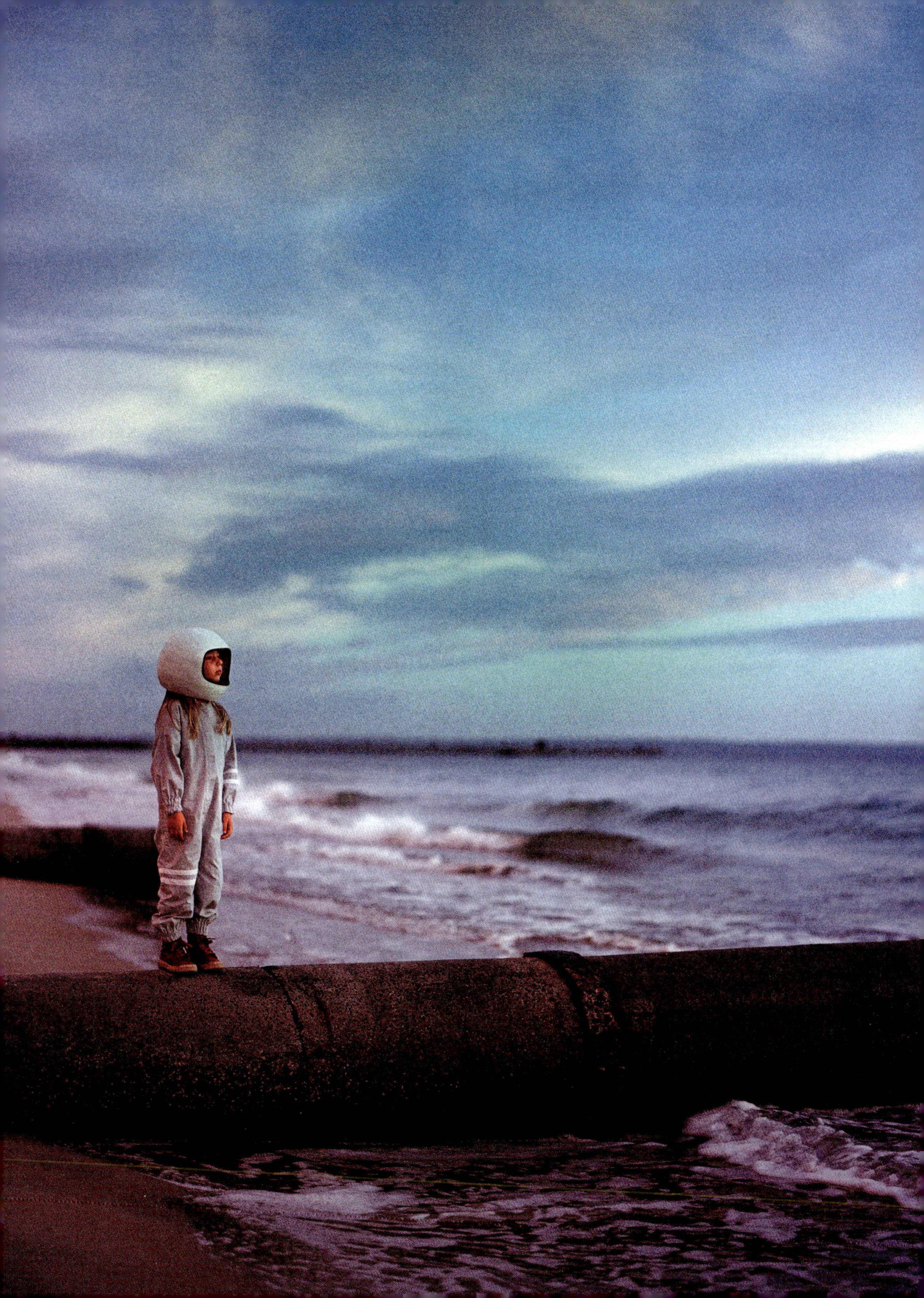

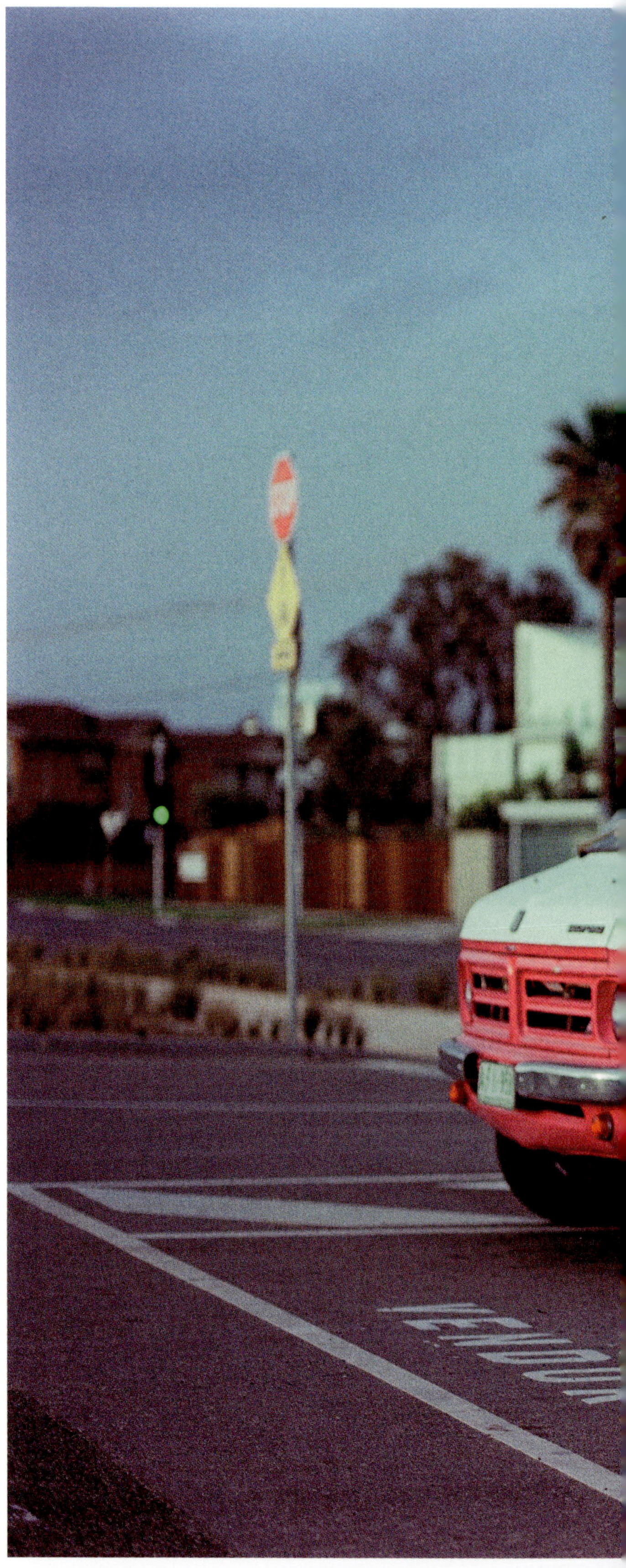

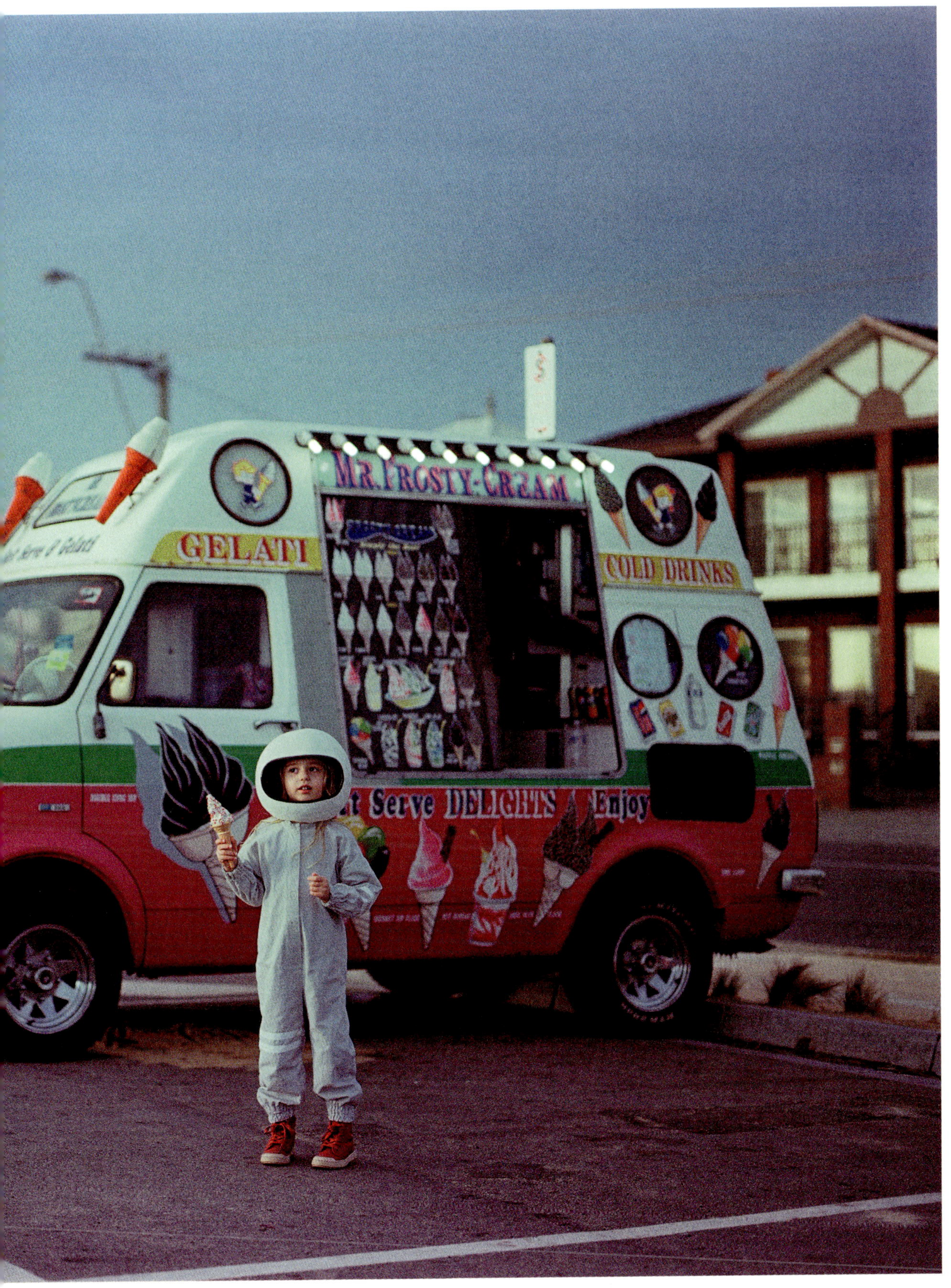
MR.FROSTY-CREAM
GELATI
COLD DRINKS
t Serve DELIGHTS
Enjoy

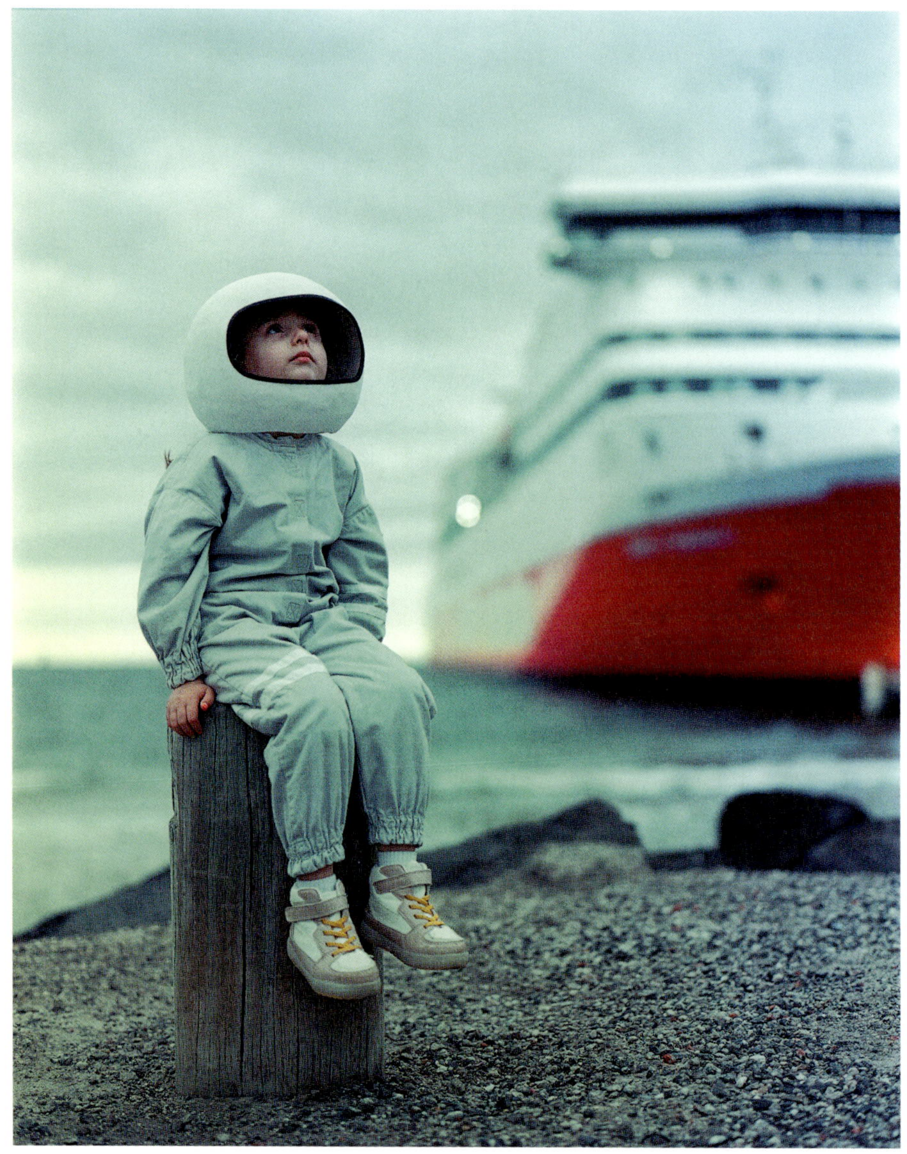

The Hull

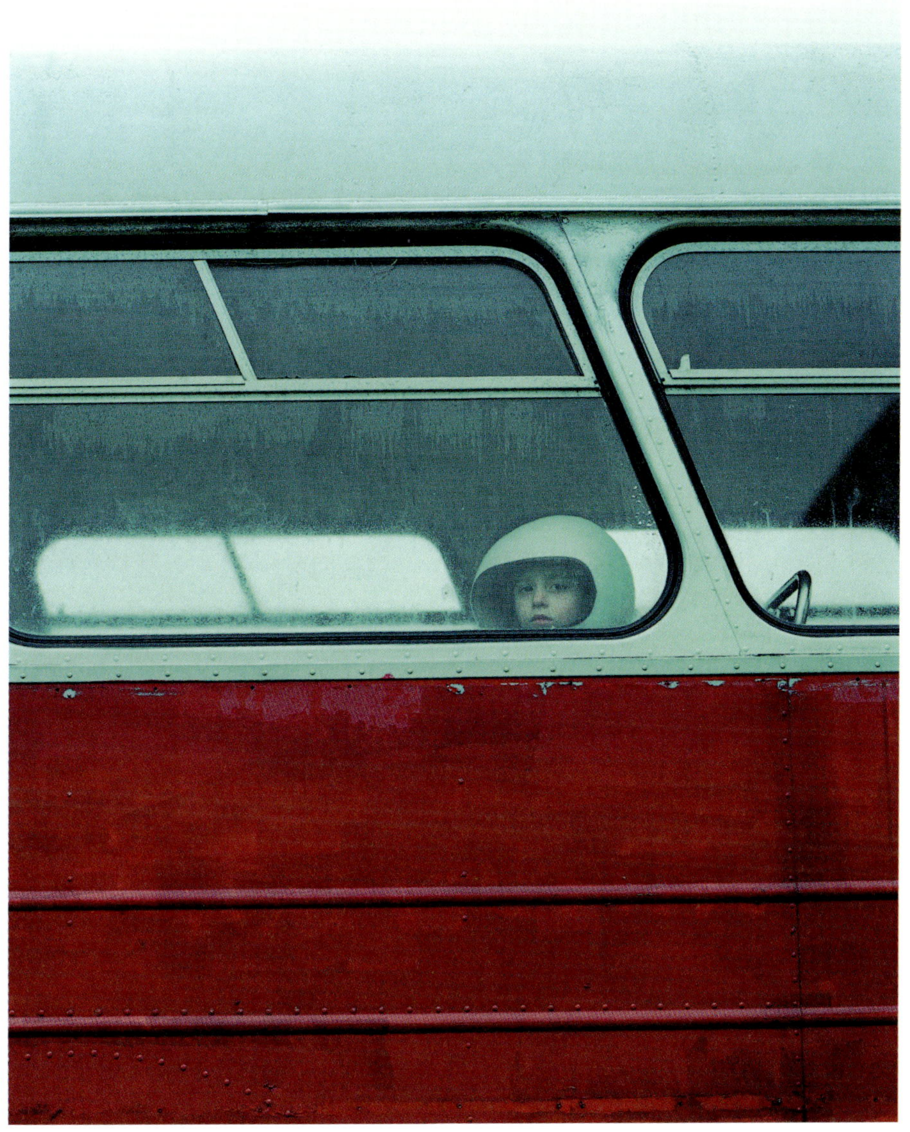

These flashes of brightness,
of luminosity, suggest a world
heading into darkness. And that
triggers a protective instinct in us.

Evening Express

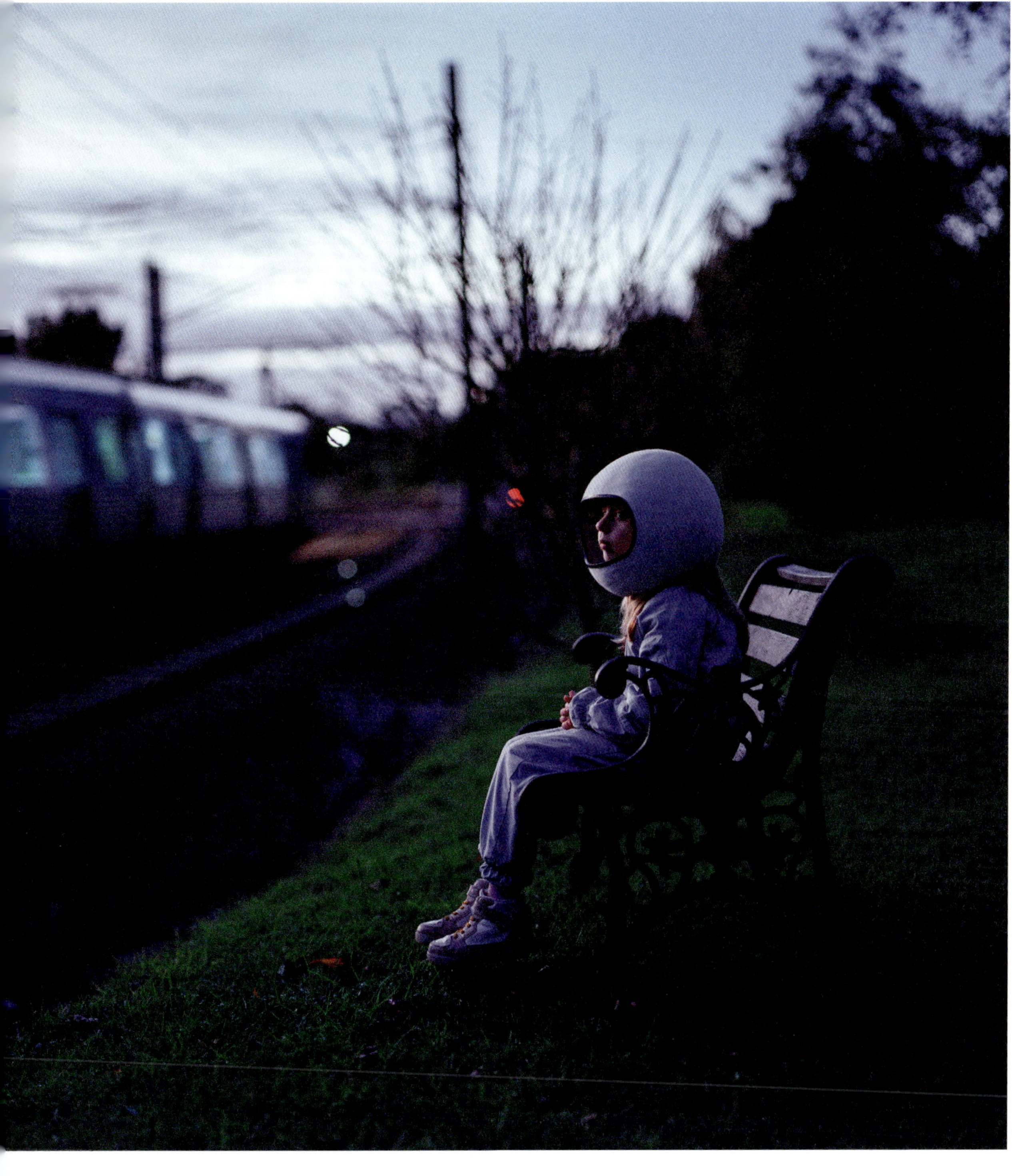

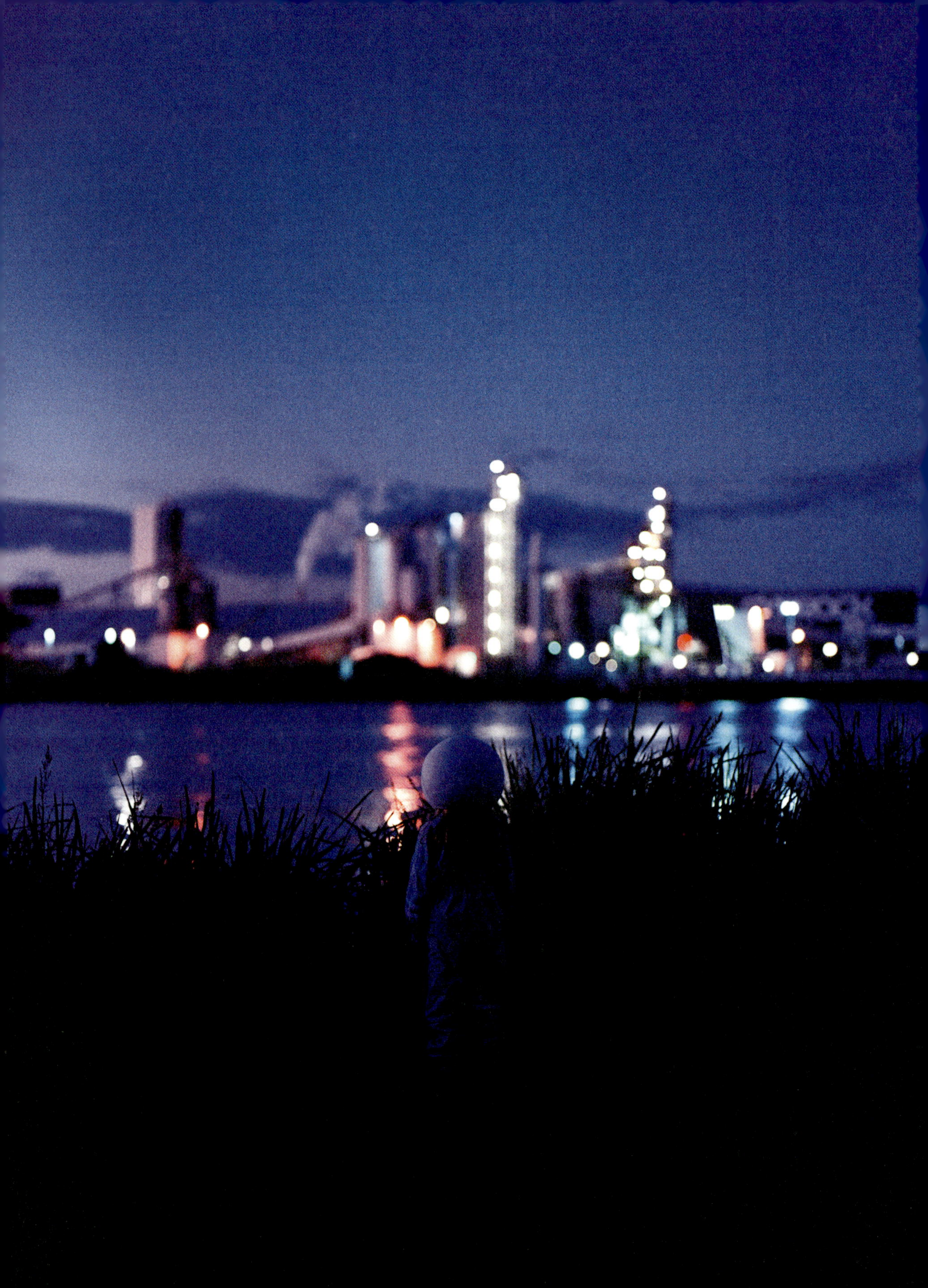

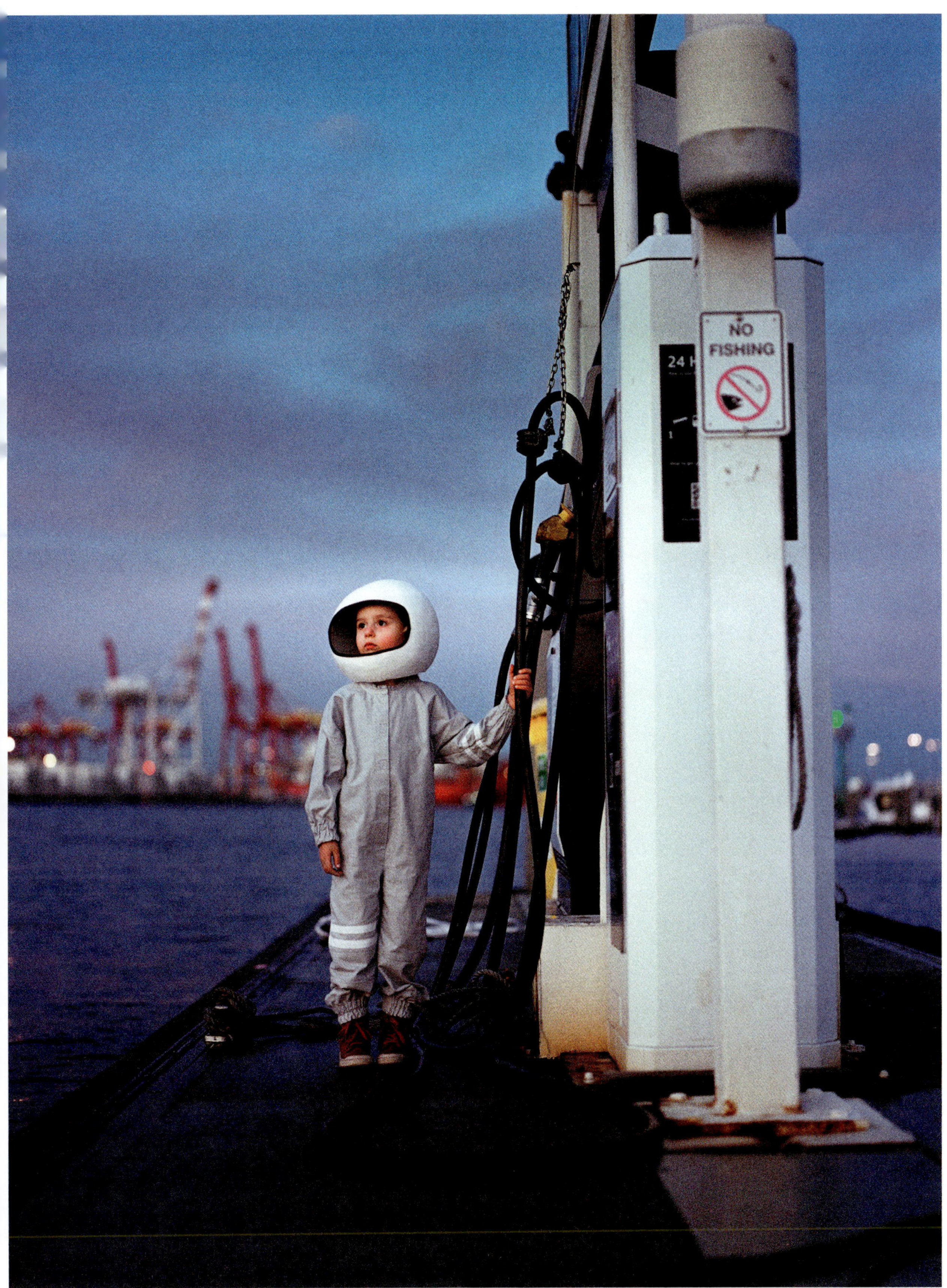
NO
FISHING

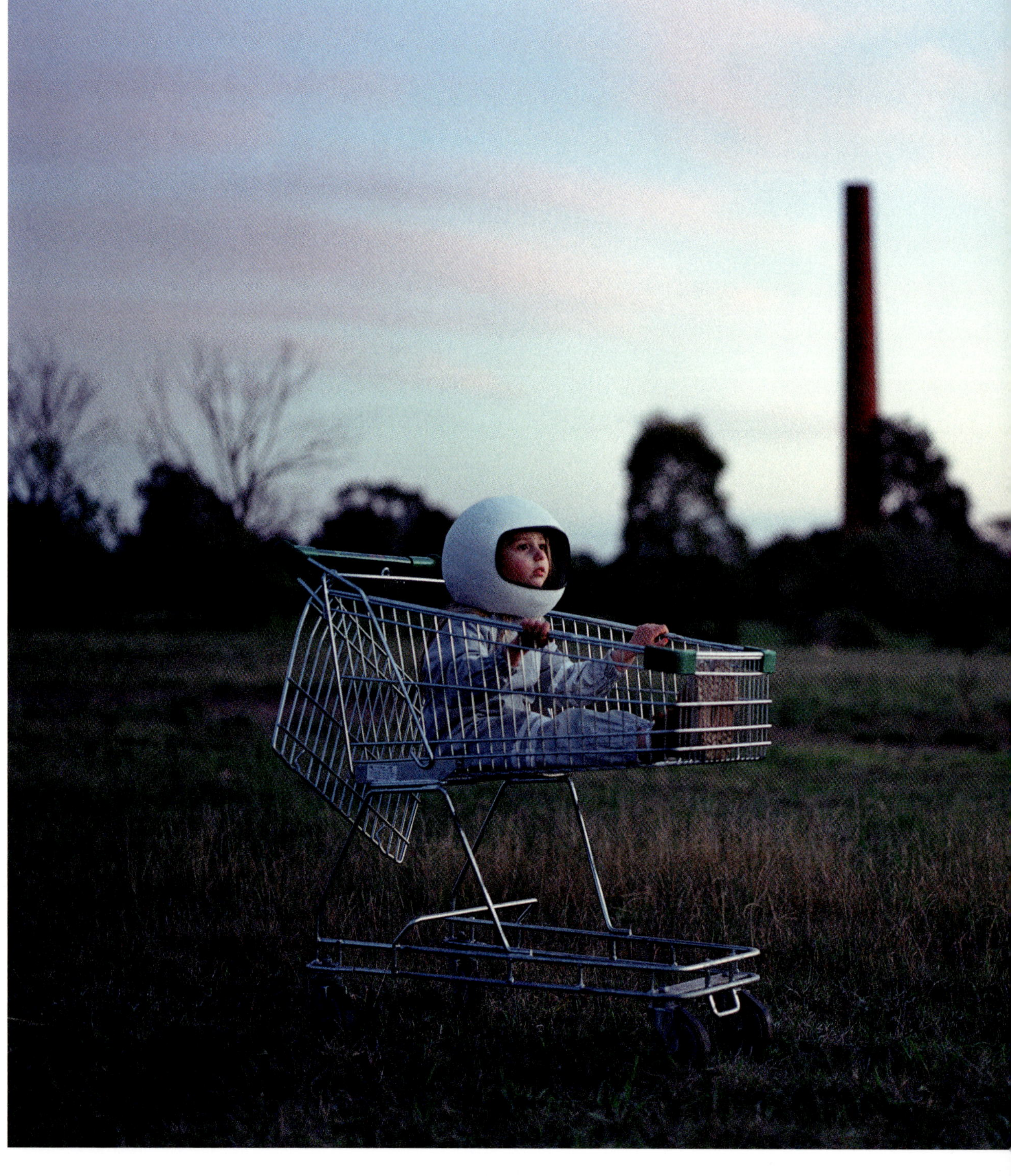

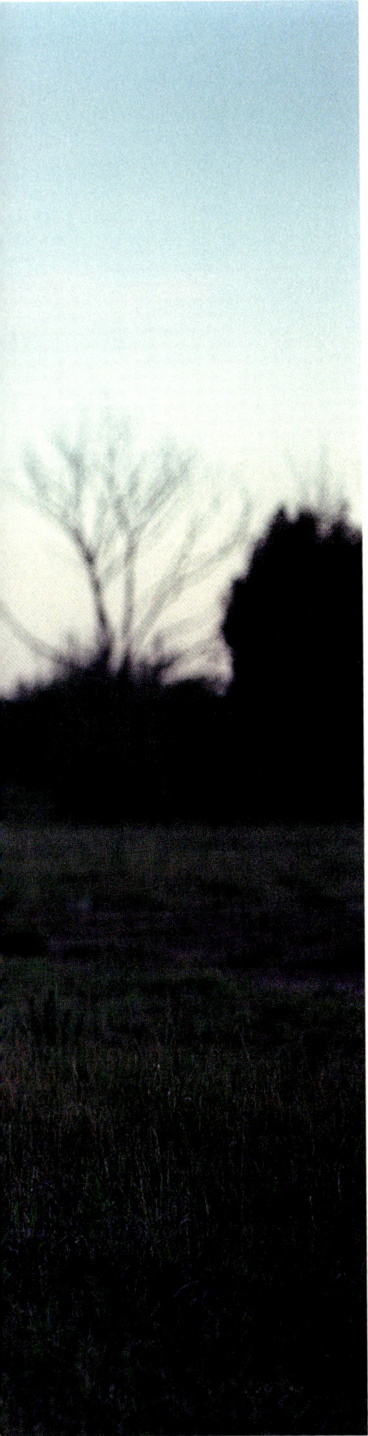

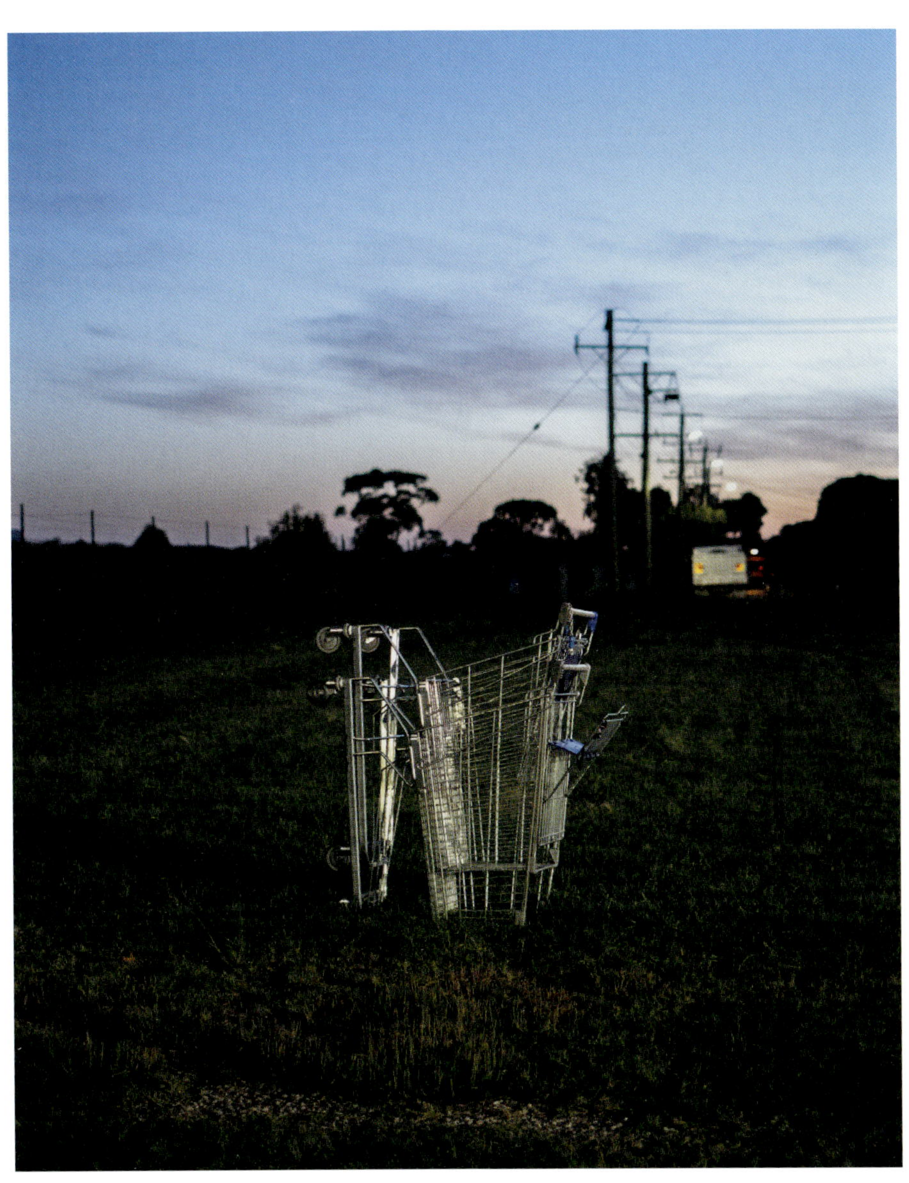

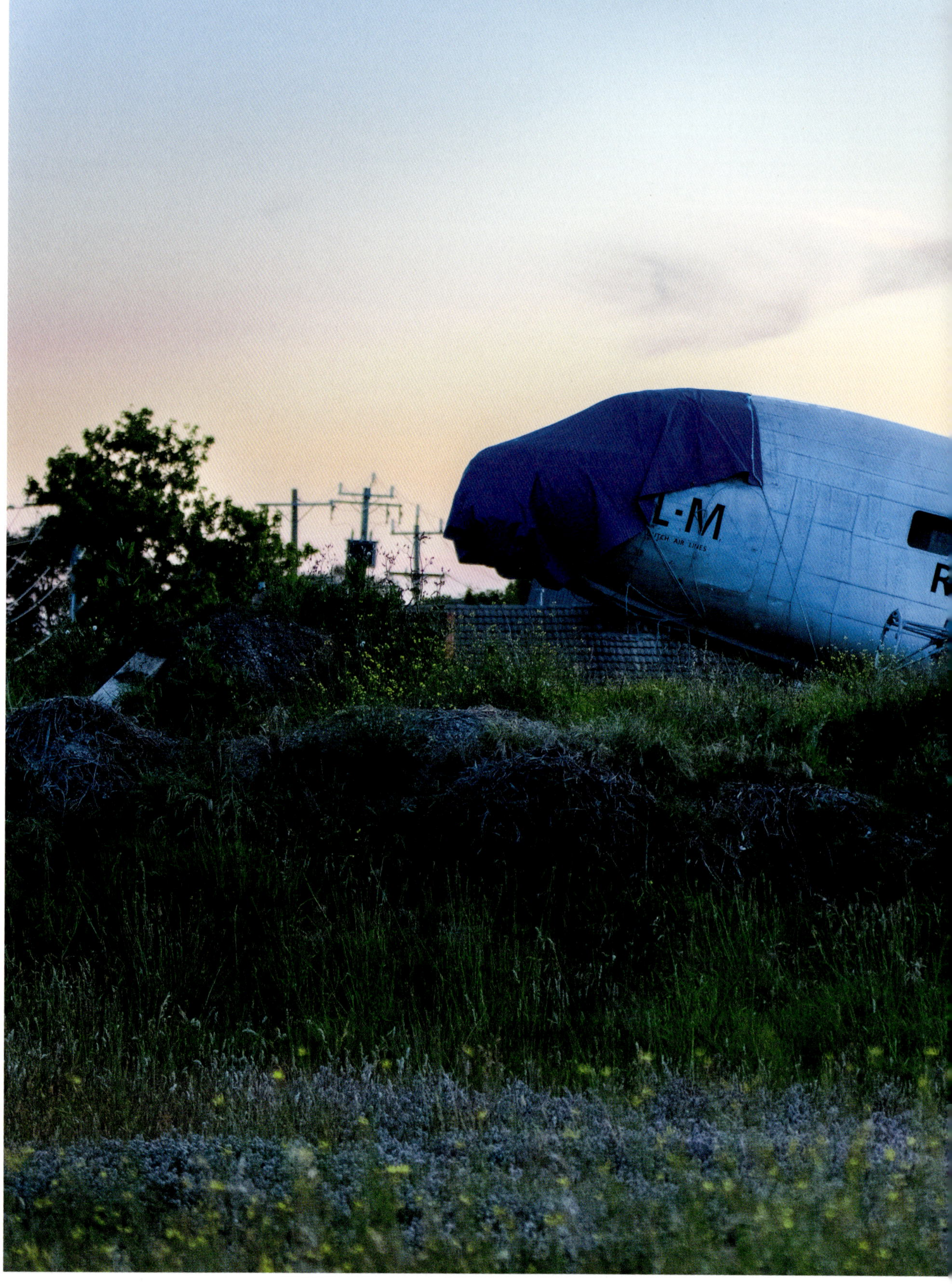
L·M

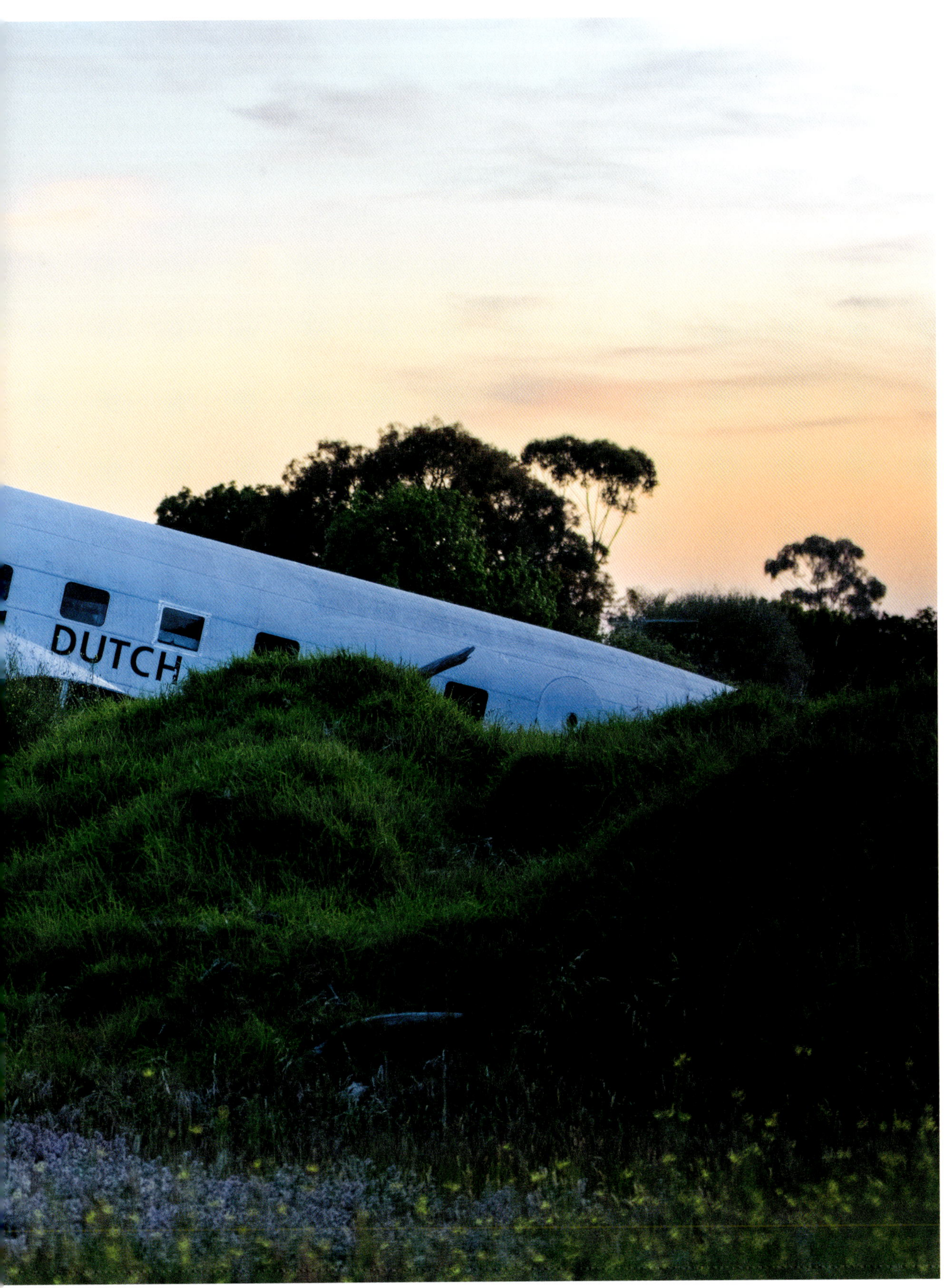
DUTCH

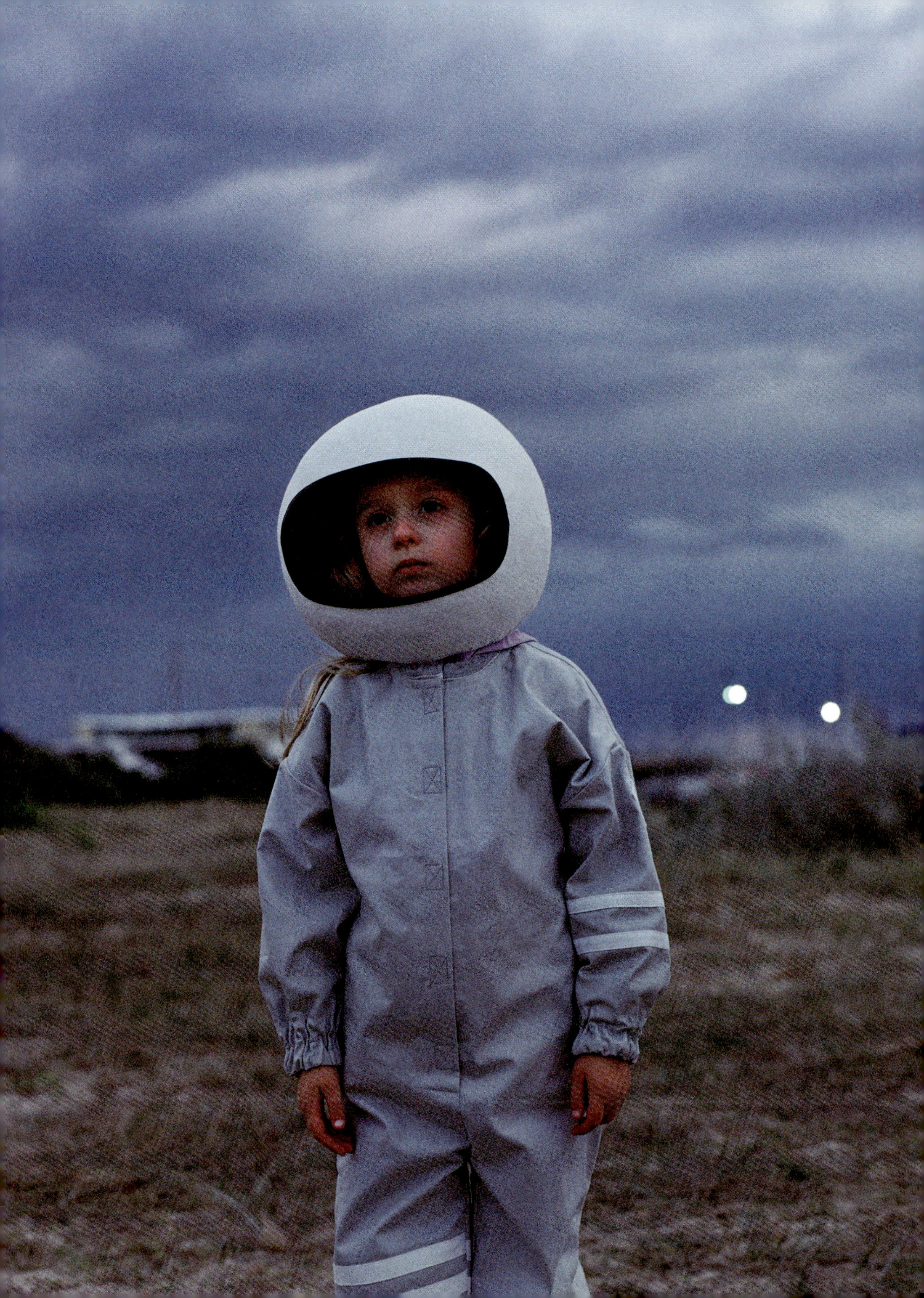

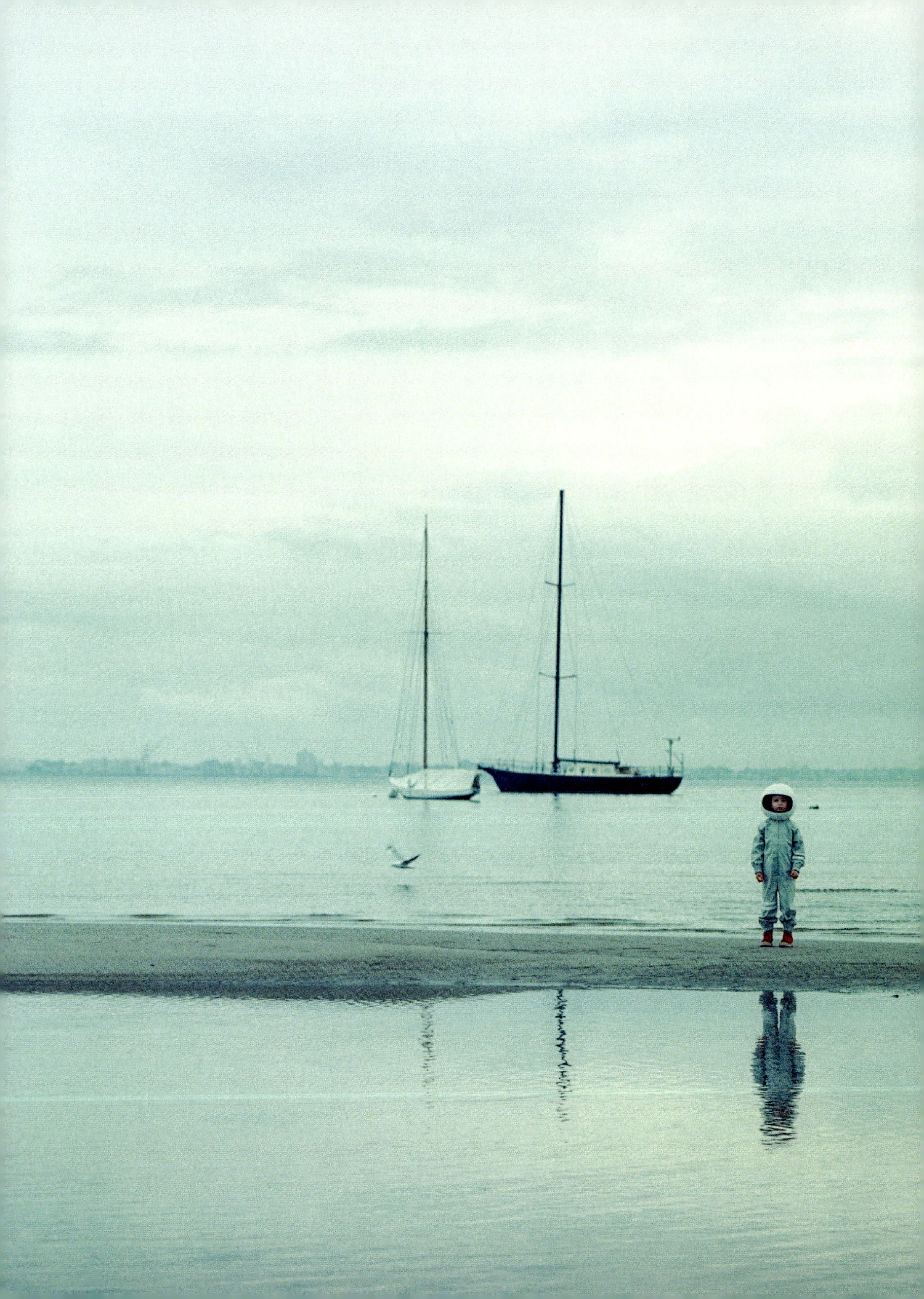

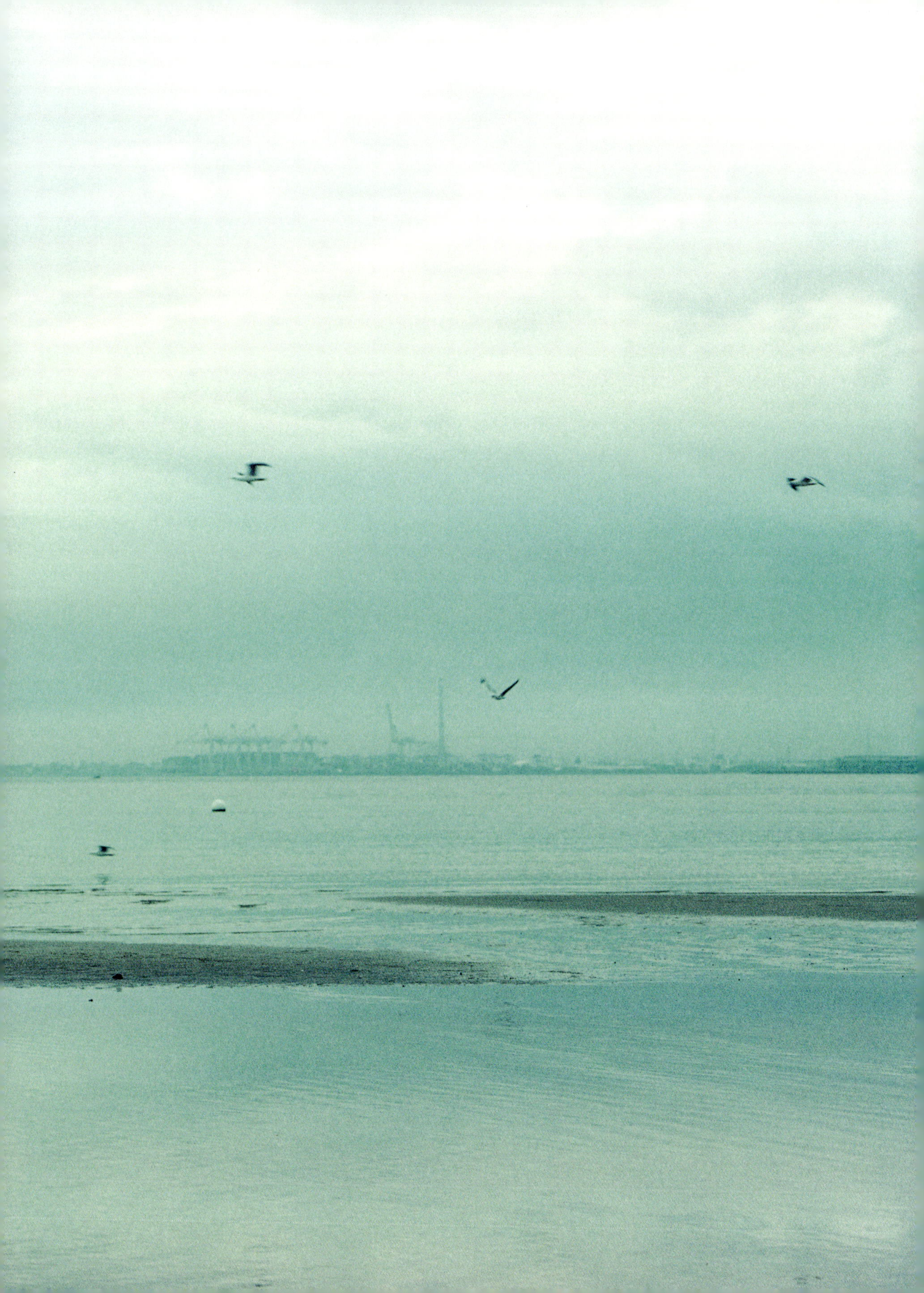

Concept, images and image selection
Andrew Rovenko

Text
Tom Morton-Smith

Copy-editing
Heather Sills

Graphic design
Bart Luijten

If you have any questions or comments about the material in this book,
please do not hesitate to contact our editorial team: art@lannoo.com

ISBN: 9789059963726
D/2026/45/61
THEMA: AJCD

www.lannoopublishers.com